Beneath Wings
of an Angel

Healing the Child Within
A spiritual healing journey
to recovery from domestic violence

Janice Romney Farnsworth

Beneath Wings of an Angel

Copyright© 2003 by Janice Farnsworth

ISBN: 0-9747644-7-7

Published by

Synergy Books

2525 W Anderson Lane, Suite 540
Austin, Texas 78757

Tel: 512.407.8876
Fax: 512.478.2117

E-mail: info@turnkeypress.com
Web: www.turnkeypress.com

Dedication

With love, gratitude and admiration, I dedicate my life's work to those who made it possible. Without you, Mom, my children and I would not have the life we live today; words cannot describe the gratitude in my heart.

If there are windows in Heaven, Dad, I hope you can see and are proud of me today.

To my Mother, LaNon Turley, for her endless love

And in loving memory of my Father, Maxel S. Romney

Acknowledgements

With heartfelt appreciation, I thank Kitty Eatherly, who has been the force behind my writing giving me guidance and support.

For those who have shared their life with me, I am grateful for the blessings I've received from their love: My brother Douglas and his wife Kennie, and Steven and his wife Silvia. My sisters whose lives brightly shine with dignity: Susan Edwards, Sharon Morgan, Marsha Buechert, Dianne Curtis and Cheryl Belnap.

The following have been inspirations and guides throughout my life: With a special tribute to Max R. Spilsbury, (June 16, 1924—November 21, 2001) my high school director and J.S.A. Football Coach; he remains a legend in his own time, and an example to many. Berkley Lunt, my 5th grade teacher, and to my cherished friends: Belle Billingsley, Anna Marie Walser, Gayle Turley, Gena Cravey, Beverly Shupe, Patty Michaels, Mary Alvord, Kristi Sherwood, Rowena Gardner, Sheri Frazier, Patricia Stole.

I am grateful for the countless hours spent helping me with this book from Debra Spilsbury, and for the encouragement received from Anna Marie Walser, Janice Hatch, Gayle Turley, Shelley Jones, and Christine Romney.

With a special thanks to my literary publicists, Phenix & Phenix who have believed in me making this work available to those in need across the country, and to my editor Stuart Wade.

My life was forever changed with the love I share with my husband Richard. Without him this book would be only a seed and an unfulfilled dream.

My children, Robert, Darinn, Justin, Nathan, Lynsey and Westin will forever be etched in my heart and may you always know my love is with you as you continue your life journey.

Contents

Nurture & Heal Your Soul:
A workbook and supplement guide for spiritual healing

The Tapestry

My life is but a weaving
Between my God and me.
I do not choose the colors,
He worketh steadily.
Oft' times He weaveth sorrow
And I in foolish pride,
Forget He sees the upper
And I the underside.
Not till the loom is silent and
The shuttles cease to fly
Will God unroll the canvas
And explain the reason why.
The dark threads are as needful
In the skillful weavers hand
As the threads of gold and silver.
In the pattern He has planned.

Author unknown

From the Author

While rummaging through old photographs, I found baby books carefully tucked away. Each book bore the name of one child. Eagerly, I looked inside hoping to read about a mother's fondest memories. Instead, I found empty pages, reminding me of their painful childhoods and the role I, albeit unwittingly, played.

Although I'd had years to come to terms with my past, my heart had yet to heal. Sometimes the heart struggles to release that pain and oftentimes our wounds from the past feel safer hidden and untouched. For several years, I struggled with my writing because the past was sealed somewhere far away—it wasn't mine to remember or to feel until the birth of my first grandchild. I was there to witness his birth, and the moment I held him in my arms his soul whispered to mine. Devinn was not ready to enter mortality, he came sooner than was planned, leaving behind his spirit's beloved knowing that his life would be one of many challenges. So tiny and vulnerable, he needed protection and love. Suddenly, the tears began to flow releasing all the anguish that had been silenced for so many years.

In agony I wept. This baby became my baby, and I desperately wanted to give to him what I failed to give my own children and spare him life's harsh reality. I wanted to start over and live my life differently. I wanted to take him home, but I could not. I had to release him from my arms when it was time for me to return to my family.

Traveling home was long and filled with tears. In fact, most of my life had filled with tears, and yet this time, I understood the purpose of life and our individual journeys. This sweet baby had many lessons to learn, and I felt comfort in knowing that I would travel with him, not to interfere, but rather to love and guide.

Finally, my writing revealed my deepest feelings, and yet *Beneath Wings of an Angel* has been a very difficult book to write for many reasons. How do you wake up one day and decide to air your darkest secrets? My children still bear yesterday's wounds, and I do not want to add to their pain. My family, especially my mother, cannot help but be affected by what I say here. Words cannot come close to describing my feelings for my mother and I would not want to do anything to hurt her.

The feelings I had as a child and young woman were my own. I take responsibility for how I perceived my life and the mistakes I made. But this I know without a doubt: The training I received and the example of a mother who stands for truth and honor have been my saving grace.

Today, I have compassion for my plight as a battered woman, and I understand more clearly the difficulty women, children, and family members face not only with an abuser, but also with law enforcement and other government agencies. It's not that agencies don't *want* to help; sometimes, the help that is so desperately needed just isn't available. Remember this: A battered woman is not just a battered woman. She is someone's mother, sister, friend and daughter. As long as society thinks of battered women in singular terms, the ripple effect of violence inside the home, in schools, on the street and in the courts will continue. Society must pull together and get help not only from family, friends, law enforcement and government agencies, but *ecclesiastical* leaders as well.

But it is more difficult for outsiders to help unless you are willing to ask. If you are a victim of abuse or if you know of someone that is, please read this book with an open mind. Abuse in any form is not acceptable and regardless of hope, faith and prayer, abusers rarely change and if they do most generally it is because someone has forced them to be responsible for their behavior.

Four years have passed since I began writing this book, and over time I've listened to heartbreaking stories from many victims of rape and abuse and family members in the LDS faith! I am appalled. I am disheartened, and I am deeply disturbed and afraid for the many women that are still in abusive relationships. While victims suffer from severe depression, irrational guilt and extreme shame they appear to be at fault because they are failing in their church callings as well as their "wife and mother obligations" while abusers are just the opposite. Dressed in suits and white shirts, faithfully they attend all their meetings and the temple; consequently how could they possibly be abusive husbands and fathers?

This isn't always the case, but if it is happening at all it is too often. Most church leaders are *not* trained in domestic violence—they can't begin to understand the complexities of the battered woman syndrome, but as long as women remain subjugated in a patriarchal society, their mental, emotional and spiritual well-being is greatly at risk. Long before an abusive relationship, women relinquish their power, and if riddled with guilt and shame, they permit teachings of purity and worthiness to deepen their wounds. Lacking in awareness and personal power in broken spirit they continue down a frightening path. They aren't the only ones suffering—what about their children?

Long after my divorce, the despair, helplessness, and guilt I felt over my children spun me into a darker world of depression and prescription drug dependency. *Nothing* compares to a mother's sorrow when faced with the unthinkable sin of allowing her children to physically/mentally and emotionally experience the wrath of their father. For many years, my pain went from the soles of my feet to the crown of my head into my last breath—and I couldn't imagine it ever fading or going away.

The heart can be a place where many secrets hide. Some we may never tell, while others, distant and faded as they may seem, have a way of changing our destiny and playing with our fate.

Could it be then that the present is only a reflection of the past we continue to live today? Sometimes, I believe it can be. Just as a beautiful melody can last throughout time, so can living with buried, negative emotions hidden and silenced within the heart.

Many of us are emotionally crippled, doing our best to find a wholeness that seems to elude us. This is what my writing is about, finding spiritual and emotional wholeness by facing and cleansing the darkness within.

Even though writing this book has not been easy, I know this is my soul's most sacred promise—to help bring healing to those who suffer. I can only pray many hearts will be touched and my soul's redemption will be found in sharing my story with others.

Blessed be,
Janice

Preface

As an introduction, I feel that it is important you understand certain aspects about my life, because even though my story is not about my Mormon heritage, my religious beliefs played an important role in events that happened to me.

In 1953, I was born in the Mormon Colonies in old Mexico. My Great-grandfather practiced polygamy, as did my Grandfather later in his life, which is how I came to be born in Mexico. Polygamy was a principle taught and lived by Mormon Church leaders and their members at that time in the Church's history. Mormon polygamists were persecuted and driven from their homes, until finally, many were forced to flee the country to avoid legal prosecution.

My Great-grandfather had four wives. In order to keep his families together and avoid a jail term, they joined a group of similar refugees that fled across the New Mexico/Mexico border in 1885 and settled what is now known as the Mormon Colonies.

My forefathers may have been obedient and God-fearing people. They certainly endured the most controversial, turbulent and violent times in the history of the Latter Day Saints Church, and perhaps they really believed in what they were doing.

At the least, I can say that the women they married were devoted women of faith. No matter how difficult their journeys or how sorrowful their lot; they were obedient women who believed their Prophet was a man of God.

They also believed this man would not ask of them what God did not command of him. Their lives revolved around obedience and unquestioning loyalty while following the counsel and guidance of their leaders, no matter what sacrifice they were asked to make.

Although a manifesto was issued in 1890, and polygamy was no longer to be practiced, polygamy and its concept have cast dark shadows on subsequent generations. I can't help but wonder about the underlying message polygamy placed upon Mormon women. I know that many of the women were embittered because of what they were asked to endure, but still they endured to the end.

Today, Mormonism still dictates a strict pattern by which members must live; any variance constitutes disobedience. Members are taught to be modest and morally clean, to obey the Word of Wisdom (abstaining from alcohol, tobacco, tea and coffee).

They must also attend church meetings, give service, hold church positions and pay a full tithing (10 percent of pre-taxed income) to the church. They are required to adhere to the words of the Prophet and to attend the temple, either to perform sacred ordinances for others or for their own endowments, which they receive when they first go through the temple.

Chastity is a powerful word taught to Mormon girls. It is the foundation by which a woman prepares herself to be a wife and mother in Zion. I remember an example of purity that was taught when I was young.

My teacher held out a beautiful rose. Perfect in its natural beauty the rose was, that is, until she started picking petals one at a time. The rose soon lost its splendor, marred by the human touch as each petal fell to the floor.

"This is what happens when young girls are improperly touched by their boyfriends," she said "They lose their virtue, and natural beauty."

Each principle of the Gospel, such as reading scriptures, prayer, and attending church meetings is a stepping-stone leading to the eternal doorway of a Celestial Marriage, but being morally clean is what allows a woman to enter and partake of the sacred ordinances to receive the promised blessings. Sacred ordinances consist of promises we make to God, each with its penalties if broken or blessings if obeyed. We are taught over and over that nothing we do in life is as important as entering through the temple doors to be sealed with our mate for all time and eternity.

The temple is the icon of the church. It symbolizes eternal salvation, faithfulness, righteousness, obedience and sacrifice; a "temple recommend" is the epitome of one's worthiness. Before a member can receive a temple recommend, which is a card signed by both the bishop and the stake president, an interview is held in which pertinent questions are asked as to their worthiness.

Being a wife and mother and living with her eternal companion is the crowning glory of womanhood for the Mormon woman. Often, her only success is found within her Celestial marriage and with her children.

Since a Mormon woman is most likely to find her own esteem in the successes of her children, it is a day of celebration when a mother's son or daughter leaves for his/her mission. Unless of course, it is when they enter the temple to be sealed to their companion.

But unlike this perfect picture of every idealistic young woman all wrapped up inside a little box tied with satin ribbon, the reality for many women is you either fit inside that box or you don't. Many who don't fit the criteria live with guilt, because they believe they have failed.

The Gospel is centered on the family. Families are taught to stay together, pray together and become an eternal family and if they do these things, they will be blessed. If they do not, then their salvation is in jeopardy.

Another tenet in Mormon Doctrine is that of God's Priesthood. Worthy males are ordained in their youth and advance as they come of age.

Since women are not ordained to this Priesthood and it is essential to eternal progression, a woman must seek the blessings received from this Holy Priesthood through her husband. Young women are taught from an early age that they should turn to the Elders of the Church when in need. Once she marries, the blessings of the priesthood are shared through her husband and it is the husband's prerogative, through his priesthood authority, to preside righteously over his family.

He is to personally interview his wife and his children on a monthly basis. If a woman feels her husband is unworthy or if they have marital problems, a woman then seeks guidance from her bishop.

In my own experience, perhaps the messages I received were mixed and confusing, but I also grew up believing that I was not to question Priesthood authority and that it was important to turn to my leaders rather than be my own authority.

I also believed that God punished those who sinned. I believed his spirit vanished the moment you did something wrong. Even though the God I learned about was a loving God, He confused me. Fire and brimstone weren't preached from the pulpit, but fear was instilled just the same.

I know that I was a deeply sensitive child filled with self-doubt and deep fears of inadequacy. It was as though my life was an unwritten book full of empty pages; I was without my own identity open to anyone teaching or leading me in any direction they chose.

In my fear of being different, I hid my shame and masked the pain, so no one would see how I really felt about myself. Because I would let no one see my wounds, my world became a kind of fairy tale, and my dreams took me into a fantasy life where I waited to be rescued by a knight in shining armor.

But in living so completely in this fantasy world, I never grew into my own identity. Instead, I became a pleaser. I learned what others wanted me to learn and to say and to be whoever they wanted me to be in my need to be accepted.

No one knew better than I that my feet were not planted firmly in reality, and I knew that my life was not of my own making. I always knew I wasn't living in reality and that I was running away from something or running toward something—I was never sure which.

It's important that I also briefly share my childhood experiences with you to illustrate how secrets of the heart separate us from our true Self and the love that inherently exists within, and this is where my story begins.

One

Secrets of the Heart

I did not lose myself all at once. I rubbed out my face over the years washing
away my pain; the same way carvings on stone are worn down by water.
-Amy Tan

In faded misty memories, I'm five years old again. I can still see the bright red lipstick marks on my bottom as I tried to wash them away, and I remember the look on my mother's face when she unexpectedly opened the bathroom door and caught me. "What are you doing?" she screamed at me. "What is all over your bottom?" I don't remember what I said, I just remember her look and the guilt I felt when she said, "Shame on you." I'm sure I said something foolish and perhaps she never knew the truth.

That afternoon, the child so filled with grace simply slipped away. My face no longer bore the rays of sunlight. Instead, shame colored my world in hues of amber gray. Over the years, the memory of childhood sexual abuse was embedded so deeply, I had virtually forgotten. Purged from my conscious mind was the memory of an older adult male while playing away from home taking me into his bathroom, and making me stand on top of the toilet seat, with my back facing him. He laughed as he made fun of me; humiliating me unmercifully, and making me feel small and helpless.

He didn't listen when I said, "No, I don't want to." He didn't care as my sobbing washed away my plea, "Just let me go home." Instead I still remember the words, "I'm not going to hurt you, just take off your clothes," and I distinctly remember bright red lipstick from a make-up kit on the bathroom counter. He told me to use the lipstick and I obeyed. Opening the tube, I painted my lips just before he placed his hands and fingers on my bottom.

Helplessly frightened, I begged him to stop, but he didn't listen. He then took the lipstick away from me. Playfully, he touched my bottom with it and asked me how it felt. Tightly closing my eyes, and holding my breath, I held back tears, but the most haunting memory of all was the moment he forced himself inside me. Bracing myself against the mirror, my little knees were trembling; pain seared through me and even though I wanted to scream, the words just wouldn't come. They felt frozen and trapped inside. Yet, to myself I swore, *"I hate him, I hate him."*

He finished. "Time for you to go home," he said just as he closed the door behind him. After pulling on my clothes, I timidly opened the door and found him waiting on the other side, "You were the one who asked for this. If you tell anyone you'll be punished, so this had better be our little secret."

Humiliated, I walked home along the dusty country road staring at my shoes and fighting back the tears. Gently I whispered, *"Don't cry; after all, it wasn't your fault."* Time and again I tried to reassure myself, *"You said no; he just wouldn't listen. But what about my bottom?"* I didn't want to go home. I felt guilty and ashamed of myself; *I know my Mom will see, what will she say? What will she think of me?"*

Today, I still see the face of this little girl, and still remember as I walked toward home a little slower than I did before I went out to play, wiping each tear away as they stained my freckled face. Somehow I knew I would have to hide my secret and never tell a soul. I was dirty now, and not from playing hide and seek, but from letting someone touch me in places that evoked deep, deep, inner shame.

As years went by, my memory of the abuse completely vanished. Soon I entered high school. Cheerleading, acting in plays, proms, riding my horse along the river and falling desperately in love were as much a part of growing up as my deepest feelings of shame.

Each lesson in my young women's class at church only solidified that I was unclean without my knowing why. I was afraid to be loved and yet more afraid that I wasn't. My boundaries had been destroyed, and yet I was taught to be morally clean so that I would be a choice spirit of my Heavenly Father. As the years went by, I lost all touch with those buried feelings, and I pulled further away from the delightful child that I must have been.

Regardless of my secret feelings, in my home there was love. My father's eyes were warm, gentle and loving. He was devoted to his family, even though his work kept him away from home most of the time. My mother was dedicated to her family and did her best to raise eight children. But open expression of feelings, good or bad, weren't encouraged and I was careful with what I said out of fear of upsetting my mother.

Even today I can distantly see myself as a child with a happy face, but my heart reaches out to that girl as I feel her loneliness. I feel compassion for the extreme sensitivity she once felt and her need to hear a word of praise.

Even though I was sensitive and easily wounded, I wasn't always a faithful and devoted little lamb. Sometimes I rebelled. I wore short skirts to school when I could get away with it, I toilet-papered the school bus and I even ditched classes, but most of all I wanted to think for myself and make my own choices. If I saw a sign that said, "Keep out," I thought it was meant for everyone but me. I didn't fit the traditional Mormon mold and at times I even "danced with sin."

I met Rex when I was a sophomore in high school. Instantly attracted to him, I didn't hesitate to let him know of my interest. Rex had also grown up in the Mormon Colonies and was home visiting during Christmas Holidays. I first met him when he was visiting a family of a close girlfriend of mine and then later on during the week at a New Year's Eve dance. I decided if anyone was going to make the first move it would have to be me. Finally, after tossing party streamers his way, which I had rolled up into tight little wads of paper, he turned around.

"If you want to dance, why don't you just ask?" Feeling a little embarrassed, I don't remember what I said, but I know we danced the night away.

Rex was much older than I and had a small child. His wife had died soon after the birth of their first child, Stacey, and because he was "too old" for me this situation was completely unacceptable to my parents. The first time my Dad became aware of my relationship with Rex, I was forbidden to date him, but that certainly didn't stop me. I was smitten with this older man, and we secretly dated when he was in town and when apart we wrote often. I was wildly in love with him and he seemed quite taken with me. If anyone has ever cared for me, I have no doubt Rex did. Yet, we lived in separate worlds. Rex lived in San Diego and was ready to fall in love and make it last forever. On the other hand, I was still living in Mexico, a student in high school and still quite young and immature, and for a time, we drifted a part.

It was nearly a year later when I saw *him*. I was awe-stricken. Irresistibly handsome, he stole my heart away. He was five years older than me and perhaps the most handsome man I have ever seen.

For several years, we secretly dated. We both knew our relationship was ill-fated from the beginning and so we dated others. My parents would have forbidden me to see him also if they were to discover our relationship. Even though I don't regret my relationship with Isidro, I do regret lying and deceiving my parents.

Girls in my hometown were forbidden to date outside their race and their faith. But I didn't understand. Isidro never once demeaned me or morally dishonored me, whereas a few of the young men, who were of my same race and religion, did!

I will always remember the night Brandon and I parked down by the river, beneath dancing stars that seemed to cover the unending sky. He said he loved me and we began to kiss. I felt he really did care about me, but soon he began forcing his hands all over my body. Repulsed, I tried to fight him off, but why did I feel powerless? Why did I feel guilty? I don't remember slapping his face, instead I remember going home sick to my stomach, fighting back tears with deep self-loathing. Even though I didn't allow him to go any further, just the fact that he tried made me feel dirty.

After coming home, I knew the moment I stepped out of the car and my feet hit the ground, the Earth would open up and Satan would grab me by the ankle and drag me into the depths of hell. Today it seems almost ironic; dating young men who were immoral wasn't the greater sin, as long as we were both of the same race and religion.

My high school days are filled with bittersweet memories. Never feeling my feet on the ground, I still went after what I wanted. Although I was a cheerleader and active in most high school activities, no one would have suspected my fear of inadequacy.

Once graduated from high school, I left home to attend college in Rexburg, Idaho, but I wanted to be home. I cared deeply for Isidro and even though I don't know that I had the courage to marry him, I never stopped loving him but several years later he married someone else.

After one semester at Rick's College in Idaho, I moved to Mesa, Arizona and enrolled at the community college. Rex and I resumed our relationship, and I would fly to San Diego and spend the weekend with him. I stayed with his brother and sister-in-law and have many cherished memories of that time during my life. My heart warmed to his daughter. Enchanting and filled with love, Stacey opened her arms and welcomed me into her life.

My parents were unaware of my relationship with Rex, and as I look back, I understand more clearly how I chased elusive dreams and danced with the forbidden—I didn't have any idea of what I really wanted.

Then one weekend I drove home. My Dad had agreed to sell my car for me. That's when he found out about my relationship with Rex. He was cleaning out the glove compartment inside my car when he came across an airline ticket. I still don't understand why, but the ticket was in the name of Mrs. Janice McNeil. Since Rex paid for the tickets, perhaps this is how the mistake was made. Even though I assured my Dad I had not eloped, he felt betrayed. I hadn't been truthful with him for several years and this deeply upset him. Many times he had told my mother that his greatest concern with me was that I wouldn't be able to take care of myself. He saw what I tried so hard to hide and he knew how troubled I really was.

When I left home at the end of the weekend, my Dad and I weren't speaking to one another. A few days later my mother called me just as my father walked into the room. My mother asked if I wanted to speak to him and I said, "No, Mom, I'm afraid he is still mad at me." I was coming home in less than a week, and what I had to say to my Dad was better said in person. I wanted to tell him how sorry I was for all the lies I had told him and that his love and approval meant the world to me.

There was urgency in Mom's voice when she said, "Janice, I think you should talk to him right now" but it was my choice to wait. That choice haunted me for many years to come. My father died that night without hearing the words I so desperately wanted to say to him.

I was just 19 years old when my father, only 48, died of a sudden heart attack. Nothing remained the same after his death. Especially the life of a make-believe princess I had created for myself. Looking back, it could have been that I suffered from depression from a very early age and at this point it worsened—but in any event, I went untreated and continued to spiral ever downward.

Believing that my father was my only anchor in life he had been my strength. He believed in me even when I could not. I adored him and he spoke of his love for me often but he also enabled my inability to be myself by constantly rescuing me from any situation that I got myself into. He was the knight in shining armor of my fantasies—slaying all my mythical dragons. I felt safe pretending to be who I thought my father wanted me to be and seeing only what I wanted to see until my fantasy died along with my father.

After the funeral, I moved back to Utah, and later on Rex planned a trip for us. He wanted to ask me to marry him, but I changed my mind often. As soon as I would say I would go with him, I would change my mind and say no.

Finally, he gave up. I knew that I had been unfair but I couldn't explain to him how I felt. Maybe I blamed Rex for the pain between my father and me. I know I grieved over my father's death and a day didn't go by without feeling deep remorse that he died before I made peace with him. If I continued my relationship with Rex, would my father not feel betrayed from beyond the grave?

It didn't take long before I began writing to someone who was serving a mission for our church. We had dated during high school, and if I were to be truthful about my feelings toward him, I would have to say that I felt sure my father would approve of him and this influenced my feelings.

When my missionary returned home we dated and even talked about marriage, but it didn't work out and I felt betrayed and lied to.

Over the next few years, I was attracted to bad relationships just as moths are attracted to a burning flame. Moths are unable to fly once their wings are scorched. I, on the other hand, was only wounded with a broken heart and able to search for yet another unsatisfactory relationship in which I would ultimately find rejection.

I kept a diary for many years, and one day I opened my book and began to read. My writing startled me—the unhappiness, loss of direction, loneliness and desperation flowed through the ink and onto the pages. Repeatedly I wrote, *"If I just stay obedient, God will bless me.*

Years later, I could not find the stability I longed for. I was unhappy and lived in the past. In time, my anger turned me against God. The only thing that kept me going was the belief that if I could just find someone to love me, my life would be different.

When I didn't find what I was looking for in Utah, I moved to Phoenix. I rented a one-bedroom house close to my work. I loved the warmth of the sun and the smell of orange blossoms, and in time, my spirits were lifted and I felt hopeful. For the first time, I was experiencing myself in a way that gave me a sense of freedom. I was going to live my life without expecting God to bless me or punish me and I no longer felt that I had to be married.

I found clerical work in a home for unwed mothers and actually enjoyed the work I was doing. My eyes opened to a whole different world, one that wasn't pristine and perfect from the outside. This world included young girls pregnant from rape or incest and the people trying to help them. Most of the girls were only 14 years old and yet they were young mothers just trying to finish high school and cope with their emotional trauma.

One afternoon I returned home from work to find my apartment had been vandalized. A police officer responded to my call, but it was obvious he was more interested in me than filling out his report. He was blonde with incredible blue eyes and skin beautifully bronzed from the Arizona sun. I was as attracted to him as he was to me and I was extremely flattered when he invited me to a party given by one of the officers that he worked with. I wasn't the least bit concerned that I didn't really know him. He was a police officer. I couldn't be any safer—or so I believed.

He picked me up Friday night after work, and we drove across Phoenix to his friend's condo. The party was crowded with people drinking alcohol and having a great time. I was uncomfortable with the fact that I didn't drink. Stan brought me a soft drink instead, but it wasn't long before I felt light-headed and wanted to lie down. He offered to take me upstairs, but I insisted on going home. We drove back to my place, and since I still felt dizzy, he carried me into my bedroom and placed me on my bed. He began undressing me and I tried to stop him. Grabbing hold of my arms, he pinned them above my head and aggressively started kissing me. He was rough and made my lips bleed. I was terrified!

I struggled against his brutal force when he violently began ripping off my clothing. His body weight was suffocating, and I was petrified, screaming at the same time, "Stop, you're hurting me." He put his hand over my mouth and the next thing I remembered were early morning sunrays filtering through my bedroom window.

As I awoke, I touched my body, and in my nakedness, froze for just a moment. I hurt and my body ached. My heart raced and my thoughts ran wild. What had happened last night? My head was foggy, and I could only remember bits and pieces of the night before. Nothing made sense, and when reality finally hit me like a ton of bricks, I realized I had been raped.

What had I ever done that was so sinister that I deserved rejection from everyone I dated? And now rape? Hot water flowing into my bathtub rinsed my body clean, but it didn't take away the physical pain or remove the inner filth that seemed to be a part of me. Still shocked and confused, I realized how naïve I had been.

Just the night before, I had left home with a wonderful date feeling all grown up and ready to take on the world, but this morning I woke up defiled and shattered not only as a woman, but also in my faith.

Finally, I confided in Karen, a friend at work, and she had to explain things I didn't understand. She told me about date rape. Karen explained that there is a drug given to rape victims so they don't remember what happened. In naïveté, I was startled. I had never heard of anything like that before. Karen, years younger than I had grown up in a world much different than mine. The excruciating pain I felt for days confused me, but Karen didn't hesitate to say, "You've also been sodomized."

"I'll have to admit, I needed her to explain that word to me also."

She said, "Janice, you have to do something."

"But what, Karen? Aren't I to blame?"

She was stunned.

"Were you born yesterday?" she asked.

Karen helped me go through the process of filing rape charges against the officer, but it wasn't successful because all of his buddies at work gave him alibis and said they had never seen me. I was shocked when I received word that the county attorney's office would not file charges against the officer. Having bathed, and not having reported the rape for several days, I was without the physical evidence needed and had no choice but to drop the charges and get on with my life. I vowed never to allow myself that humiliation, embarrassment and utter frustration that victimized me all over again. Growing up in a small, country community hadn't prepared me for this even though I don't think anyone is prepared regardless of their background—the legal system can be brutally unjust to victims.

Nothing I did ended with a positive result. Then I told myself, *"Just put it away Janice, like a game you no longer want to play, pretend it doesn't matter and it will go away."*

Two months later, I realized I was pregnant. The emotional trauma from that terrifying night and the helplessness I felt caused extreme turmoil, and I felt more alone than I had ever felt before. Afraid of facing the ugliness in me, my only thought was, *"How can I tell my mother?"* The reason for my pregnancy didn't seem to matter, I felt dirty and that I was somehow to blame. I had never met my date before and never saw him after that night, but he changed my life forever.

Weeks went by, and I agonized over the situation in which I found myself. I seemed to be more of a failure than I had been before. If anyone were ever to know about this, it would shatter their image of me forever. Even though, in my heart of hearts, I was sure I wasn't to blame, my remaining feelings from my past destroyed my ability to face my family.

Nighttime offered little relief, and often I would awaken screaming without being able to make a sound. Paralyzed with fear, I soon realized my nightmares had more to do with my past. Perhaps, present emotional trauma triggered abandoned and long-forgotten memories as they sprang forth rapidly, growing as tiny tangled vines consuming all light. Shame, the one feeling I had hidden since I was a child was staring me in the face.

I didn't remember everything, yet I still knew that I had been deeply hurt as a child. I remembered being in a bathroom with a tube of bright red lipstick, but when I felt hands and fingers touching me, I felt threatened and desperately wanted the memory to stop. Grabbing at hands that were no longer there felt repulsive. Feelings of sexual stimulation sent me into a spiraling spin of shame and in vain I cried, "Please, God, just make this stop." Feelings of guilt carried me to a frightening place where I didn't want to be.

I tried getting in touch with the Bishop of the ward I was in, but he never returned my calls. I guess I was considered inactive and, therefore, not someone of his flock. I was not permitted to talk about personal matters with the counselors at work, and yet I tried many times to reach one that I admired later in the evening at her home. She had a small family and put me off enough times that I stopped calling her. Without knowing where else to turn, I looked in the Yellow Pages. I found a number under Planned Parenthood, so I called and made an appointment. At first I felt relieved, believing they would have the answers I needed.

My appointment was in the evening after work. First I had to take a pregnancy test. Several days later when the test results were finished, I had another appointment. The woman I saw didn't see my situation as a sinful one, but rather one that I could change. Stunned, I sat quite still in my chair as she talked about alternative solutions.

"Why are you so afraid?" she asked.

"Don't you offer unwed mothers help such as pre-natal care or adoption?" I answered.

Unfortunately, the only solution Planned Parenthood had was to terminate the pregnancy. It wasn't a baby she said, just an undeveloped fetus without any feeling. I felt life drain out of me as panic set in. Sickened that I was sitting in this woman's office, I just wanted to go back to being a naïve young girl without these problems. Still in shock, I couldn't believe I was even pregnant. In a heartbeat my life had completely changed and yet even today I can hear her say, "You do not have to carry a pregnancy which is a result of rape."

What I once considered life within now appeared only to be a mass of cells without any life at all. Yet I was repulsed when I heard the word abortion. While I was still naïve enough to somewhat believe what she said, I wasn't naïve enough not to know what a terrible sin it would be if I went along with her advice.

After leaving Planned Parenthood, I went home and thought about the only solution I had been offered. During the following days, I functioned as if in a fog. Nothing seemed real. Over and over I thought about the night I was raped. I wanted to remember so that I could absolve myself from guilt.

If I wasn't to blame then why did I feel so guilty? I wanted this baby as much as I knew I could never go through with the pregnancy.

During a restless night, I knew that I couldn't wait any longer. I reached for the phone with enough courage to call Gena, my closest girlfriend from high school. She was living in Provo, Utah and the second she heard my voice, she said, "Jan, what's wrong?"

She was stunned when I told her. I couldn't stop crying long enough to talk to her, but she understood me enough to say, "Jan I will do anything I can for you, but please don't have an abortion."

I had already been given a referral to a doctor who would perform the procedure and I knew the choice I had made was the only choice I had. Within a few days I made an appointment with this doctor. His office was just like any other—I could even pretend I was there for a routine check-up. As the doctor explained the procedure, I closed my eyes and tried to fight back the tears but they flowed from such a deep place inside me that I couldn't stop them.

During the '70s, abortion was a two-day procedure. The first day, they inserted something to make me dilate. Later that night I felt contractions just like the doctor said I would. My body was trying to expel the fetus. In agony,

I lay awake, sobs wracked my body, and I felt emotionally exhausted before sunrise. Even if I wanted to change my mind, it was too late. I had all night to feel the torment of my most difficult choice. I mourned the coming death of my baby as anguish tore at my soul. My only thoughts were that now God must surely be angry with me; I had finally given Him reason to punish me and I felt for sure my soul was damned.

The day before the abortion procedure, Gena flew in from Provo to be with me. The following morning I was wheeled into a room I remember very little about. The operating room was cold and sterile. Lights showered the room with an eerie brightness and all I could see were people with gloves dressed in white saying, "It will be over soon."

I could hear the noise of the suction and I could feel just enough sensation to remember it the rest of my life.

I wasn't the only one in the clinic that morning. Other young women were seated in the waiting room when I first arrived; no one spoke a word to each other and after the procedure, I remained in a recovery room for a short period of time. As the anesthesia wore off, I looked around; women just like me lay on separate beds not speaking a word to each other either.

Gloom permeated the room, which reminded me, of another time when people gather together: when someone has died, a hushed silence fills the room. If a word is spoken, it's barely whispered. Grief is shared from heart to heart but in somberness no one really knows what to say. I wanted to share a part of me that morning with a woman close by, knowing that my heart's deepest sorrow could never be shared with another human being that hadn't been in a similar room where life is ended even if no one knows without a doubt when life begins.

Yet, my grieving went too deep. There was nothing to share for no one else but me would have to learn how to live with what I had just done. I also felt something inside me die the morning of the abortion, a part of me that loves, cares and nurtures even the most insignificant creature that is living, and nothing can ever ease the heartache I feel for what I have done. Later that night, while trying to fall asleep in heart wrenching sorrow, I begged God to forgive me. Regardless of the circumstances, I felt taking a life was unforgivable and even if God forgives a sin like mine, what would it take to be forgiven?

Gena and I never mentioned what had happened. I know she grieved with me, but we didn't know what to say to one another. Perhaps there was nothing to say. The following day, she hugged me as we said goodbye at the airport. We shared tears, the kind that kindred spirits weep when they have always known each other's secrets, their dreams and all of their human fragilities and still love without hesitation.

Several weeks later I went home to visit my mother and there was a "fireside" held at the chapel that night. I was sitting in the front pew when the lights went out and the movie started. Soft music began to play and immediately I knew what the film was about. I wanted to run, but I knew I couldn't. Instead, I slithered into my seat, closing my eyes wanting to be anywhere else but there. Excruciating guilt welled up inside, and I knew that I had to leave as I fought back tears. Darkness closed in on me as if I was about to suffocate. I felt lights surrounding me with every eye watching. Of course, no one else knew what I was going through, but I knew this film was just for me. Right in front of me was a screen that appeared enormous. A young pregnant girl was seeking guidance; abortion was a choice she had been given. As the film progressed the message given was that abortion is a sin akin to murder. The message was clear…"Taking the life of an unborn child is a heinous sin and one that you may *never* be forgiven for."

Each spoken word flowed through me like a winter's chill—the words "heinous sin" played over and over like a broken phonograph record playing inside my head. How many times during my life had I heard the word heinous? Enough to know that heinous means evil, wicked, and abominable—I felt wicked, evil, repulsive and disgusting—that sin was the same as me, and even if God might be willing to forgive me, how could I possibly forgive myself?

Calmly, I rose from my seat. Methodically, I walked to the door as if nothing was wrong. My heart was pounding and my legs felt weak, as I desperately tried to keep myself from screaming. Tears had already soaked my face by the time I walked through the chapel doors, and I hung my head in shame wanting to die if for no other reason than to rid myself of the pain.

Fighting the cold night air, I walked home desperately trying to erase the images from my mind. I didn't even have to close my eyes to see the fetus recoil in its attempt to survive; this little clump of cells felt the pain inflicted by the instruments used to destroy its life.

Unable to silence my sobs, I gripped my arms around me. When I could no longer stand to see the images, emotional pain began to rise as a mighty tidal wave. I asked myself a thousand times, tormented by this question I could not answer, *"What have I done?"* Wishing with all my heart that I had stayed at home instead of attending the fireside, I continued walking. With each step, numbness took over. I wasn't crying anymore; in fact, I wasn't feeling any emotion at all. I felt dead inside.

Abortion was rarely if ever talked about. I knew so little. The only sex education I remember was abstention, and guilt if you didn't, but the leaders of the church decided young girls all over the world needed to see for themselves the horror of abortion. That night, I was certainly reliving the horror of my own abortion. What I hadn't seen beyond the sheets covering my body, someone else had captured on film.

The film showed the fetus as it was developing through each phase. During the abortion procedure, limbs were literally ripped from the body as the fetus was torn from the womb. I felt nauseous and emotionally traumatized by what I saw. That little lump of cells was actually a baby with fingers: toes, legs and arms, and I could even see the heart beat.

I had been in my fourth month of pregnancy when the doctor performed my abortion and what I saw in the film that night nearly destroyed me.

Perhaps many will say, "You deserved it after what you did," but nothing anyone can say would be any worse than what I have said to myself.

But not once did I ever hear the words, "You were raped, it wasn't your fault."

From that day on, I knew I could never be forgiven, and subconsciously I went out of my way to find those who would punish myself. Because something inside of me had died with the abortion, I became someone I didn't even recognize. Everything about me changed, including my values.

Within a few months, I moved away from my little one-bedroom house, yearning to start my life over, hoping I could somehow become the daughter my father always said I was. I wanted him to be proud of me, and I knew he could see my life on Earth as he watched from somewhere in Heaven. What was he thinking of me? I often wondered if I would have had the strength to tell my father if he had been living. Would I have trusted his love enough to know that he would never turn away from me?

After moving to Mesa, Arizona I found a new job and apartment. Fate was starting another chapter in my life, but once again it was being written with unresolved heartache and secrets from my past. I did what I had always done, buried my deepest feelings and started over.

I became promiscuous. I looked for and found men to date that would hurt me. After work I would stop at a nightclub, and I would always find someone to flirt with. This was a new me. Flirtatious without any intention to say no when the guy asked to take me home knowing exactly what he wanted. Today, I cringe at my scandalous behavior, and even though I felt used by the men I was with, perhaps what I didn't realize at the time was that I was only using them in transferring the pain I felt.

When I was young, I couldn't understand why God was punishing me but on the day of the abortion I became someone who deserved to be punished and abandoned by a God who, I had been taught, would not tolerate the least degree of sin. This traumatic procedure was a never-ending nightmare of anguish. I grieved in a way that I never got over, and my life was never the same. But this little secret was placed somewhere deep inside along with my unfinished grieving for my father, my failures and my childhood secret of sexual abuse.

Two

Should love hurt?

Love is symbolic of warmth and friendship. Love is also being who you are and allowing others to be who they are without forcing change but never, never should love hurt.

It was a Sunday afternoon, and I was sitting in Sunday worship. Across the aisle was a man who kept drawing my attention. As our eyes met, I felt our mutual attraction, but it made me uneasy. It was as though an inner voice was whispering, "You know him, but stay away from him."

Bobby and I lived in the same apartment complex and after seeing him in church, we met later again that week by the pool. That uneasy feeling didn't leave me, but something about the way he talked to me as he said, "When I first saw you, I saw the sadness in your eyes," made me think twice about my feelings. I was ready to throw caution to the wind he seemed so caring.

We were both raised in devout Mormon families and even though he had been inactive, he seemed to have turned his life around. Recently divorced, he was going to church every Sunday, paying his tithes and obeying the Word of Wisdom. More than anything, he wanted to be married in the temple.

In the weeks that followed, we spent quite a bit of time together. One evening, we had gone out to dinner, and the waiter spilled water on me. As the waiter mumbled an apology, he quickly tried to clean up the mess he made. Even though my dress was wet, I laughed and told him not to worry about it, but Bobby didn't think it was funny and told him so.

"You're a damn fool," he said. With that insult the waiter was clearly embarrassed, and frankly, I was shocked by his rudeness. I told Bobby that he had embarrassed the waiter and he shouldn't have. We finished our dinner in silence.

When we got to the car, I sat close to him. Once we were ready to leave, he put the car into drive when he should have put it in reverse and drove over a cement block. The car rocked back and forth until all four wheels rested on the ground. I laughed because it seemed so funny, but he didn't laugh. Instead he was angry with me. He said I tried to humiliate him. When I innocently said he was being silly, a darker side of him emerged.

Abruptly, he turned and shouted in my face, "Shut the fuck up." I immediately moved over in the seat as he continued yelling at me.

"Don't ever laugh at me, bitch."

Jolted by his reaction, I defended myself.

"I wasn't laughing at you."

"Like hell you weren't. Do you think you're better than me?"

Shocked more than anything, I argued with him until he leaned over just far enough to scare me, "Go fuck yourself bitch, no one insults me in front of other people."

I glared back and demanded that he just take me home.

He drove to my apartment complex, stopped the car and said nothing. I half expected him to walk me to my door, but felt relieved when he said, "What in the hell are you waiting for?"

In disbelief, I answered him, "I guess I'm not waiting for anything, Bobby." Opening the door on my own, I placed my feet on the pavement grateful that he stayed behind.

Bobby called me the following day at work to say he was sorry, but I wasn't interested in an apology, I didn't want to see him again, but at noon he came by the office with flowers in hand. He spent the next hour, over lunch, telling me how sorry he was for the way he behaved. Tearfully, he justified his behavior as he said: "I was completely out of line, I had a bad day at work and I'm sorry I took it out on you." He also explained that every woman he had ever been with had betrayed him and he was afraid I would do the same. By the time he drove me back to the office, all was forgiven.

There were two sides to Bobby, and he kept me guessing as to which one would show up when we were together. At times he was easy to be with, but in a heartbeat he could change, and I always felt on edge. Still, I continued to see him.

Several months later, Bobby made reservations at a local restaurant. That night he asked me to marry him. At first I didn't have an answer. There was a part of me that wanted to say yes and another part that didn't. Hidden in a secluded booth, I was persuaded by his sincerity and I felt sorry for him. No one had understood his pain. No one had cared about him. He had been a victim of child abuse and even though he had a volatile temper, I believed there was another side to him, one that would emerge once he felt safe with love.

The night air was cool as we left the restaurant. Bobby put his arm around me as we hurried to his car. He seemed excited about our future, but he was also insistent that we not wait. Suddenly I felt nervous. He had yet to place a ring on my finger, but I had just agreed to marry him. Perhaps it was the night air or maybe the urgency with which he spoke of our wedding date that sent a chill through me. I didn't want to rush into marriage, but Bobby was in a hurry! How I felt didn't matter.

After we had been engaged for a few weeks, I knew I needed to share my secret with him. Maybe I just needed to absolve my soul. My secret weighed heavily upon me, and I had been taught that there was only one way to be forgiven and that was through confession to the appropriate authorities. Bobby demanded absolute honesty from me, and I believed that by being honest with him he would learn to trust me.

Carefully, without telling him why, I explained that I needed to see our Bishop before I could agree to a wedding date. Suspiciously, he wanted to know why, but I wasn't ready to tell him.

After making an appointment, I went to see my Bishop. Knowing the reason for my appointment, the Bishop had arranged our meeting to be that of an official Church Court.

I really didn't know what to expect, but sitting before God's adjudicators on the eve of my judgment only reinforced my need to be punished. Three chairs were placed next to each other at the front of the room with one single chair placed in the middle facing the other three. The Bishop and his two counselors took their seats and told me to take mine. As I looked into the penetrating eyes of my Bishop—to me an almighty force—I felt myself disintegrate into a disgraceful little girl. It seemed to take forever for the words to come. At first, I didn't know where to start but once I did, I poured my heart out. I wept, as they remained silent, waiting for their response.

My Bishop was a forgiving man, and I sensed his compassion. He was kind and gentle when he asked pertinent questions, but one of his counselors couldn't quite conceive of any woman doing what I had done—aborting my child. I could see it in his facial expressions, and when I described certain details his eyes grew wide. He raised his eyebrows so high; they nearly flew off his face. Then he wanted more intimate details.

Even though I explained that my pregnancy was a result of date rape, he kept repeating the same question, "But you agreed to go out with this guy, didn't you?" and "After you went to his place you invited him into your apartment, didn't you?"

"Are you sure you didn't drink that night or act in any way that would lead him on?"

Humiliated beyond words, I felt like he was insinuating I couldn't be raped if I invited the rapist into my home.

I felt the tears would never stop as I waited outside the office while the three men, who held my fate in their hands, made a decision. The events of the church court replayed in my mind and I felt confused.

Once they had agreed upon their decision, I was summoned into the Bishop's office. That night disciplinary action was taken against me. It was the decision of the Court that I was to be disfellowshipped, which is a method by which a member's name still remains on church records but they are forbidden to partake of the sacrament or participate in Church callings for six months.

Even though I accepted their decision that night, I felt shunned, and the most devastating thing I felt was that in God's eyes I was still a sinner until I could atone, or feel sufficient sorrow to pay the price for my sins. As I walked away that night, I realized just how well acquainted I had become with sorrow and how the feelings of unworthiness had walked every step of the way with me since I was a child. What I desperately sought that night was to feel the healing power of my Savior's love. Longing to feel His gentle hands drying my tears, my heart was empty knowing that I would never be in His arms because I was a sinner.

I left the Bishop's office and drove home. I parked outside my apartment but instead of going home, I walked the short distance to Bobby's apartment. I knew he would be waiting to hear from me. As soon as I neared his door, a feeling of caution came over me. The moment I raised my hand to knock on his door, I quickly turned away but before I had the chance to run, the door opened and Bobby was staring me in the face. His eyes were stone cold and I knew that he was angry. Harshly, he told me to come in. That was the last thing I wanted to do, so I said it was late, and I would talk to him the following day.

He grabbed me by the arm and said, "Don't play your fucking games with me," as he jerked me inside.

Frightened, I told him to get his hands off me, but instead he threw me across the room, locking the dead bolt to the door behind. Then he forced me to sit down. Standing over me, Bobby demanded to know exactly why I went to see the Bishop.

My heart raced. I felt unsafe and threatened. My instinctive reaction was to say something that would calm him down, so I lied when I answered him, "The Bishop was busy and we never got a chance to meet." He jumped in my face, grabbing me by the shoulders, shaking me.

"You're a lying bitch," he yelled, "I saw your car over there for more than two hours."

Pushing him away, I answered, "This is insane, Bobby, and I don't even know what you want from me." By this time I was really frightened.

"You bitch. You know exactly what I want," he shouted. Terrified, I begged, "Please don't do this Bobby! I can't talk to you when you are like this."

Slapping me across the face, he yelled, "You're a lying whore," Still ranting, he demanded I tell him.

"What's the matter, stupid, cat got your tongue?"

He had me pinned against my chair. I felt like his prisoner being threatened, interrogated and humiliated. I tried in vain to convince him I hadn't spoken with the Bishop. I was frightened. His behavior was so irrational and volatile my only thought was to escape.

Back and forth he paced, stopping only to get in my face, "You'll pay for this, bitch," he bellowed.

He grabbed my shoulders and shook me violently, demanding an answer.

"Get your hands off me," I screamed.

But he didn't. With his face in mine, I saw the evil in his eyes and at that moment, I saw Bobby as a stick of dynamite, and anything I said could ignite the fuse, but I had no other choice, I had to tell him that I had been disfellowshipped.

"Just back off Bobby, and I'll tell you."

I don't know if I was more frightened or angry. He held me against my will and forced me to share my deepest hurt with him, a raging maniac, when he really didn't share in my pain.

Bobby moved far enough away and then I told him. "I can't marry you in the temple, Bobby, at least not for six months."

Swiftly, he lunged at me, I ducked and his fist barely missed my face as his hand slammed into the couch behind me. "You fucked men, didn't you, and then you had an abortion?"

He wanted to rip my face off; I could see it in his eyes. Fighting back against his own rage, he wanted to pound me into the ground.

What a fool I must have been. An hour had passed since I'd first knocked on Bobby's door, and I was just now realizing he already knew what I tried so hard to conceal.

With my heart racing, I asked Bobby how he knew. "I've never trusted you from the beginning," he said. "I knew you were a lying cunt underneath that perfect, rich little girl you pretend to be. Tonight you've proven who you really are."

He waved his arms self-righteously, and shook his fists at me as he explained that for the first time I was being forced to see myself as I really was. It was his duty, he said, to follow me that afternoon when I met with the Bishop. Then he quietly listened behind closed doors to every word spoken.

Feeling betrayed, and humiliated, I tried to stand up. I was through listening to him, and I was angry. Instantly reacting, he grabbed me and shoved me against the chair, "You're not getting out of here!" he yelled. Hurtling insults and demanding answers from me he wouldn't even let me answer. He wanted me to know how cheap and disgusting I was.

"You lied to me," he yelled repeatedly, "I thought you were decent but you're not." "At a loss for anything to say, I begged him to stop yelling at me. What I said only added fuel to the fire.

"Fucking whore," he said. Grabbing me by the hair he dragged me from the couch and threw me to the floor.

"How can you ever make this up to me?" he hollered with his face in mine.

Kicking and screaming, I struggled against him as he bashed my head against the floor. Paralyzed with fear, my mind was spinning but no matter what I said, he would mock me unmercifully.

"Please don't hurt me," he would sneer in my face. "Poor little bitch! What's the matter? You afraid of me?"

Pinning my hands above my head, he held me down, laughing because I begged him to let me go. But all too soon, his laughter turned chilling.

With his face inches from mine, he said I deserved to be punished for killing an unborn baby. He said I deserved to be punished for whoring around and cheating him out of a temple marriage. He threatened to tell my sisters about my abortion—he wanted to make sure everyone knew that it was I who was guilty of immorality.

He knew he had me, as my body went limp, and I stopped fighting him. For hours he had forced me listen to him rant. All the emotions pent up inside me exploded. I was hurting, but not from Bobby physically restraining me or bashing my head against the floor. Everything he said about me was true. My head was spinning, and I felt nauseous. I saw the same repulsive reaction earlier that night in the Bishop's office. With tears streaming down my face, I wept.

Slowly, Bobby lessened his grip on me.

"Go to hell, Bobby," I whimpered.

In disgust, Bobby lifted his body off mine and moved away from me. For a second, I thought I had a chance. I tried to get up and run for the door but he grabbed me and knocked me to the floor raging, "Where in the hell do you think you're going?"

Screaming for help, he clamped his hand over my mouth, and then, instantly, with both hands he reached around my neck trying to choke the life out of me. Gasping for air, I struggled. Wildly thrashing, I thought I was going to die. Loud pounding on the door stopped him as a neighbor yelled, "Is everything alright in there?"

Bobby let go of me and then hollered, "Nothing is wrong, so mind your own damn business." The neighbor walked away but Bobby also let me up from the floor.

As soon as he moved far enough away from the door, I made a break for it. With my heart pounding, I fumbled to unlock the deadbolt then I grabbed the doorknob. The second it opened; I was out of there. Terrified, I made my way back to my apartment and immediately locked the door behind me. Unable to believe I was finally home, I was also stunned and shocked at his behavior. I was outraged, shaking, and trying to absorb the intensity of the fear I felt for several hours when the phone rang.

On the other end of the line was a man whom I had dated in Utah. He had been given my telephone number from a mutual friend of ours. Recently, he moved from Utah to Phoenix to study for a degree in International Banking and he wanted to see me.

Bryce meant a lot to me, he had that wholesome, clean-cut missionary appearance, but I wasn't the same person he once knew, and I couldn't help but wonder what he would think of me if he knew the truth.

Needing to talk to someone, I poured my heart out to him telling him what Bobby had just done to me. Still shaking, it was difficult to talk to him but I was relieved and grateful that he had called.

"Please promise me that you'll never go near him again," he said and then with softness and genuine concern in his voice he said, "Janice, be grateful that you have seen what he is really like before it was too late. Now you can walk away from him."

"Can't we get together," he repeated, but I convinced myself that I didn't deserve him because of who I really was. Without explaining, I answered him, "It's too late, Bryce. I'm not the same person you used to know."

That night, I turned away from a man who was kind and gentle because I honestly had convinced myself that Bobby was the only one who would have me.

Bobby's cruelty and vicious words terrified me, but I must have felt I deserved what he said because I went back to him. I truly believed that underneath my pretty face was a despicable woman, and even though my reasoning defies all logic, I know that my feelings had been trapped inside long enough. Perhaps that is why I allowed him to hurt me enough to make me feel my pain. Maybe, I even believed that enough punishment would give me the right to be forgiven.

The next day after work, I stopped by his apartment. Still sullen and unfriendly, he opened the door.

Standing before him, I said words I didn't mean. "I'm sorry I lied to you, Bobby."

A deep sense of betrayal swelled inside me as I choked back my tears. As if to calm my beating heart, silently I whispered, *"This is my only choice."* In my heart I knew that no other man would marry me. I also needed to hear Bobby promise me that he would *never* tell another soul about my abortion.

Even though Bobby was moody, we spent the rest of the evening talking. He admitted his temper was a problem, "But I can change, Janice, it just takes the right woman for me to want to try."

"Don't you see?" he said. "I've wanted a temple wedding all of my life—when I met you, I believed it would happen."

He also wanted his father to be proud of him knowing that he had turned his life around. How better else than to attend the temple.

What I really wanted was assurance that no one else would have the chance to condemn me; Bobby gave me his word that he wouldn't tell anyone about my abortion.

Even though I was terrified of Bobby's temper, I convinced myself that what happened the night before was just another isolated incident and that it wouldn't happen again. I also made him promise that he would NEVER hurt me again, no matter how angry he became. He said, "I never intended to hurt you in the first place." Once again he asked if I would marry him.

My answer was yes.

Early the next evening, he handed me a tiny black box, and I knew it was a ring. Nervously, I opened the lid and tucked inside a pocket of velvet was a gold band with a sparkling exquisite marquis diamond.

Trying to show my excitement, I put my arms around him as my inner voice said, *"Say no Janice, just say no."* In my heart I must have known I was making a serious mistake but briefly, I let him hold me close. I didn't love him, even though I fooled myself into believing I did.

Every night after work, we walked around the temple grounds, a favorite place of ours, and planned our future. Beneath the starlit sky, Bobby said I was the woman that would change his life. Holding hands, as we walked through fragrant gardens filled with blooming flowers, we talked for hours. The air was brisk, so he put his arms around me shielding me from the cold. He wanted me to know all about him. His mother died when he was four. He lived with relatives that sexually and physically abused him. Later on, his father remarried, but that didn't end the violence in his life. To escape the abuse and a stepmother he detested, he ran away from home at the age of 14. Later, he joined the Navy, eventually becoming a Navy Seal during the Vietnam War.

Seeing tears fill his eyes, I believed he had a heart. I gently held his hand, telling him how sorry I was for the life he had lived. At that moment, I believed I could make things up to him.

Springtime is one of the loveliest times in Arizona, and I soaked in the attention he showered on me along with the sun. My heart, parched and withered from betrayal, felt nourished in the warmth of romance and a sense of belonging. Seeing this other side to him, I believed that all I had to do was nurture this side and he would change.

We spent a few days in the White Mountains sightseeing and hiking. One morning, I looked in the mirror, and the reflection I saw revealed a glow that hadn't been there before. Later on, Bobby took a photo of me standing beneath a tall pine tree.

One candid photograph, which I held on to for many years, revealed something lost and forgotten—a beautiful young woman still clinging to her hopes and dreams.

Once away from the cool mountain air, the valley brought me back to reality. No matter how hard I tried to love Bobby, I only brought out his anger, and he never let me forget it. Because of his volatile temper, I broke off our engagement several times, but he would come back begging my forgiveness. In tears, once again, he would recall memories of childhood abuse. In time, this became the only part of his heart he entrusted with me; in fact, it was our only means of bonding, one wounded heart with another.

One evening we were at the park, and I said something that offended him. He raised his voice and got in my face; I jumped up quickly and ran. He ran after me and blocked my way before I could open my car door. In the blink of an eye, he grabbed my keys. I begged him to let me go home. I was tired of fighting with him. He immediately threw me against the car pounding his fists into my chest.

With all my strength, I tried to push him away, but we struggled. Raging, he shouted, "What in the hell do you think you're doing? You're not going anywhere until I'm through with you."

He was hurting me as he twisted my face and held it against the window. "Make one sound, cunt, and I'll bash your head through this glass."

Pinned against the side of my car, I was terrified. He had my face tightly gripped in his hands, and I knew he meant what he said.

Fear raced through me. I was unable to break free as I struggled against him. Twisting my face, he dug his nails further into my checks. It was late in the evening and no one was around, but I screamed for help anyway. That's when he threw my keys as far as he could.

"Bitch, see if you can find your own fucking keys," He shouted, as he turned and walked away. It was dark by then, and with tears blurring my vision, I had a hard time finding my keys. I searched for them long enough to really be angry when I found them. Swearing to myself that my relationship with Bobby was over, he was a jerk. I was sick of his behavior.

The phone was ringing when I arrived home, but I didn't answer it. The next morning I left for work. When I returned home, he was parked next to my apartment. He yelled out his window for me to stop, but I didn't. Instead, I drove around Mesa for several hours until I thought he had left.

There was no sign of Bobby the next morning when I left for work.

Within an hour a dozen red roses arrived at the front desk with a card that read, "Janice, please forgive me. I love you."

For several days, a dozen red roses arrived at the same time, with his hand-scribbled notes, begging my forgiveness. Finally, I gave in and called him.

Bobby and I met for lunch that day, and he apologized incessantly for the way he behaved. Making excuses, he said he was terrified of losing me. When I abruptly left without settling our differences, he felt threatened.

"Don't ever walk away from me when you are mad and I won't get angry." He made it sound as though it was my fault he lost his temper.

Tears welled in his eyes as he held my hand and said softly spoken, "I can't live without you, Janice. Please don't be angry."

He spent my entire lunch hour making promises and convincing me that this time he meant all of them.

I went back to work that afternoon, and over the next couple of days he called me repeatedly at my office. Finally, he showed up one night when I was working late. Alone in the office, I was startled when he pounded on the door. I opened the door to a desperate man. Unshaven, it appeared as though he hadn't slept for days.

"Please let me in. Just talk to me, that's all I need and then I'll leave."

I walked away from the door, allowing him to enter.

Sobbing, he claimed he hadn't been to work for days. "Please, Janice, I'll do anything to keep you."

"You need to go home, Bobby. Tomorrow we can talk."

"I have nothing left to live for if I've lost you," he said.

He went on to cry his heart out and I was afraid he wouldn't leave—I wasn't sure what he was going to do, but finally he stood up from his chair and walked out of the office with his shoulders bent, sullen and broken-hearted.

The next day was Saturday. He called early in the morning to tell me that he would give me time.

"I know you're angry and you don't trust me," he said, "I have a problem, but I'm willing to go for counseling."

Later that afternoon, I tried to call my mother in Mexico to tell her the wedding was off. I had enough of Bobby. He pushed me too far, and I didn't want to try anymore. I was ready to give his ring back.

Instead of getting my mother, I reached my younger sister who let me know that my mother had made a trip to El Paso to finish buying items for my reception then Dianne said, "Janice, Mom has everything planned, aren't you excited?"

I didn't know how to answer. I put the phone down, and sat in my kitchen feeling the pressure. My thoughts were running wild. All I could think of was how I was going to break off my engagement now that the invitations had been sent and the arrangements made. I just couldn't tell her I didn't want to marry Bobby. Instead, that afternoon I fooled myself into believing that after the wedding it would be much easier to end my marriage if it didn't work out.

Three

Luna de Miel

Tonight is my wedding night, and now that I'm his wife, surely he'll love me and honor the vows we shared.

ince childhood, I dreamed of my wedding day, and finally that moment arrived. Nothing else seemed as important to me as being a wife and mother and to live happily ever after in a cottage filled with love.

On June 17, 1978, the morning of my wedding, yet another feeling of caution and dread came over me. As I sat on the edge of my bed, my eyes fixed on my wedding gown.

As if in a trance, my fingers lingered over its softness. Shouldn't my heart beat with excitement and anticipation? Shouldn't my face reflect a bride's radiant glow? I wondered.

This was to be my wedding day. A day once asleep in quiet slumber had finally awakened no longer to a dream, but reality.

Knowing it was too late to change my mind, I quickly silenced my foolish heart.

My thoughts returned to my sister's wedding gown, simple in design and yet splendid in its sweet and sacred reverence.

Wild and frantic thoughts pulsated through my heart. How had I arrived at this day so ill prepared in really knowing what was best for me?

Why did Bobby and I meet?

The feelings of familiarity, fear and attraction seemed to pull me into his world. A force beyond my understanding spoke of another time, perhaps unfinished business between two souls. I didn't love Bobby, I never have but I was drawn to him as though I didn't have a choice.

Bobby and I met in late January 1978, and became engaged in March of the same year. Three months later, I was planning to walk down the aisle and become his wife.

But on that day, I wanted to flee from the altar, proclaiming, "This is wrong."

But I didn't.

I ignored every warning sign. Mute and afraid, I gathered my dress close to my breast and prayed for blessings, miracles, and happy endings.

Susan, my oldest sister, was my Matron of Honor and my four younger sisters, all dressed in pale yellow, were my bridesmaids. I wanted my family to be proud of me. I had already made my choice and somehow it *had* to be the right one. I didn't want to be the one who always failed. Silencing my doubts, I tried on my veil as I held the gown up to myself. Still, my mind wandered far away. Softly, I wiped away my tears, telling myself they didn't mean anything, brides are notoriously nervous on their wedding day. But nothing felt real, least of all my feelings.

My deepest sorrow on my wedding day was the absence of my father. It had been four years since his death, but I was still his daughter and he belonged with me on my wedding day. Why had God taken him when I desperately needed him? For a minute, I thought about God. Who was He anyway? Did He really answer prayers? Did He love His children when they were bad or only when they behaved? For quite some time I had been angry with God and now I mourned the loss of my father, as if he passed away just yesterday.

The morning flew by, and soon it was time to meet with my family at the chapel. As I walked into the foyer, I once again felt a silent reminder that I didn't have to marry Bobby, the choice was still mine to make, but I was without the courage to run. Instead, with the organ playing, I walked down the aisle and confronted a man with two different faces. One face desperately desired to conquer his demons and the other side was an inner child of rage. Holding my brother's arm, I felt my world slip away, as Bobby's hand reached out to me.

Slowly, we faced the Bishop as Bobby promised to love, honor and cherish me as his wife, and in return I promised to obey him as my lawfully wed husband, and with those words I looked into his eyes and said, "I do."

Our evening was filled with excitement. Relatives painted Bobby's car with the words, "Just Married," and tied the traditional tin cans to the bumper.

Once the guests had left, Bobby and I gathered a few of our belongings and left for California.

It was late into the evening when his driving made me nervous enough to timidly speak. "Honey, don't you think you're driving a little too fast?"

He hit the brakes so suddenly that the car came to a screeching halt in the middle of the freeway.

The smell of burnt rubber permeated the air, and soda cans and melting ice spilled onto the floor of the back seat. Before I had a chance to react, he grabbed me by the hair and bashed my head against the dashboard.

"Fucking bitch," he yelled. "Don't you ever tell me how to drive again, do you understand?"

Scared out of my wits, I immediately pulled away from him.

Quickly, he surveyed the back seat of his car and became livid at the sight.

"Don't stand there looking stupid, bitch. Get the fuck out of my car and clean up the damn mess you caused."

The second my feet touched the ground I wanted to run. But where would I go? It was late at night and we were in the middle of the desert so I climbed into the back seat, furious and humiliated, holding back tears as I cleaned out the car. My head was hurting, and I felt the swelling from the bruises that were already starting to form while he drove the rest of the way in silence. I didn't dare say a word.

Early the next morning, we arrived in Anaheim. We checked into a motel, and I felt the hostility between us. I couldn't believe the terrible mistake I had made when I married him. There I was in the motel lobby, on my honeymoon, wishing the bridegroom would die of a sudden heart attack. This was worse than anything I had ever imagined.

Bobby refused to sleep with me on our wedding night, and during the day he hardly touched me. He was still angry because we weren't married in the temple. That first night, he destroyed any hope I had for a dreamlike honeymoon, and I stewed alone in bed planning his demise. I hated him, but I also wanted him to talk to me. I needed him to tell me why he behaved this way. Instead, he slept soundly while I tossed and turned all night.

After a few days at Disneyland, we drove to San Diego. We only stayed over one night, but I loved the view of the ocean and longed for my husband's gentle touch as proof that he loved me. But Bobby had a way of bringing me back to reality. He had purchased armloads of fireworks and put them in my care. I tucked Bobby's little treasures into a drawer inside the motel room without thinking about it, part of my habit of tidying up any room the minute I walked into it. In our hurry to pack and leave, I forgot they were there. So did Bobby.

We were an hour outside Mesa when Bobby suddenly remembered his fireworks, but it was too late. Nervously, I had to tell him I left them behind. That's when the real fireworks lit up the inside of the car.

"Stupid bitch," Bobby yelled, slamming on the brakes and banging his fists against the steering wheel. "There was only one thing I asked of you, and you fucked it up."

This time, I was prepared. I was already sitting close to the door. On the way home I didn't pretend to be a loving wife sitting next to her loving husband. No one wanted our honeymoon over more than I did. I started counting the minutes until we would be home.

The instant he put his key inside the lock and opened the apartment door, I felt sick. I didn't want to go inside. Memories of the night he kept me locked inside were on instant replay. Suddenly, even the smell of his apartment nauseated me. Quickly, I turned the lights on before carrying my luggage inside. Sitting on the edge of the bed, I felt empty. Too exhausted to even think, I felt numb. My honeymoon was nothing like I had anticipated. I honestly thought that nothing could be worse than our ruined honeymoon, but married life soon proved me wrong.

While dating, Bobby appeared to be a man of success. He dressed impeccably in designer suits and shoes that cost more than my whole wardrobe. The diamond on his finger always drew attention. He bragged about his success in commercial real estate and from the time we met, he lavished me with flowers, gifts and dinners out, but a few days after we returned from our honeymoon, he was penniless.

We argued over money; in fact, we argued over everything. No matter what I did, he complained and found constant fault in me.

"How could I have married someone so senseless," he sneered. "There isn't anything you do in which you use your head."

One night, Bobby wanted rice with his dinner. I poured water into a pan, filled it with rice and then left the room. When I checked back, the kitchen was filled with smoke. No matter how hard I tried, I couldn't air out the apartment quick enough.

Unfortunately, Bobby came home early, and that's when the yelling began. "I work hard all day while you sit on your fat ass doing nothing," he complained.

The awful smell only seemed to fuel his foul mood. I sensed the worst was yet to come, so I did everything I could to hasten dinner. He had me running around the kitchen, making excuses while he stayed on my tail.

"Lazy stupid bitch," he swore as he tried to get a drink, but the sink was filled with dirty dishes.

Furiously, he threw the glass against the wall. He shoved me, yelling, "Get the hell out of my kitchen before you burn the house down!"

His insults made me feel about an inch high and I got defensive. He didn't like that. With one swift shove, he sent me stumbling over my own feet. I fell, and he stood over me. I looked up just as his foot lifted and he swiftly kicked me. My hip felt the impact, and I doubled over in pain.

Crawling backwards, I screamed at him to stop. His blows were severe as I desperately tried to escape the next blow.

As I struggled to stand on my feet, he kicked me down again. Screaming, I begged him to stop and in horror, I asked him over and over, "What have I done?"

"You've been nothing but a disappointment to me," he hollered as he swiftly kicked me one last time.

Curled in a fetal position and sobbing hysterically, Bobby finally left me alone. I got up from the floor, looked around the kitchen and felt numb.

What had I done? Tears wet my face as I stood in our tiny kitchen. Shock and fear raced through me.

Bobby was volatile; I knew that before I married him, but I honestly believed once I became his wife, he wouldn't feel so threatened about losing me. What he had just done completely baffled me.

But after several months of constant faultfinding and bickering, his mood finally changed.

He was pleasant to be around and started taking me out to dinner and buying small gifts for me. We would double date with friends from our church, but it never failed: As soon as we were around other people he would put me down.

One afternoon, he was going over the bills we couldn't pay and accused me of causing our financial problems.

He demanded to know what I had done with his money. "What *can* you do right?" he demanded, but I didn't dare open my mouth. "Answer me when I speak to you, bitch."

I was afraid to say anything, realizing that no matter what I said, he would fly off the handle.

He stood up and stepped directly on top of my feet, jabbing me in the shoulders yelling, "You think you're smarter than me, don't you?"

Quivering, I stared back at him.

"Answer me," he bellowed. Still, I didn't say a word. He pounded against my shoulders while still holding me in place with his feet. I couldn't move and the humiliation and rage were building.

I wanted to spit in his face.

Finally, I said, "Jerk, get off my feet!"

That's when he shoved me hard enough to send me flying backwards.

Hitting hard against the floor, I tried to stand, but he grabbed me by the hair as he dragged me over to the chair.

Shoving me into the seat he demanded that I see how broke we were.

He humiliated me. I was nothing but a spendthrift, a spoiled little whore, and a baby killer that he detested, but since this wasn't his fault, he wasn't going to make sure our bills were paid.

"Fix the problem—or else!" he raged as he whacked the back of my head.

The following day, I took our bills, including rent, telephone and utilities and asked our Bishop if we could be helped from the ward welfare fund. The church paid our bills, and I was grateful but also extremely humiliated for having to ask for it.

Bobby hated liars, and according to him, I was the only liar in the house. But he had his own secrets.

He had failed to tell me that he had filed a petition for bankruptcy several months before our marriage. I found court papers he had hidden in a drawer.

He'd also neglected to inform me that he was still legally married when he first met me; he said it had been a year since his divorce was final.

I didn't dare confront him with what I knew. When he was angry, his eyes glazed over. He became evil incarnate.

One night, I closed the bathroom door, whether I locked it or the door was already locked when I shut it I don't remember, but Bobby watched me go in and close the door. He lightly knocked on the door and asked me what was I doing.

"What do you think I'm doing, for Heaven's sake?" I answered sarcastically.

Suddenly, he started beating on the door, demanding I open it immediately.

"What's wrong with you?" I screamed back at him.

When I didn't open it, he broke the door down and grabbed me by the hair, calling me a "fucking whore."

He knocked me off the toilet seat, and my head hit the side of the water tank, painfully bruising the side of my face.

Tears poured down my face. He stood over me, yelling that I was sneaky and perverted and that I was never to close the bathroom door again.

Bobby walked out of the bathroom leaving me completed stunned. I wanted to hurt him in return, but I knew what would happen if I tried. I was trapped inside that bathroom and if I made him angrier, I would have no way to escape.

Every time he hurt me, I wanted him to see me cry. I wanted him to feel my pain. I wanted him to feel bad for what he had done, but instead of feeling bad he ridiculed me for crying. "Poor little baby," he would sneer. "You just want me to feel sorry for you don't you but I don't." Instead he was angry that I was so weak. "Is that why you had an abortion?" Tauntingly he would ask.

"You don't have the guts to face anything you've ever done do you?"

I hated him every time he brought up my abortion.

"What do you think your family would say if they knew your secret?"

Panic would set in as I begged, "You wouldn't dare tell anyone in my family. You promised me you wouldn't."

Almost daily, I planned how I was going to get away from him.

It was although he knew my plans. He emptied my wallet of any spare money I had. He kept the spare key to his car and would take away my apartment key every time we had an argument.

In the meantime, when bills came in the mail, I started hiding them from him. I also kept the house immaculately clean and his shirts pressed without a single wrinkle. I never stayed at the grocery store too long and never talked for more than a few minutes on the phone. Early on, I picked up on every little thing that would tick him off, and then tried to eliminate that problem before it happened. But I wasn't always able to foresee what would set him off.

Prior to my marriage, I had been diagnosed with cervical cancer. My doctor scheduled me for surgery to have a small portion of my cervix removed two months after I was married.

After the surgery, I was brought back to my room and Madeline, a friend, stopped by to see me.

We were visiting when Bobby walked in the room. As soon as he saw her there, he picked up a chair by the door, threw it against the wall and walked out.

I was so embarrassed, I tried to make excuses for him, but my friend knew Bobby and said, "Janice, either he changes or you will be as miserable as my mother was in her marriage."

A few days later, I was home from the hospital, but unable to do much of anything, so our apartment wasn't always clean. Bobby was irritable and complaining that I wasn't doing my job. Then one night, just after I climbed into bed, he started caressing my body as he attempted to remove my nightgown. Quickly, I tried to stop him; he knew I wasn't to have intercourse.

Because I resisted his advances, he got angry and then he took me by force. "Isn't this what little whores really want?" he asked as he rolled over on top of me.

Desperately, I tried to keep my legs together, but he held my arms above my head and said, "Spread your legs, bitch, before I spread them for you." I struggled against him and begged him to stop but he didn't.

As he forced himself inside me, the pain was intense.

"How does this feel?" he whispered in my ear.

In agonizing pain, I squirmed in every direction trying to stop him. But he was heavier than I.

"Is this what you asked for the night you were raped?" Enraged, I wanted to scratch his eyes out. I loathed him for what he was doing to me but I couldn't stop him. Once he was satisfied, he rolled over.

I could feel the blood beneath me staining the sheets. Quickly, I gathered the top sheet and placed it between my legs as I hobbled into the bathroom, but within seconds the blood flowing from me created a puddle on the bathroom floor. I was too frightened to leave the bathroom so I tried to stop the bleeding myself. Sitting in a pool of blood on the cold bathroom floor, I sobbed and shook violently. Rocking back and forth, I felt like I was losing my mind and I knew Bobby would never let me reach the phone and call for help.

Finally, the bleeding seemed to subside, and I went back to bed. For days afterward, I bled heavily, but was too embarrassed to tell my doctor. When I went in for my six-week check up, my doctor said I had been foolish not to call him.

Once I was able to work, I found a job working part time for an attorney in Tempe, Arizona. Bobby had made me quit my job at a law firm a few weeks before our wedding, but we needed more income.

One morning as I was dressing for work, he came into the bathroom and stared at me. Nervously, I continued brushing my hair.

He sarcastically commented about my weight, even though I was underweight if anything.

He continued making insulting remarks and when that didn't provoke me he said, "You've always been spoiled and that makes you think you're better than me doesn't it?"

Irritated, I answered him, "For Heaven's sake, Bobby, I'm just trying to get ready for work."

"Want to be smart with me and put me down, bitch? Try it, and you'll be damn sorry."

I told him to stop it and just get out of the bathroom. That was all it took. He grabbed me around the neck and bashed my face into the sink. He took hold of my hair and pulled my face up, telling me to take a good look at myself. "What do you see, fucking cunt?"

Afraid, I didn't answer him, so he shoved my face closer to the mirror and answered for me. "A whore that calls herself a Mormon."

Tears streaming down my face, I looked at myself in the mirror, my lip was bruised and cut and my nose was bleeding. I swore back at him, calling him a son of a bitch. "Look what you've done to me, Bobby. And you say I'm sick?"

We struggled in the bathroom, as he yanked my hair and punched me a few times. "Leave me alone," I screamed and screamed while struggling to get away from him.

He had me trapped in the bathroom and I was terrified. Loud screaming only bounced off the walls but when he saw blood dripping from my face and the bruising he quit beating me. He then ordered me out of the bathroom and into our bedroom. I did as I was told.

Breathless and extremely agitated, he threatened me, "If you even try and leave this room, I'll beat the hell out of you."

I lay on the bed sobbing while promising that I wouldn't cause any more trouble with him. Holding myself close, I sought comfort in hushed silence. I cried but I was too afraid to do anything.

Feelings of entrapment engulfed me. I wanted to leave him but I didn't know how.

Where would I go? Whom could I call? Wild, but wildly scattered, thoughts overwhelmed me. I just wanted Bobby to be nice—I wasn't trying to fight with him but everything I did triggered deep rage in him.

And, if I did anything to remind him of his mother, such as leaving empty Coke cans inside his car, he would fly off the handle, accusing me of being a slob.

I was sick of being insulted and demeaned by my husband—certainly I didn't deserve the insulting remarks and name-calling, even if I wasn't a perfect wife.

Since Bobby was far from a perfect husband, I argued right along with him. I fought back when he hurt me and I joined with him in name-calling, but I felt badly about it.

Time and again, I was humiliated when others, especially my sisters, overheard Bobby and me attempt to out-scream one another.

Perhaps, if I could just stop reacting and walk away from him he would stop. Thinking this way only made me feel worse—I didn't want to ignore him or walk away, I wanted him to stop humiliating and hurting me.

I must have cried myself to sleep, but when I awoke, I felt extremely discouraged.

The room held an eerie feeling of evil.

My lip was swollen and my head still ached. Carefully, I tiptoed to the closed door. Bobby was watching TV in the living room.

I felt brave enough to quietly open the bedroom window and run. The night air was cool, and the parking lot was empty. Alone and frightened, I walked up and down the street not knowing where to go.

Choking back tears, I swore at my husband. I loathed him and I was scared to death of him.

Without really having a place to go, I entered a fast-food restaurant. Sitting alone in a booth, I didn't have enough money to buy so much as a drink, and I felt stupid just sitting there.

After I had sat inside the restaurant for a while, my courage to leave him mellowed. Besides, I didn't have a quarter to call anyone but even if I did I wouldn't have used it. An hour later, foolishly, I returned home.

When I checked the window, it was locked, so I had to knock on the front door but Bobby wouldn't answer it. I sat by the pool for a couple of hours until he finally came outside, left the door wide open and went back in. He didn't say anything when I walked in, and kept his eyes glued to a movie he was watching.

As I was dressing for bed, he came into the bedroom.

Bracing his arms against the doorframe, he laughed and said, "You're sure a dumb bitch. What are you trying to prove?"

In defeat, I said, "What do you want from me?"

"A wife, bitch, not a whore and not someone stupid."

"It's always my fault isn't it, Bobby?"

Sneering, he said, "No one that knows you would ever believe you aren't the cause of our problems."

I was so sick of having him throw "my problems" into my face. I turned away from him and pulled down the covers to get in bed.

"What in the hell do you think you're doing?"

"I'm going to bed because I'm tired."

"Get your fucking ass out of my bed. You left me, remember? You may think you're good at playing games, but no one plays them better than me. Now get the hell out of my room. I don't care where you sleep, but it won't be in here."

With my pillow, I made a bed on the couch, but he stayed in the living room with the TV blaring most of the night.

One afternoon, Bobby couldn't find a client's earnest money deposit. He accused me of losing it. He stormed into the house trashing everything in sight. Frightened, I started looking for it with him. The check wasn't anywhere. I always panicked when he was like this and I had good reason. He grabbed me by the arm and began twisting it. He demanded to know what I had done with the check.

"Let go of me," I begged. "I haven't seen it."

Slapping my face, he yelled, "Find that fucking check, or else!"

He let go of my arm and shoved me into the bedroom. He pulled a drawer out and dumped the contents on the floor. Shoving me to my knees, he towered over me demanding that I search through scattered papers.

When I didn't find it, he grabbed me by the arm and threw me across the room.

"Just find it!" he yelled.

My heart pounding, I rifled through the closet, throwing things around the room. I even tried begging him to calm down. I was scared, but he was blocking the doorway trapping me inside.

Like a chicken with its head cut off, I scurried around the bedroom. Searching inside drawers and pulling books off the shelves, I became hysterical knowing that I wasn't going to find it.

Sobbing, I pleaded, "I've never seen the check, Bobby. I didn't put it anywhere."

That's when he struck me. The sting of his hand reeled my head and instantly brought tears to my eyes. My check burned, and instinctively, I wanted to fight back. Instead, I clenched my fists, and closed my eyes waiting for the next blow.

I turned around to face him, tears streaming down my face.

"I don't know where it is!"

Bobby grabbed a huge handful of my hair and threw me to the floor.

Kicking me, he said, "I'm going to kill you, bitch, if you've fucked up my deal."

Then the phone rang. He stopped yelling long enough to answer it. It was the escrow officer, asking Bobby if he had located the client's check.

I heard Bobby tell him that he was still looking, and that he would soon leave for the office. The moment he put the phone down, he returned to stand over me.

Irate, he said I made him look like a fool. Bobby paced the floor, extremely agitated.

Trembling, I waited until he leaned close into my face and said, "Bitch, if that check is lost, you're dead."

I was sobbing as he walked toward the door. When I heard the door close behind him, I bawled. I touched my face; it felt tender and sore as I brushed away my tears. My back hurt and it was difficult to move.

Outraged, I ran into the bathroom to wash my face.

Then I knew what I had to do. A light clicked on inside my brain. I didn't have to take it; I could get the hell out.

I grabbed a suitcase and threw in some clothes as fast as I could, scared half to death that he would catch me before I had time to escape.

Each time I threw a sweater or pair of jeans into my suitcase, I panicked and ran around in circles.

My adrenaline was pumping, and I was shaking like a leaf. I ran to the window, trying to see outside to the parking lot, and then I hurried back into the bedroom and continued emptying out my drawers. Then it dawned on me: I wasn't prepared to leave. I had no money, no car and nowhere to go.

Suddenly, the front door flew open. His intrusion brought me back to reality, and I couldn't hide my suitcase fast enough.

Furiously he threw me onto the bed, grabbing me by the hair. He put his face in mine and said, "You filthy cunt. If you leave me, I swear I'll tell everyone you had an abortion."

I stared back at him, wanting to spit in his face.

He demanded I answer him. "How does it feel knowing you killed a baby? How can you live with yourself?"

I wanted to scream back at him, "I can't, Bobby. I hate myself. Can't you see that?"

My hands ached to reach up and slap his face. I was so angry with myself for not running out the front door screaming for help. Did it really matter whether I had a place to go? Sleeping on the streets would have been safer.

How could anyone hurt another person the way he would hurt me? God, I hated him! I was emotionally exhausted from hurting so deep. Inside my heart my wounds were bleeding.

Throwing my head back against the bed, he released his hold and walked out of the room.

Once I heard the front door slam, I knew he was gone. No longer scared, my anguish and sorrow broke through a dam of repression. In agony, I prayed, "What's wrong with you, God? Why won't you help me?"

Unable to stop the tears, I cried until I was exhausted. I stayed in bed the rest of the afternoon. When I awoke, it was dark in my bedroom. The sun was setting, and I felt night drawing near. Gloom filtered out the soft glow of the sun, just before it dipped beneath the Earth, and I felt damp with desolation.

I'm not living anymore, I sobbed. I felt dead inside, as fear and darkness enveloped me.

Later that night, Bobby returned home with a beautiful bouquet of red roses, as if that would erase the horror he'd caused.

He was despicable, and yet each time he put his arms around me, I allowed him—and I pretended to love him as I returned his cold embrace. He apologized for his atrocious behavior that afternoon and casually admitted that the check he accused me of losing had been clipped to a file inside his briefcase.

Silently, I whispered, "*Just don't feel anything Janice, least of all your pain.*"

Madeline was my only close friend. I started calling her when I needed a place to stay overnight. But as soon as Bobby found out I was with her, he would show up at her house threatening her if I didn't come home with him.

One afternoon when I refused to go home with him, he calmly turned away and left. He later called to accuse me of having sex with Madeline. "That's why you've run to her isn't it?"

I would hang up and he would call back. The phone never stopped ringing, but I was afraid that if I didn't answer he would return. I stayed with Madeline for several days, but I felt guilty involving her. I knew that I couldn't stay with her forever, and I didn't have a way to get to work. I called my boss to tell him I was sick, but I couldn't keep that up forever, either.

I was ready to file for divorce. I knew of a Mormon attorney and called his office to make an appointment. That afternoon, I went in and explained my situation and he explained his fee. I wasn't sure I could pay it, but I said that somehow I would get the money. I asked this attorney how single men would see me once I was divorced

Leaning back into his plush chair, he said, "Divorced women are like used cars. Men that can afford to buy new ones never shop in the used car lot, so chances are women like you remarry lemons just like they did in the first place."

"Then maybe I should fix the lemon I've got rather than trading him in for something worse, since a decent man would now consider me a used car."

He smiled and said, "Probably."

I went back to Madeline's townhouse feeling more confused than before. On the third day, I saw Bobby's gray Lincoln coming around the corner. I ran inside just as he slammed on his brakes.

Bobby jumped out of his car and opened his trunk while we were peeking out her window. Throwing all my clothes on her front lawn, screaming obscenities, he yelled, "You're a sick bitch. Now, you're fucking Madeline," loud enough for everyone to hear.

The neighbors flocked to their windows, and some ran out their front door watching him rant and rave, while my shoes, clothes and underwear were flying out of his trunk. Once he was through dumping my wardrobe, he made the same grand exit out of the parking lot with his car tires burning rubber as he flew over speed bumps and around corners.

At first, Madeline and I looked at each other in complete shock, and then we started laughing.

We were in stitches at what we had just witnessed. Madeline's lawn had once been green, but it was now covered in white.

I went running around in the middle of all my clothes waving my arms in the air screaming, "Madeline, it snowed in Arizona, but only in your front yard!"

Then I sat down and cried. The whole scene was so incredibly funny, yet so incredibly sick.

What I remember about Madeline was that she had grown up in an abusive home, and she wasn't much stronger than I. Even though she remembered the abuse her mother went through, she also remembered that her father changed once he became active in the Mormon Church. Madeline and I talked about this at great lengths. She felt Bobby had the potential to change. Between the two of us, I was convinced it was too soon to give up on my marriage.

Later that day, I called Bobby and told him I was ready to come home. He cried that afternoon telling me he was so afraid of losing me. It was his fear that made him toss my clothes on Madeline's front yard. It was my inability to love him that made him react violently. He hugged me, and we both cried, pledging our love and commitment to one another. He was going to change; he promised again and again to never hurt me again. To my everlasting regret, I believed him.

The memory still sickens me, but that afternoon we picked up my clothing and stuffed it inside his trunk. Believing in his sincerity, we drove away from Madeline's townhouse.

Sitting close to the man who had insulted me and battered me both physically and emotionally since the day we met defied all logic, but emotional neediness defies all strength and courage—and that's why Bobby had such a hold on me.

Several days later, Bobby slammed the door behind him. He was home from work and things hadn't gone well for him and I was to blame.

"Get the hell out of my life," he said. "What have you done today to make life better for me?" he shouted.

I couldn't answer him fast enough. I tried to think of something to say. Then I told him that I was sorry he had such a bad day.

"Go to hell, bitch, you're not sorry about anything."

Scared of what he was going to do next, I slowly walked toward the door grabbing hold of my purse on the kitchen table.

"What do you think you're doing?" he yelled as he jumped in front of me.

"I'm leaving, Bobby."

Shoving me backwards he shouted, "Like hell you are."

I struggled against him, trying to get away. I broke free long enough to grab the phone but he yanked the cord from the outlet. He slammed me up against the wall, and I screamed. My neighbor, Cindy, heard the noise from our apartment and she called the police. Cindy then pounded on our front door shouting at Bobby that the police were on their way. Bobby let go of me, and I ran outside the apartment. From a pay phone I called my sister and she came to get me.

The police had to knock down our front door. Bobby refused to open it, and fearing I was still inside, they took drastic measures. Bobby was arrested that afternoon, and later on I spoke to the arresting officer. He told me I needed to come to the police department and press charges against Bobby.

I asked how long they could keep him locked up, and they said maybe a couple of hours. That wasn't long enough. Even if I pressed charges there was still no guarantee that Bobby wouldn't be out before I made it home. I was terrified of what he would do to me so I refused to do it.

"Don't ever call us again," I was warned. "Don't waste our time if you're not willing to press charges."

Even though I didn't call 911, Bobby still blamed me that he had been arrested. He was livid when he said, "If you ever put me behind bars, you'll regret it."

He reminded me that he had been in the Navy Seals during the Vietnam War and killing meant nothing to him—he could twist my neck in a heartbeat.

Later that evening, Bobby appeared at my sister's. I was the only one at home that night when I heard someone pounding against the door. Knowing that I shouldn't, I opened it. Bobby immediately entered grabbing me by the hair. For the first time since I met him, I knew he had been drinking. With his face in mine he threatened me. I would never be safe. He would destroy me and tell everyone about my abortion. Then he started pulling me out the front door yelling that I was his wife and he would hurt anyone that came between us.

Struggling against him, I begged him to stop.

"Just get help, Bobby," I cried.

Terrified, I didn't want to get inside his car. I hated the sight of his car, but he had power over me. Once inside, I didn't dare say a word. I wasn't about to beg for mercy; instead I was terrified of what he was going to do next.

Neither of us said a word to each other. Empty cans of beer rolled around on the back floor. Between periods of intense silence he would blame me for his problems.

"You've betrayed me, Janice," he said with tears streaming down his face. "I can't live without you, but you are destroying me."

The moment we arrived in the apartment parking lot, he threatened me with my life if I made a sound and I didn't. That night he didn't speak to me and I was grateful. Several days later he returned home with a bouquet of yellow roses.

Even though I may have been sexually naïve growing up, I knew something was wrong with my husband's sexual behavior. Bobby was not only unloving outside the bedroom, he was unable to be sexually intimate.

Bobby wasn't interested in a loving relationship. I expected some foreplay or at least a tiny spark of passion between the two of us. Perhaps I was unrealistic, maybe I watched too many romantic movies, but I felt degraded doing things his way.

When he wanted sex, what he really wanted was for me to perform oral sex.

He would make the first advance and then he wouldn't touch me. At first, this confused me, but it didn't take long for me to understand that I wasn't to expect pleasure in our lovemaking, unless I was purely selfish.

I adamantly objected many times. It just didn't feel right, and I wasn't being selfish. I thought sex was an act of love between two people.

We constantly argued over the way he wanted sex. For an excuse, he said my body didn't do enough for him, and I actually believed something was wrong with me.

But one night I was indignant and unwilling to do as he said. It was repulsive to me, and it felt disgusting to have him hold my head in a certain position while being rudely persuaded to perform oral sex.

Reluctantly, he turned over, as though he was going to sleep. Suddenly I felt his foot kicking me in the middle of my back. He knocked me onto the floor and held me captive backed into a corner.

Punching me in the stomach, he said, "Who the hell do you think you are?"

"Please don't do this, Bobby," I begged. Grabbing the back of my head by the hair, he made me look him straight in the face. "You're nothing but a cunt, remember? You're a whore that spreads her legs for strangers. Even if you don't want me, you're not strong enough to refuse me, now get your ass back in bed."

Bobby crawled over the bed to his side, waiting for me to submit myself to him.

Degraded beyond words, I wanted to run but it was dark outside. Where would I go even if I could escape from him? What about my clothes? Could I get to them before he turned on me again?

I knew I couldn't. After I reluctantly climbed back into bed, he forced me to perform oral sex. Fighting back tears, I slowly did as I was told, while I kept gagging, which made him irate.

He grabbed my head and pushed my mouth down as far as it would go. Even when he ejaculated, he still refused to lessen his grip on me. I struggled against him, humiliated.

When he was ready, he released his hold on me. Trembling with anger, I turned my back on him.

He leaned over my shoulder and whispered, "There now, was that so bad bitch?"

I tried to silently cry myself to sleep. But sleep didn't come very easily that night. I lay awake tossing and turning hating my body and feeling repulsed by the taste in my mouth. Feeling completely destroyed as a human being, I realized how close I was to murder. With the rage I felt, I knew I was capable of killing my husband.

How had my life turned to this? Tears streaming down my face, my pillow soaked and my head pounding, I tried to understand myself. Was this relationship all I deserved? Was God really that angry with me? Or had he simply abandoned me because I had sinned?

I gently touched my face. I didn't think it was so grotesque, and as my hands followed every contour of my body, my skin felt soft and curvaceous and tightly toned.

A voice inside me wanted to scream, *"What's so wrong with me?"*

One afternoon, sick of being blamed for everything, I stood up to him when he started throwing unpaid bills in my face. Shaking like a leaf, but indignant that I was being blamed, I shouted, "The only reason we don't have any money is because you aren't making any."

Slowly, he took a few steps toward me, like a wild cat sneaking up on his prey, but I didn't move away from him. I was going to fight back this time.

Looking me straight in the eye, he sarcastically said, "Do you want to repeat what you just said?"

At that moment I did, so I answered him, "When you bring home a paycheck, Bobby, our bills will be paid."

First, he hit me with both hands against my shoulders, shoving me backward, and then he dared me to say it one more time. That's when I regretted opening my mouth. I frantically tried to take the words back. I really was sorry for saying them, not because they weren't true, but because I had provoked him.

With one blow, he knocked me to the floor and started throwing punches. Terrified, I was screaming, but this didn't stop him. Bobby was out of control. He beat me from the neck down with his fists.

The wind knocked out of me, I lay helpless as he kicked me one last time and told me to get up. Humiliated, I slowly picked myself up off the floor. By his tone, I knew he was finished for now and I was free to walk away.

The sun was sinking below the Earth as my heart was sinking below the deepest portion of my being. What a poor wretched woman I had become, trapped like a bird whose freedom had been taken away. I desperately wanted love, and I was tired of living on the hope that tomorrow he would be someone different. I wanted to fly away on moonlit beams to a place that offered me a minute's peace, but instead of taking power away from him, a timid voice, one that I knew to be my enemy, silenced any courage I had. In its place was left a whining little girl frantically begging for someone to answer her, *"Where will I go, how will I ever get away from him?"*

I walked into the bathroom, unable to look at myself, as I meticulously got dressed for bed. Pouring my thoughts into what I was doing, feeling too tired to think or run, and hurting over every inch of my body, I finally glanced into the mirror and saw the bruises. I touched my body and felt the physical pain, but nothing compared to my despair. I crawled meekly into bed, silently praying that by morning this nightmare would go away. Somehow, I would come up with a plan.

I waited until he was asleep. I carefully got out of bed and searched through his briefcase until I found a check. Would it be enough to cover a plane ticket? I didn't care. I took the check and carefully tucked it in a pair of shoes.

The next morning, he awoke and dressed for work feeling satisfied that I had nowhere else to go. But this time he was wrong. I felt brave enough to ask a neighbor I barely knew to give me a ride to the airport. I bought a one-way ticket to Salt Lake City. I would stay with my sister until I could figure things out.

Four

Before it's too late

Listen to the whispering in your heart; listen before it's too late. There's only one choice to make—do it for yourself!

My sister, Diane, was attending Brigham Young University in Provo, and my mother was visiting with her family in the Utah area. Once I arrived, I confessed to my Mother the terrible mess my life was in.

I must have been undecided, even though I swore I would never return to him, because I called Bobby a few days later. I wanted him to know that I was far enough away from him and this time I wasn't coming home.

I didn't owe him the courtesy of a phone call, but perhaps I just wanted to hear him beg for mercy or say how sorry he was.

It's possible that in my delusional thinking I really didn't want a divorce; I just wanted him to change. But the memory of his violent temper, his rage and the beatings spoke for themselves.

Bobby wasn't going to change and I knew that from the deepest part of my being. Over the next few days, we spent hours on the phone talking, but a silent voice kept on whispering, *"Leave him, Janice and you will be okay."*

His remorse and the sound of his weeping didn't change my mind at first. I had made up my mind, and I wasn't coming home. That's when he threatened to kill himself. I had sensed his despondency, and I really believed he would, so I gave him my sister's phone number.

A day or two later, I was still in Provo with my sister when I received a phone call from Mesa. The voice on the other end was a counselor in the Bishopric. Bobby had been to see him "more repentant and humble," he said, than anyone he had counseled with before.

"Your husband is severely depressed and I'm quite worried about him, he is threatening suicide." He went on to say, "He deeply regrets the harm he caused you."

"But Janice," he said, "Bobby loves you. He hasn't stopped crying or left his apartment since you left him."

He also agreed with me when he said, "Your husband does have problems, but he is willing to work on them."

He seemed to know my husband better than I did, but still I didn't know that I believed him and I was afraid. I continued to pour my heart out to Brother Dunhill. I told him how volatile and abusive Bobby was, and asked him how he could guarantee my personal safety if I returned?

I didn't really want to return, but Bobby had a sick hold on me. He was in my head, controlling how I felt and what I did. I was the weak and he was the conqueror. When he told me I was helpless, I believed. When he told me I was stupid, I believed. But when he told me I would never escape from him, I didn't want to believe.

After months of living with someone as erratic and explosive as my husband, I had somehow found the courage to leave. It was the right thing to do and I knew it. At first my husband had almost convinced me that I was the crazy one. I needed to fix myself. But even if I had problems, I didn't feel safe with him, so I didn't understand why someone else had enough power over me to convince me that I should return.

Where was my voice? What had happened to my strength?

I didn't understand, but deep inside I had no doubt that if I returned to Bobby, I would never again find the courage to leave him.

It took nearly a week of many phone calls before Brother Dunhill convinced me our marriage was worth a second chance.

"You just can't walk out on him without giving him a second chance."

He pleaded with me to be forgiving, and by doing so I could help save Bobby's soul. He told me about the first time he met Bobby and how impressed he was that this man was willing to do anything just to turn his life around and be active in the church.

But most of all, he said, Bobby wanted a temple marriage. He reminded me that to be married in the temple, Bobby would have to be worthy; therefore, he would need to get his life in order.

"This is something you can both work toward," he said and reminded me that I had my own problems to work on before I would be in good graces with God.

He was right; my membership had not been fully restored.

Then he said, "Shouldn't this be a time you work on your problems together? Bobby is willing, shouldn't you be also?"

I didn't want to return, and I knew that I shouldn't. I agonized over the decision and for once I needed to hear, "Janice, follow your heart, you know what you need to do," but I had been so conditioned during my life to listen and follow the counsel of my Church leaders that I didn't listen to myself.

Still undecided, I sought the advice of my Uncle, who lived just outside Provo.

He was also a Bishop, and I was sure he had enough experience to understand my situation. I don't remember whether my Uncle made a phone call to Brother Dunhill, and because of that he trusted in the Brother's advice, or whether he felt that if Bobby was sincerely repentant our marriage was worth saving.

In any event, he counseled me to return.

Later that week, reluctant and frightened, I boarded the plane.

When the plane landed in Arizona, Bobby was waiting. In his hands was a beautiful bouquet of red roses, with delicate sprigs of baby's breath.

"I love you," he said, "and I promise never to hurt you again."

Bobby was elated to have me home. He had a gift for me, wrapped in an expensive box from a department store, one I knew we could never afford. A stunning silk nightgown lay carefully inside. He made love to me, caressing my body and telling me how beautiful I was. He was so sorry for his behavior— he wanted to start our marriage over again.

But disconnection notices and unpaid bills were also sitting on the kitchen table, and I had to wonder if the rent had even been paid.

In the weeks that followed, we had an interview with our Bishop and we were told that in a year, providing we did as we were told, we could be sealed in God's Temple.

This was the goal we were told to work toward, and the blessings we would receive from entering God's Temple would improve and bless our family.

We were advised to faithfully attend our church meetings, hold family home evening, pay our tithing and be active in church callings. The Bishop agreed to pay for our counseling from the ward budget, but we would have to meet with a church-approved psychiatrist.

Bobby was anxious to go; he thought counseling would help me. During our first session, Bobby used the hour to complain about what bothered him about me. The following session, the psychiatrist gently told Bobby he had a few problems to work on himself. Bobby jumped from his chair and started shaking his fist at the psychiatrist. He accused him of taking my side.

"What the fuck do you know? You don't live with this bitch," Bobby shouted at him. "You may have a degree hanging on your wall, but you're dumber than shit."

After that, Dr. Hunt didn't dare refer to Bobby's problems. It was apparent to me that Dr. Hunt didn't have any more guts than I did to stand up against Bobby, so we started focusing on my failures as a wife that made my husband angry.

One afternoon, Dr. Hunt had me come in alone. During our session, he explained to me that Bobby was controlling me by his behavior. He recommended I do something different when Bobby became angry to throw him off guard. When our session ended, I was completely confused.

One week later, Bobby came with me to our next session. Dr. Hunt let us both know that what we needed to work on was "behavior modification." He explained to Bobby that he would have to work with me. Then he turned to me and said, "It is imperative that you not react in the same way when Bobby loses his temper."

I wanted to know how that could be possible when Bobby was beating me.

"Well," he paused for a moment, scratching his head and toying with his eyeglasses, "What do you normally do when Bobby raises his voice? Do you argue back with him?"

"Sometimes," I answered. I leaned closer to his desk really wanting to know what magic cure he had for Bobby's violent behavior. A little apprehensively, I asked, "What are you suggesting I do, Dr. Hunt?"

"I don't know," he answered, "but you can whistle a tune or recite poetry, that should throw him off guard."

Suddenly, the mental scene of me reciting poetry flashed before me, and just the thought of me whistling a tune when Bobby got in my face, made that suggestion not only ludicrous, but also life threatening.

Bobby nearly rolled off his chair with laughter. He told the psychiatrist that he knew for sure he was crazy.

"First of all," he said, "I don't need your help. Work with this bitch, she's the one with the problem."

We both walked out of his office completely baffled. I had to wonder who needed more help, this doctor or me. Needless to say, I never returned and neither did Bobby.

Life with Bobby really didn't change. But my membership in the Church was fully restored and within five months of our marriage I was pregnant. I wanted to feel joy, but the feelings weren't there. The afternoon that I received the test results from my doctor's office, I was torn between excitement and fear.

Bobby was five years older than I was and for years he desperately wanted a child. I felt that having a baby would save our marriage. I must have believed that somehow the baby would do what I had not been able to accomplish— softening Bobby's anger.

Later that evening, I shared my news with Bobby and his reaction frightened me. I put my arms around him and gently kissed him as I said, "Honey, I'm pregnant."

He pulled away from me and said, "Am I supposed to trust that you won't kill this baby like you did the last one?"

His coldness spoiled another moment in my life that I had always dreamed of. He had robbed me of precious moments that should have been filled with joy. I turned away to hide my tears. I didn't want him to see how deeply he had hurt me again.

Even though I was desperately unhappy, I was good at pretending otherwise. I was excited about being an expectant mother. What would it be like to give life to this baby, carry it inside me and feel it move? The world around me silenced for just a second. I sat quietly outside by the pool, feeling the heat of the Arizona sun. The air, filled with sweet fragrant orange blossoms, reminded me of the days when I first arrived in Arizona. My hopes and dreams soon shattered, and the choices that followed changed my life forever. Reality, as cruel as it can sometimes be, reminded me how precarious elusive dreams really are, but on that day, I promised God that I would not fail Him as a mother.

Bargaining with God was my last hope and I prayed to the only one who understood my needs. *"Please God, let this be a new beginning."*

No matter how much my husband reminded me of my failings, I knew I would be a loving mother. For weeks, all I could talk about was "the baby," and how excited I was about becoming a mother.

The marital tide changed, and for a while Bobby seemed bewildered, as if he didn't know how to behave. He stopped finding fault in me; in fact, he was calm when he spoke. He left every day for the office instead of staying home. We had friends over for dinner, and we went out to movies. The change felt like a breath of spring air flowing through open windows in a still basement. I felt hopeful. I even believed Bobby was settling down. During this time in my marriage, I was happy. Any loving touch from my husband warmed my heart, and I gave thanks each night for soft-spoken words of kindness—how I hungered for love.

I was still working part time, and I splurged once in awhile buying baby clothes and preparing a nursery. Without feeling the tension at home, I was excited to show him anything new I had purchased for the baby. I felt free to come and go. I honestly believed Bobby would never hurt his unborn child. I even believed he felt a greater respect for me.

One hot July afternoon, when I was seven-and-a-half months pregnant, Bobby wanted me to go for a ride with him. We had just entered the freeway when he said, "I know you're planning on leaving me."

"Whatever makes you think that?" I exclaimed.

Bobby and I were getting along. He was nice. I certainly wasn't planning a way to escape, so I denied it.

"You're a fucking liar, bitch," he screamed at me.

Before I could absorb what was happening, he struck me across the face. I immediately panicked. I had been in the same situation before and hated being trapped in the car worse than a closed off room when he was explosive. I begged him to stop the car. All he did was yell louder, weaving in and out of traffic. I tried to grab the keys from the ignition, but he grabbed my hand before I could. I tried to break free and he slammed on the brakes pulling off to the side of the road. He slugged me hard enough in the side of my stomach to knock the wind out of me as he pulled back on to the freeway. Terrified that he had hurt the baby, I froze in my seat. I didn't dare move, but I couldn't stop screaming while Bobby was yelling, "Shut the fuck up or I'll kill us both."

Within minutes, he exited the freeway and found a deserted street with an empty field and apartment complex close by. He pulled over, yelling, "Get the fuck out of my car."

At first, I refused. Then, thinking of the alternative, I leapt out. He immediately threw the car into reverse. Then burning his tires, he drove right for me. I screamed at him to stop, terrified that he would run over me.

An empty field stood a short distance away from the apartment complex. I ran toward the apartment building screaming for help. Bobby slammed on his brakes and jumped from the car chasing me.

I was far enough ahead that Bobby stopped and turned back. I hid inside the apartment's courtyard until I thought he had left.

Then I started walking home, but home was miles away and I was without even a dime to make a phone call.

Finally, I sat down on the curb. I didn't know what else to do, but I was scared. My stomach was cramping as though labor had started and I was extremely exhausted. I was so concerned for my baby's welfare that the tears started flowing. Sudden relief flooded me when finally I felt the baby kick.

Sobbing, I talked to the baby telling him how sorry I was for the terrible mess our lives were in.

It was scorching hot that day, and I knew I wouldn't make it very far walking, so I waited. Sweat was dripping down my face, and I was furious at Bobby. A few hours had passed when I finally spotted his car. I waited until he drove up beside me. We were both still angry and we continued to argue, but

I got back inside the car. On the way home, he gave me an ultimatum.

"I would rather see you dead than allow you to ever leave with my baby."

"You're crazy, Bobby. Is this your sick way of warning me?" I screamed back.

"Take it anyway you want, bitch, but you will never leave with my child. Once the baby is born you can get the hell out of my life for all I care, but you will never leave with my baby."

Heartsick that I was back in the same old situation with Bobby, I had to admit to myself that nothing had changed. I despised Bobby even more knowing he was capable of endangering not only me, but also our unborn child. During the night, I started feeling bad. The cramps I felt earlier intensified, but I thought all I needed was more rest. The next morning was Sunday, and I told Bobby I didn't feel like attending church.

"You're not staying home," he said and demanded I get dressed and show up to church with him. I did as I was told.

By noon I was feeling contractions. We left church early, and Bobby drove me to the hospital where I was admitted. My doctor was notified and for several hours the nurses monitored my contractions until they determined I was in labor

I listened as the nurses spoke amongst themselves, "She's too small. I don't think she is full term." But when my doctor arrived, he didn't seem concerned. After 12 hours, the doctor broke my water to increase the intensity of my contractions, and it worked.

My baby was seven-and-a-half weeks early. Robby wasn't breathing and had turned blue. They worked on him for a moment, and then the nurses rushed him out of the delivery room. I was frightened, but no one would tell me what was happening. Later, a nurse told me my baby wasn't breathing on his own.

As soon as I was in my room, my doctor came in and said my baby's condition was critical. He was on oxygen, but it was imperative that they air-evacuate him to St. Joseph's Hospital in Phoenix, where they were better equipped to handle premature births. I had a few minutes before the helicopter arrived.

More in shock than anything, it was difficult to grasp the seriousness of my baby's condition. I shed many tears and felt so helpless. When I saw him in his isolette, I couldn't believe how tiny he was. I desperately wanted to hold him, but all I could do was touch his little hands and feel his tiny toes. All too soon, the nurses wheeled him away. I couldn't believe how quickly everything had turned upside down. All night I prayed and never stopped begging God to let my baby live.

Robby suffered from hyaline membrane disease, also known as Respiratory Distress Syndrome. RDS occurs in babies with incomplete lung development and it is the most common disease of premature infants.

As soon as I was released from Mesa Lutheran Hospital, Bobby and I rushed over to St. Joseph's. Even though Robby was tiny, he wasn't the smallest infant in the Neonatal Intensive Care Unit. Robby almost appeared full term in size next to one tiny infant, Willie, who wasn't more than two pounds, and quite often the nurses thumped his little chest with their finger to keep his heart beating.

I felt so terribly guilty when I watched my infant son struggle for each breath he took. He had tubes and wires connected from him to monitors, and within days his condition took a turn for the worse. His doctor reassured me that this was to be expected.

I quit my job to be with my baby as often as I could. Within two weeks, I was able to hold Robby for the first time outside the safety of his incubator. The nurse would lift him out, careful not to disturb the wires and other connections he had, and place him in my arms. I spent many long hours inside the NICU while rocking my baby and listening to the monitors.

I was completely unprepared for his premature birth, but was amazed at the skillful care he received from specialists. I will always be grateful for the love his nurses gave to him when I could not do more than touch his little fingers. Often, my heart felt overwhelmed with emotions that seemed to engulf me in pain.

Gradually, Robby improved. His stay was less than four weeks, but Robby was still so tiny when we brought him home that I hardly slept at night, afraid he would stop breathing. I kept his bassinet right next to my bed and often I would fall asleep with my hand inside his bed so I could touch his little chest to make sure he was still breathing.

Bobby was supportive during this time. He stopped complaining and finding fault with me. Perhaps he felt a twinge of guilt, if that's possible, that our baby was born premature. Even though I held my feelings close to me, since it never served me well to confide in Bobby, I couldn't help but feel resentful and angry with him that he caused unnecessary harm the day before. Was he to blame? Was I?

A year had passed since Bobby and I said our wedding vows and Bobby finally got the moment he had been waiting for his temple ceremony. More than anything else, he wanted to be married in the temple with the ceremony he believed would seal us together for all eternity. Since I not only had myself to think about, but the baby as well, I believed it was the right thing for us to do.

We both made appointments to see our Bishop. Bobby's appointment was separate from mine, but in my interview it was mentioned that a wife could soften the heart of her husband and by my willingness to enter God's Temple, I would be blessed. Responsibility was placed on my shoulders to be kind, patient, forgiving and endure the trials God placed before me.

Five

For all Eternity

Is there magic inside a sacred room that softens hearts and changes anger into love and a house into a safe haven?

I'll never forget the morning my husband and I knelt at the altar, and our baby son was gently placed between us. We joined hands and reverently listened to each spoken word. The ceremony was different from that of our civil marriage. *This* ceremony felt sacred and filled with many promises.

Looking into my husband's eyes, I desperately wanted to believe in everything I had been told. On this, my temple sealing day, I was an obedient spirit daughter of my Father in Heaven. Kneeling before God and Heavenly Angels, I was fulfilling one of the most sacred teachings of my youth. I paid my tithing and was devoted to my church callings. Finally, I felt worthy enough to say, "God no longer has any reason to punish me. My sins have been wiped clean, and I have been faithful and obedient in all things."

It was a wonderful feeling to look around the room lavishly decorated in such extraordinary elegance. Its exquisiteness was equal only to a mansion in Heaven with crystal chandeliers and richness in every ornate detail that filled the room. Its rich beauty mesmerized the eye of the beholder and I felt lost in the room's secret mysteries. It was so easy for me to pretend and believe in prophetic words of eternal family promises in such elaborate surroundings. For a moment, I was carried away. For a moment, I was a bride starting her life over.

I remember standing in front of a mirror that echoed my image forever.

This mirror symbolized eternity—the room symbolized purity—how could we leave this place and not be changed?

Later that morning we left with our families. Bobby was holding my hand as I held our son and we walked down the front stairs of the temple. I believed with all my heart that his heart had been miraculously softened after our experience that morning, just as I had been promised it would be. We had dinner with our families and then it was time for everyone to leave. Bobby and I returned to our home. I felt changed, and even though I can't really say what he was thinking, I know he was kinder to me that day.

Divorce seemed further away as an option. The birth of our son changed the dynamics of our relationship, and our temple sealing seemed to give me what I needed to believe that our relationship was as it should be between husband and wife.

Each day, I awoke with the same burdens; yet I made my way throughout the day, as a Mormon wife should. I did all the right things and my home portrayed the ideals I had been taught. I was sugary sweet when I spoke of my husband. We both had church callings and I felt included for the first time in the ward we belonged to. I wasn't a restricted member of the church; I was just like everyone else—married in the temple and starting a family. I had also been called to serve in the Young Women's Presidency in our ward. I loved working with the young girls.

My life seemed different. I even made friends with another woman my age and we did things together. I really believed Bobby had changed during that time.

Just months after Robby was born, Bobby closed a real estate contract that gave us enough money to put a down payment on a home and assume an existing mortgage. I fixed up a nursery and tried to find some normalcy in my life. We lived in a cul-de-sac with a lake at the end of the street and now that we had a home, I had a false sense of security.

But then the fighting started all over again. First it was over little things. Bobby said I spent too much time away from home. He didn't like it that I had to go to church meetings during the week. He didn't like it that I spent time with the young girls from my class.

One afternoon, I was at a presidency meeting, and Bobby was home with Robby. He called me hysterical. He said that he was trying to light a fire in the fireplace and he spilled lighter fluid. The carpet had caught on fire. Of course, I left immediately. When I got home, I found burned spots on the carpet, nothing serious, and more than likely burned on purpose. He told me he was trying to teach me a lesson of what could happen if I forgot what my priorities should be.

It became increasingly difficult to carry out my responsibilities as a counselor in the presidency and also as a teacher. I worried constantly every minute that I was called away from home. I quit leaving with my girlfriend to go shopping. Bobby resented me when I did. He said that I didn't have the right to be enjoying myself while he was working.

Three months after the birth of my son I was pregnant again, complicating my situation even more. Robby wasn't sleeping through the night and sleepless nights lessened my coping ability. This was a difficult time for me because nothing was stable in my life. In the beginning, I was resentful that I was pregnant. I didn't want another baby that soon.

Bobby hated my body. In fact, he hated everything about me. When he wouldn't come to bed at night, I didn't mind the fact that often he didn't want to sleep with me. Many nights he would fall asleep on the couch and never wake up until the following morning.

I begged Bobby to start counseling again. His answer was always the same. "Why should I go? I'm not the one with the problem." So I tried harder to please him. That confused me. Why did I want to please him when I didn't even like him most of the time?

We lived close to Bobby's identical twin brother, Glynn and his wife. Soon, we became involved in their problems. Glynn was an alcoholic. At first, this bothered me because they looked identical. What made them appear different was Glynn's lighter hair color, and Bobby's moustache. But their faces and mannerisms were identical—the way they walked, talked and laughed. I couldn't stand Glynn. He lost his temper in a heartbeat and he was rude, abrasive, cold, cruel, insensitive and extremely selfish.

Actually, Glynn was a reality check for me, but since I wasn't willing to admit the truth about my own husband, I didn't recognize it, so I did what I always did: I saw what I wanted to see and discarded the rest. I made a mental list and found certain little things about them that were different. For instance, Bobby always went to church, Glynn didn't. Bobby never touched alcohol, and Glynn never left it alone. Bobby came home at night, Glynn disappeared from time to time and no one knew where he was until the police called. Glynn beat his wife when he was drunk; Bobby beat me, but never under the influence of any drug. Glynn had been married eight times before, and I believed Bobby had only been married once before. But I still had a hard time looking Glynn straight in the face and not seeing Bobby.

As much as I wanted to stay home with Robby, I wasn't able to. Bobby's commissions were few and far between. I found another job with an attorney in Scottsdale. His practice was limited to "domestic relations," and I typed many divorce petitions and filed them with the court. I would read through each file, amazed at the stuff that was there.

One husband, whose wife had sued him for divorce, burst through the office doors cussing up a storm and demanding to see the S.O.B. who was destroying his life. When he wasn't permitted to see the attorney, he grabbed chairs throwing them around the room. I thought to myself, "What a jerk, no wonder she is divorcing him."

Once I started experiencing difficulties with my second pregnancy, I had to quit working. This time, both my doctor and I were aware of the chance that I could give birth prematurely, so I was put on bed rest at the first sign of complications.

I had an apricot teacup poodle named Yackie and she always slept by my side when I had to stay in bed. We became close and I felt her love and loyalty. She was my tiniest and sweetest warrior—she was there to protect me. If Bobby was in a bad mood, he could hardly get past her without her baring her teeth. She also seemed to understand what I was unable to say to anyone else and she was the only companion that wouldn't scream at me or tell me I was fat.

It was quite obvious that Yackie didn't like Bobby. From the day we brought her home, she growled at him. Later on, no matter how hard we tried to house-train her, she would do her little thing in front of our bedroom door. Bobby angrily spanked her with his hands when she did this. Often, he was too rough, and I was afraid for Yackie. One morning, Bobby complained that the inside of his shoe was wet. I didn't have an explanation and neither did he. The incident was forgotten until the next morning when he slipped on one of his favorite expensive brown shoes and all hell broke loose. Bobby came storming out of the closet swearing he was going to kill that "damn dog."

I broke into a run hoping to find the dog before he did. Neither one of us found her that morning, so Bobby spent his time cleaning up doggie poop from the inside of his shoe. Silently, I snickered; praising my little dog for doing something I would have never had the guts to do. After that incident, Bobby found doggie poop on top of his pillow. Yackie was a smart little dog, but she wasn't aware of Bobby's real temper; she hadn't been with us long enough, and even though I found it rather amusing, Bobby didn't.

Within a few days, Yackie escaped from the open door and we couldn't find her. Bobby spent an hour looking all over the neighborhood, not because he loved her but because it was his money that had paid for her. He had lost his patience by the time he finally found her. I watched Bobby from our upstairs bedroom window as he entered our neighbor's backyard and exit with my dog running in front of him. He picked her up by the neck, yelling as he swiftly hit her repeatedly on the back end. Yackie furiously fought against him as she tried to free her self from his grip.

Watching this helpless teeny dog, I fought back my tears. Feeling panic swell inside me, I didn't know what to do but as she continued to struggle I knew that she was only making the situation worse for herself.

"You're hurting her," I screamed. "Please let her go," I begged but he only seemed angered by my interference.

Horrified, I watched as he held her by the neck swinging her around in the air while punching her severely in each side. He didn't stop hitting her until he was standing in our front yard, then suddenly he dropped her.

"Run, Yackie run," I screamed as I turned and swiftly ran down the stairs.

Just as I threw open the front door, I saw him kick Yackie as she went flying through the air. Once she hit the ground she didn't move. For a few seconds I waited to see her get up, but she didn't.

I knew that Yackie was dead.

Heartbroken, I ran to her side screaming, "How could you kill my dog?"

Bobby pushed me aside, picked the dog up and threw her in my face and told me to bury the damn thing; it was her fault for getting out. I buried her in the backyard with tears, bitterness and extreme resentment for a heartless husband.

As I got closer to full term, I was taken off bed rest, but struggled with depression and was unable emotionally to cope with stress. Bobby kept Robby with him most of the time.

Bobby had verbally abused me so much about the way I kept house that I became obsessed with it. I wore out vacuum cleaners. The carpet pile couldn't have lines in it and if I saw footprints during any time of the day, I would haul out that vacuum cleaner and vacuum those prints away. I scrubbed the bathrooms until they appeared as though no one used them. I would keep an eye on both of them throughout the day.

One morning, I went into the kitchen and started cleaning. Everything appeared filthy to me, and yet it was not. I tore everything from the pantry shelves littering my kitchen floor with a huge mess, and then I scrubbed the shelves with tears streaming down my face. Soon my tears turned into wracking sobs. I sat in the middle of my floor sobbing my heart out with swollen ankles and a stomach that made my husband laugh at me when I undressed in front of him. I hated myself, but I also hated the mess I made in my kitchen.

Somehow, I made it through my second pregnancy—I don't know how— but nine months passed rather quickly.

Even though my baby was four weeks early, Darinn was healthy. But once he was home from the hospital, this baby cried nonstop. He was constantly fussy, and his non-stop crying frayed my nerves, but a routine checkup with his pediatrician revealed an ear infection.

I felt guilty for the feelings I had while I was pregnant. The baby wasn't to blame and I wanted to make that up to him.

I held him and sang soft lullabies.

I let dirty laundry pile up. My kitchen didn't have that "Mr. Clean" look to it, and that bothered Bobby.

It took time, but he didn't treat Darinn the same as he did Robby.

He was cruel to Darinn. If I ever had to discipline Robby, Bobby would immediately take it out on Darinn. From the time Darinn was a baby, Bobby told him over and again that his mommy didn't want him before he was born.

When the baby was only a few months old, Bobby insisted I walk away from him and let him cry because I was spoiling him by holding him. I ignored his warning until he grabbed Darinn from my arms and ran into the bedroom locking the door behind him. He stayed inside that room as I listened to my baby scream for what seemed to be hours.

I pleaded with him to let me in.

"He's just a baby," I said as I knelt sobbing by the door.

The door flew open and Bobby grabbed me by the hair. Dragging me toward the stairs, he screamed, "I've warned you for the last time to keep your fucking mouth shut."

I tried to hold on to the railing, but with his superior strength he yanked me away and threw me down a flight of stairs.

"I'll never let a bitch like you ruin my fucking kids," he screamed as he watched me hitting each step. "You're not fit to be anyone's mother."

Stunned, I lay aching at the bottom of the stairs. My shoulder hurt and I had carpet burns on my face when reality struck me like a bolt of lightning. My husband hadn't changed; I had only created a more difficult situation for myself.

As outraged as I was, I wanted to sprawl on the floor in my own misery.

Instead, an overwhelming sense of betrayal raced through my veins.

I jumped to my feet screaming like a banshee, "I am crazy." I yelled at the top of my lungs, "To live with you Bobby, I would have to be crazy."

Before the reality of the repercussions for saying that hit me, I heard Bobby's thundering feet as he raced down the stairs. I may have been crazy for marrying him, but I wasn't that crazy. At least I knew when to run for my life.

Racing for the front door, my heart nearly leapt from my chest as I grabbed the door handle. It opened and I was out of there, leaving the door wide open.

Bobby didn't follow me. Instead, the door slammed behind me. I heard the locks click tightly into place and I knew I would be left outside for as long as it took him to open the door and allow me to come inside my own home.

Even though Bobby was cold and distant from the beginning, now he didn't seem to have any feeling for me at all. Constantly disrespectful, he hardly spoke a kind word and he easily lost his patience when either baby cried.

Darinn was nearly nine months old when Bobby picked him up because he was crying. First he tried soothing him. He gave him a bottle and walked with him but Darinn wouldn't stop crying.

Timidly, I asked Bobby to let me have him. I knew that it wouldn't take long before Bobby lost his temper. But he only shoved me aside and then started violently shaking the baby. Frightened, Darinn screamed louder.

In a fit of rage, Bobby threw Darinn hard enough that the baby bounced off the bed and hit the floor. Racing toward him, I picked him up as Bobby stood there staring at him. At first, nothing seemed to be really wrong with him. I laid him down on the bed and then we both saw—his little arm was broken.

"Look what you've done to this baby," I screamed.

Instantly, Bobby slapped me across the face; he swore he'd beat the hell out of me if I ever accused him of hurting the baby.

"It was an accident, bitch, an accident. That's all it was." We rushed Darinn to the emergency room and the doctor put on a cast.

I never told a soul that Bobby broke the baby's arm.

I am so sorry for this. Even though it sounds so meaningless today, I didn't say a word about Bobby's volatile temper when I should have.

I should have screamed at the top of my lungs, "Someone get this man away from me and my children before he kills one of us," but I didn't.

I was weak and scared.

Standing in the ER next to my cruel and vindictive husband, who had me by the arm, I was terrified—I had to go home with Bobby that night, I didn't know where else I would go.

Six

With time, it only gets worse

Battering isn't an isolated incident. If it happens once it will happen again and again. And with time, it doesn't get any easier—the heart never accepts the pain and the mind never accepts the lies and deception.

It was a blistering summer afternoon, hot as it always is during August in Mesa, when Bobby and I took the boys for a ride.

Abruptly, something I said irritated him. He started yelling at me in the middle of traffic.

Our windows were rolled down, due to the lack of air-conditioning in our car, and I was embarrassed.

When we stopped at a red light, I tried to quiet him down while he raged at my stupidity. The light soon changed to green and recklessly he kept driving and we both continued to argue.

I always felt I needed to defend myself—prove to him that I wasn't an imbecile.

"I'm not stupid, Bobby," I said, "Why do you always say that?"

"Because you don't have a brain. You act stupid and you fuck up my life." Finally, just to shut him up, I agreed with him.

With a little sarcasm in my voice, I said, "You're right, Bobby, I'm not as bright as you—I'm dumb and stupid and I've made a mess of your life—I'm sorry."

In one quick move, he reached over and slapped me. "Fucking bitch," he yelled, "get out of my car."

I rolled up my window in a hurry. "You can't leave me here in the middle of the street," I cried. "What about the kids?"

The argument we were having turned into an ugly, violent scene. He swerved in and out of traffic. Yelled at the kids and me. They were both screaming, and I was really scared.

"Stop this car, Bobby, you're going to get us all killed."

"Whose fault is it?"

"I'm sorry, Bobby, I know it's mine, but just stop until you can calm down." He hated it when I told him to calm down. He lost it and started hitting me then he pulled to the side of the road.

"Get out," he yelled, as he tried pushing me. Frantic, I wouldn't open my door, instead I begged him saying, "I can't, not without my kids."

"They don't belong to you, bitch. Now get the hell out," as he shoved me toward the door. Humiliated beyond words in the middle of traffic, passengers were staring like they had never seen a couple fighting before. I wanted to scream at them, *"What are you looking at?"* But I didn't. Instead, I reached for the door handle, tears streaming down my face; I got out of the car.

"Bitch," he said, just before he drove off, "get the hell out of my life and don't ever come home."

I watched the car disappear out of sight. Standing in traffic, I was boiling mad and bawling like a baby. Then I started walking. I walked and walked but not toward home. I walked in circles not knowing where I would go. Scared for my babies and hurting beyond measure, I wanted to pound my fists into my chest. Something inside was going to explode. Bobby was using my children to hurt me, and it didn't bother him. I knew I would have to go home sooner or later—he had my children. I didn't have my purse with me and I wasn't about to stop at anyone's home and call Bobby. And I certainly wasn't going to call anyone else I knew.

It took me nearly three hours walking in the heat of the afternoon sun until I finally reached the edge of my driveway. The car was parked in the garage, but the front doors to the house were locked. I stood outside knocking on the door begging Bobby to let me in.

He finally answered, opening the door only a crack. "What the hell do you want?"

Quietly, I answered him, "I want in, Bobby."

He stared at me for a moment, and then left the door open. Muttering under his breath he said, "Suit yourself, bitch."

A few days later, we received a foreclosure notice in the mail. Bobby hit the ceiling. "What in the hell are we going to do?" he screamed at me.

Waving the certified letter in my face, he blamed me for the mess we were in. "Go to hell, Bobby," I screamed back. "Whose fault is it? Mine? You didn't want me to work, remember?"

Then he let me have it. Bobby hit me across the face, knocking me to the ground. Feeling the sting, tears sprang to my eyes. Hating him, I didn't dare stand up or react in anyway. Curled in a fetal position, I couldn't help but silence my rage with self-blame. Stupid me, why hadn't I learned to keep my mouth shut? But then I thought to myself: Because it wouldn't have made any difference, Bobby would hit me anyway.

Some time later, I remember strapping Robby and Darinn into their car seats and leaving for Circle K to pick up more empty boxes to move.

I was exhausted that morning. I had been up most of the night with both babies. I searched through smelly garbage finding old discarded boxes and then piled them into the trunk and backseat of my car. Both kids were fussy, and my nerves were frazzled. If I had only stopped to feel my pain or sense the alarm bells ringing in my head maybe I would have realized that I was on stress overload.

The minute I drove into our garage, I took Darinn out of his car seat and released Robby from his. Unable to carry babies, milk and boxes into the house, I opted to leave Rob in the car for just a few seconds.

As soon as I put the milk in the refrigerator, Darinn started crying and Bobby yelled at me. We got into an argument, and I completely forgot about Robby.

Minutes later, I panicked when I looked around and didn't see Rob in the room with us. I ran into the garage, but it was empty. No car, no Rob, just an empty garage. I ran frantically down the street, but there was no sign of my car or baby.

My first thought was that someone had stolen my car, but the second I turned around to run back home, I saw a tiny fraction of the back end of my car's trunk, just before it sank to the bottom of the lake on the other side of our street.

Rob had taken the gear out of park and the car rolled down the embankment and into the lake.

I screamed for help, and a nearby neighbor and Bobby heard me. Bobby and the neighbor jumped into the lake and started swimming toward the car. I ran into the house and dialed 911. Soon police cars and fire trucks lined my street. The car was at the bottom of the lake before anyone was able to break the back window and bring Robby up to the surface.

Miraculously, Robby was unhurt in the accident.

Once my baby was safely in my arms, a news reporter from a local television station wanted to interview me. He caught Bobby on camera, but I quickly ran into the house. I wasn't sure what the law did to mothers who left their baby inside a parked car, but I was too ashamed to talk to anyone.

Later that night, I wept as I held Robby tight. I couldn't believe I left my baby alone even for a few seconds.

How could I have been so irresponsible? In spite of this near tragedy, I didn't listen to the alarms going off in my head telling me something serious was going to happen if I continued living this way.

Our insurance company refused to pay for our water-damaged car, so we found an attorney that would file a lawsuit against them on our behalf. We had our car repaired as best we could afford, but the interior smelled mildewed and dank, and the car never ran again without belching exhaust like a chimney. In fact, most of the time it didn't run at all. Consequently, Bobby spent less time selling real estate, than he did before.

I hated my life, and the tension was building between Bobby and me. He was always underfoot. I wanted him as far away from me as possible, but he smothered me with his foul moods and deplorable temper. Several months later, I borrowed money from my brother and my mother to put down on another mortgage, which Bobby assumed.

We were given six months before the foreclosure sale on the house we were in, but since we found another home, we decided to move right away. Bobby found someone else to assume our mortgage, and the buyer was supposed to make up the back payments.

The four of us moved this time to the other side of town. Bobby went to work for another real estate company, and we continued to fight a lot.

Soon after, I discovered that I was pregnant with my third baby. Bobby had also been in an automobile accident, rupturing a disk. For several months he was in physical therapy and not working. Making an appointment with our Bishop, I went in to see him alone.

I broke down. Pouring my heart out, I told him of the abuse and Bobby's inability to support his family. The counsel I was given was to keep doing my best.

"We don't believe in divorce," he said, but I do agree that you and Bobby need counseling." I tried to explain that counseling hadn't worked in the past, but I was encouraged to attend the temple and pay my tithes and offerings and we would be blessed.

However, he was willing to give us assistance. Completely dependent on Church Welfare, I thought I had reached the lowest point in my entire life.

It was so humiliating to take my food order and drive to the Church Storehouse. I would have to hand over the approved form to a person who was in charge that day. They would walk with me, making sure I only picked those items on my list. That didn't make me feel any better, and if I saw someone there from my ward volunteering, I would drive home without picking up my desperately needed food.

I was in my seventh month when labor started. My doctor put me on bed rest. For weeks I stayed in bed and nearly lost my mind. My house was unkempt, with dirty dishes everywhere. My two little ones got into everything and Bobby complained of constant pain.

Friends in my ward helped out. They brought meals into our home and several sisters took turns caring for Robby and Darinn. Another friend, Patty, spent time at my house cleaning and doing laundry. She would sit by my bed folding clothing. We laughed as though life was wonderful. Perhaps it was for her, but with a broken spirit, emotionally, I was dying inside.

Finally, Bobby's doctor recommended surgery. While I was still on bed rest, Bobby was admitted to the hospital.

At the same time, Glynn and his wife split up.

She left him in the middle of the night. Glynn had been drinking heavily, and was without a place to go. No one else in his family would help him. Bobby wasn't home and I didn't want Glynn inside my home, but he invited himself anyway when he showed up on my front door step.

One evening after I had just put the kids to bed, I heard a terrible noise out in front. It almost sounded like a plane had crashed in my front yard. I ran to the window and saw red lights flashing. Glynn's car was halfway in our driveway, badly damaged from a head-on collision.

Glynn had run a red light, hitting another vehicle and then he'd fled the scene of the accident. It was amazing that his car even ran, but the radiator had been destroyed and steam was everywhere.

Scared half to death, I made a dash for the front door and locked it. Glynn was beating on my door begging me to let him in. Cops were outside their car doors with their guns raised yelling at him to stop dead in his tracks. I cowered behind my door. The police arrested Glynn that night, but I knew he would be released the next morning, as he always was, and would expect to stay at my house.

That night, when I shouldn't have been out of bed, I packed Glynn's belongings and put them in a box.

I had never been this cruel to anyone in my life before. I didn't have the courage to stand up to Bobby, but somehow I found myself packing Glynn's things and placing them outside the front door with a note that read, "Don't even think about coming in, you're not welcome."

That was a huge step for me, but I felt so terribly guilty, I cried all day worrying about where he would go. Glynn must have walked home from the police station late the next day.

He saw his clothes and the note, yet still pounded on my door. I wouldn't answer it. He left and went down the street to find a pay telephone.

The phone rang and I answered. When I learned it was Glynn, I told him I was sorry, but I couldn't let him stay with us. I had had enough trouble without him.

Between returning to my front door and calling several times, he finally gave up. He picked up his belongings, and then I watched him walk away, feeling like the worst jerk on the face of the Earth.

Bobby was released from the hospital and was given a prescription for Percodan, a pain medication. He popped them every few hours because he said he was in so much pain. Fortunately, I was in my eighth month, and my doctor said I was released from bed rest.

Still, I was not to overdo it, but Bobby was home and he demanded certain things be done. Since we had to have food, I was the one that made the trips to the Church Storehouse. I was the one that had to care for Rob and Darinn, cook and clean.

I wanted to scream at Bobby for not helping me but I didn't dare, I knew he was depressed. He hardly ever left the house. He was taking large doses of his pain medication and a friend supplied him with other painkillers when his prescription ran out. As he grew more despondent, his rage surfaced more often, and it didn't matter what I did because it was always wrong. Some days, it was the way I answered him and others it was the way I fixed his meals. I tiptoed around the house and kept my mouth shut when he yelled at me, and never once did I dare talk back.

One evening, he was furious at the way I cooked his rice. He had a fetish about his rice, but I would forget every time that I wasn't supposed to open the lid and stir it.

Screaming in my face, he yelled, "How many times do I have to tell you how to do things right?"

Ignoring him, I turned to walk away.

"Fucking bitch, don't walk away when I'm talking to you."

Then he pushed me against the counter. I tried to resist, but the more I struggled, the angrier he became. Slapping me in the face, he grabbed my hair. With his other hand, he took hold of the pan of rice and dumped it on the top of my head.

Stunned, I screamed in horror as hot, steaming rice covered my head, face and shoulders.

"You deserved this," said Bobby. Then he walked away.

With my fingers, I reached into my hair. The top of my head hurt—I knew it had been burned, and so I carefully rinsed my hair with cold water.

"I hate you, Bobby," I swore under my breath. *"How could you do this?"*

I tried to smooth Aloe Vera on my face to stop the burning. I also stayed in the bathroom knowing that Bobby didn't care—he certainly wasn't feeling my humiliation or the anger I felt. But the most chilling memory of all was lying in bed that night pretending I still loved him.

He had sex with me. I let him touch me, while secretly loathing everything about him. I didn't have a right to say no to him, but I resisted him in every possible way with my rigid body. I thought, certainly he knows why I'm not responding to him, but obviously he didn't care.

Fighting back tears, I closed my eyes. I couldn't bear to see his face. But once he fell asleep, I didn't hold back my bitter tears. Without a sound, I cried unleashing years of pain. I longed to feel the arms of someone who loved me, and to feel comforted in knowing I was cherished in the light of day or still of the night. Instead, my heart was empty knowing that never once did I feel loved, least of all by my husband.

If I ever felt that Bobby had the potential to kill me, it was during this period of our marriage. He was severely depressed all the time and taking Percodan for his pain. I didn't have any proof, but I felt certain a friend of his supplied him with other illicit drugs. Bobby had unidentifiable pill containers—I had no idea what was in them, but he yelled at me to stay out of his business when I asked what they were for.

One afternoon, he came home with a prescription his doctor had written for him. I watched Bobby as he took a pen and tried to change the amount of the refill at the bottom of the prescription. Then he handed it to me, demanding that I take it to the pharmacy to have it filled.

He said, "Don't you dare come home without the amount of refills I have marked on this prescription."

"You're crazy, Bobby," I said. "That's illegal, I'll get in trouble." Shoving me against the wall, he put his hands around my neck threatening to squeeze the breath out of me. Then he pulled me toward the door, shoved me outside, and told me told me to make sure I did it right.

I handed the prescription to the pharmacist, my heart pounding as he looked closely at it. He walked away, and then he returned and called me up to the window. "Did you do this?" he asked.

"Do what?" I innocently replied.

"Forge a different amount of refills?"

I adamantly denied that I had, which was true.

"I believe you didn't do it, but you know who did and this was a stupid act on your part."

He told me to take it back and have the doctor re-issue another one. He explained that a doctor, by law, could only prescribe so many refills at one time of a controlled drug such as Percodan. Bobby had foolishly changed the refill number to an 8.

Humbled to the stature of a real fool, I walked out of there. The minute the night air hit my face, I remembered Bobby's warning: "Don't come home without my pills."

Now, what was I to do? Without any choice, I walked home. I walked through the door, with my invisible coat of armor acting brave, and yelled at Bobby that he almost had me put in jail and he could go to hell before I would ever do it again. He didn't move a muscle, and I walked as fast as I could to the bedroom and picked up the phone as if I was dialing someone.

Bobby never came back in the bedroom. Instead, he waited until he was sure I wasn't on the phone, and then called his doctor from the kitchen and said he lost the prescription he had been given and could he please call one in by phone. Bobby even went to the pharmacy to pick up the prescription himself.

Later during the week, he was complaining about my inability to work or take care of the house, and even though I knew I shouldn't, I screamed back at him, letting him know he had failed me. Our home was in foreclosure, he was out of work and we were on welfare. I was due at any time and I was enraged. I'd had enough but at that moment, I broke a battered woman's most cardinal rule; never make your husband angry when he has access to any kind of weapon.

He grabbed a golf club, and before I could run, he hit me just below my knees. With shattering pain I fell to the floor, but the second blow came before I could move. As I crawled across the floor, he hit me again and again.

The boys were playing with their toys, and I screamed at them to run into their rooms and lock the door. They didn't hesitate. They ran as fast as their little legs could carry them and quickly slammed the bedroom door. Bobby never stopped hitting me. Suddenly, my pain didn't matter. My only thoughts were, *"What if he hits the baby?"*

I doubled over screaming as I tried to protect my unborn baby. Immediately, I felt a blow across my back.

Bobby screamed, "Get up, bitch," but I didn't move. He wouldn't stop beating me.

One leg and hip was feeling the brunt of each forceful swing and I screamed over and over begging him to stop. My back, hip and leg were severely throbbing with pain, but Bobby laughed and said, "If you could only see how pathetic you look. You're a stupid weak bitch that doesn't know when to stop."

Once he stopped swinging that awful club at me, he threw it across the room and walked away. I could hear my boys crying behind their door, and screaming for their Daddy to stop, but I couldn't go to them. On hands and knees, I crawled into the bathroom unable to stand.

This was a turning point for me.

I wasn't angry with Bobby like I had been in the past, because I expected his abuse. I had lived that way for so many years; it had become part of a sick marital ritual. This time, in all my wounded pain, I was angry with myself.

I grabbed a pair of scissors from the bathroom drawer. Not knowing exactly what I was going to do with them, I screamed at Bobby, begging him to answer me.

"What have you done to me?" Carefully, I slipped off my pants, but I was in terrible pain.

Half of my body was so badly beaten it looked like a slab of meat, black and blue and purple and quickly swelling. Immediately, I took off my maternity top and carefully examined my stomach. Bobby's blows had not touched the baby. I was so angry, and sobbing violently.

I wanted to hurt myself. I thought about slashing my wrists, but with a dull pair of scissors I knew that wouldn't work. In sheer desperation, I even wanted to stab myself, but it was my face that kept looking back at me every time I peeked into the mirror.

Only God knew how deeply I hated that pathetic face. I wanted her to go away, but she wouldn't stop staring at me. Silence filled the air; I couldn't hear a sound. I wasn't crying anymore; instead, I was gazing deep into my bathroom mirror and the image looking back at me was of a woman that I hated.

I wanted her to die. This hopelessly brainless woman had haunted me for years.

Helplessly, she cried out and in anger she stormed about ranting and raving, but not once did she walk out the front door and never return.

Even though I hated the sight of the pitiful woman, I knew she had won. The woman, living in the attic of my mind, was my enemy and somehow she had invaded my body and was living my life. It was me that was dying every time she took the abuse and I realized how much I deeply, deeply hated me.

I took the scissors and cut off chunks of my hair. Then I really looked hideous, and I couldn't help but let the tears begin again. In a fit of fury, I smashed the mirror and as it shattered into tiny pieces, I turned to God and once again begged him to answer me, "Why God, why is this happening to me?"

From that day on, I knew without a doubt that I would die living with my husband before I would ever find the courage to escape from him. He held me captive long enough, Leaving no longer felt like an option; instead I needed only to survive. Somehow I would learn how to survive inside a violent world.

I made my way into the kitchen, fixed a bag of ice and hobbled into my bedroom. As I tried to lie down on the bed, I hurt so badly I had to stay in one position so I placed the ice where it hurt the most. I could hear Bobby in the bathroom walking on broken glass.

"Don't even come near me," I screamed at Bobby. "I swear I'll kill you if you touch me one more time." He didn't seem to care as he wandered back into the kitchen and fixed himself a sandwich.

I could hear him open the door to the boy's bedroom. Bobby told them to come out and I knew he was bringing them into our bedroom. They were terrified as they came closer to me. They were almost too afraid to look at me when Bobby offered to take them out for a treat. "How about going with me for some ice cream," he shouted with glee, as though it was party time.

Without saying a word, my two little boys took their Daddy's hand, as he reached out for them. They both stopped and turned around to look at me. The look in their eyes stills haunts me today.

"Don't look at your Mom, she's a little crazy," he said. "Let's leave her alone to see if she can calm down. She's not really hurt, she just wants us to feel sorry for her."

All three of them walked out my bedroom door and piled into the car as Bobby drove them to Dairy Queen. "I hate you, Bobby," I mouthed the words. "Someday you will pay for what you've done to me."

Seven

A chance to leave

Did you ever just once play dress up in Mommy's high heels, putting on her make-up and dresses that were too big? In a world of dreams and fairytales, little girls have fun with make-believe, but sometimes grown up girls close their eyes to truth and pretend for as long as they can.

I wasn't living in a world of make believe. I no longer hoped that Bobby would change. I was simply trying to survive from one day to the next. Justin was born on May 25th, 1982.

Although the swelling and bruising were still there from the terrible beating Bobby had given me, they weren't as bad as in the beginning.

After I was admitted into the hospital, a nurse saw my leg and wanted an explanation. I made up some silly excuse and as she left the room she said, "If you ever want to tell me the truth, I will listen."

I didn't trust her any more than I trusted anyone else. What advice, given to me in the past, had ever served me well? The sole advice I'd received, from one Bishop to the next was, "Try a little harder, Janice. Certainly you can get along with your husband if you just try. Say your prayers, keep attending the temple, and hold family home-evening and your marriage will improve."

As a family, we seemed so normal on Sunday as we worshipped together. The only thing wrong with our marriage could be found under the description of wife beating. But I guess knocking your wife around was okay as long as the husband repented and made a promise to his Bishop that he would never hit his wife again.

The message I received was that beating your wife wasn't a sin great enough for a wife to leave her husband or one that would keep him from attending the temple, but if you failed to pay your tithing, a temple recommend would surely be denied.

One afternoon, a friend who lived in our ward told me about a job opening as an assistant marketing director for a homebuilder. I was hired and went to work full time while Bobby stayed home with the kids. After a few months, I realized I could attend night school for my real estate license while I still had a salary coming in. This was the opportunity I really needed. Within a few months, I passed my real estate exam.

Just as I was finding a little bit of success, my husband found more reasons to find fault and criticize me. I was angry because he was out of work; he was resentful because I went to work. I don't know what I hated the most, his rage, his violence or his inability to provide for his family. He always had an excuse why he wasn't successful in real estate and that excuse was always me.

A few months after Justin was born, our home was foreclosed. We found another place to live, after asking the Bishop for financial help, but within several months, the house sold and we had to move again. Bobby had his brother qualify for a loan for us and after it was approved we moved in. But that situation didn't work out, so we moved again. My sister had a twin-home, which is a building consisting of two homes that share one common wall. Marsha had recently moved and since we needed a place to live, she agreed to let us move in her place. I don't remember why, but we didn't stay there long either. Regardless of the reason for each move, I was sick of moving. That's all I had done since my wedding day.

Finally, Bobby's brother agreed to apply for another loan so we could get into a house. I was thrilled with the house and friendly neighbors surrounded us. I had quit my job as assistant Marketing Director for a new homebuilder and I was selling new homes instead. It didn't take long before I was one of the top-producing agents in the office. But Bobby was extremely jealous.

He hated that I was doing well. Soon he began criticizing my work. He said I didn't know how to fill out contracts or how to work with buyers. He was afraid I would lose them so he went with me when I met clients. Soon, he talked me into turning my buyers over to him, letting him be the selling agent.

My neighbor volunteered to watch Robby and Darinn. Even though I didn't really know Sara and her husband Craig, they seemed to be a trustworthy and religious family. Since Robby started Kindergarten, he was only at Sara's for half a day. Heidi, a friend of mine that also lived in the neighborhood, kept Justin when Bobby wasn't at home.

I had just recently listed a new home subdivision. I had approximately 150 lots to sell to prospective new homebuyers, so with a broker we set up a new office for onsite sales. I also designed sales brochures. I loved the work and sales were really going well for me, but at home, things were not going as well. Bobby was his usual self and complained constantly that I was always at work. Now that I was exclusively selling for a new homebuilder, Bobby didn't have access to my buyers.

Robby and Darinn, who had just turned five and four respectively, did not adjust to the new changes in their life. Within several months, they were both angry and didn't want to be left at Sara's. It was a struggle to get them to stay, but I had to work—even though I felt guilty leaving them.

Early in the morning when I dropped them off, they would beg me not to make them stay with "that lady." At night, they cried and often had bad dreams. Darinn started wetting the bed and Robby destroyed almost every toy he had. So much violence had gone on inside our home that I didn't pay attention to sudden changes in their behavior.

After work one day, I stopped by Sara's to pick up the boys. We were standing outside talking when Robby ran out into the street, chasing a basketball.

Craig yelled at him to get out of the street. Robby ran to me crying hysterically. He grabbed me around my knees and held onto me tightly. I was baffled at his reaction, and I told Craig that he had really frightened Robby. When Robby wouldn't stop crying, I excused us and went home.

That incident bothered me, but since I didn't understand Robby's behavior I let it go. Nearly a year had gone by since Bobby and I moved into our home on Inverness Street and almost as long since I started leaving Robby and Darinn with Sara. But within a few short days, my life was to be changed forever.

One afternoon, Donna, a friend that lived around the corner from me, paid me a visit. She thought I should know that her five-year-old son had innocently walked in on her while she was taking a shower. Before she could say anything he said, "Mommy, I love you so much I could just kiss your pee-pee."

Shocked, Donna hurried and dressed and then sat down with Alex. She wanted him to explain why he had said what he did. She had never heard him say things like this before, and it was a peculiar thing for a child to say.

Without hesitation, Alex answered her; "Because Matt does it to me all the time." Matt was the 16-year-old son of Craig and Sara. Alex continued to tell his mother how Matt and his friend would take several of the neighborhood boys to a park inside the subdivision. There was a large drainage pipe where they would all go inside and the older boys would have the younger boys fondle them and perform oral sex.

Robby and Darinn often rode their bikes in the neighborhood and Alex went with them. Usually, they were all together in a group. Heidi, my friend who watched Justin, allowed her two boys, the same age as mine, to play with the same group. That night, I took Robby and Darinn for a ride. We went for ice cream then on the way home I asked them about Alex and if he had inappropriately touched either one of them.

We talked about "good" and "bad" touches. Robby fidgeted with his ice cream smearing it all over the car. I continued talking to them when suddenly Robby crawled into a fetal position on the floor of the car and started crying.

Darinn said, "I can't tell you, Mommy. You'll be in trouble if I do." I couldn't get them to say anything, but deep in my heart I knew, without a doubt, they had been sexually abused and had both been traumatized.

All three mothers, Donna, Heidi and myself, got together and decided it was best to allow the police to investigate. Alex was the only one willing to talk and he told his Mom that Matt and his friend did it to all of the kids, including mine.

I called the police and Mona, a detective for the Mesa Police Department, was assigned to the case. She interviewed all the alleged victims and I went with my boys when it was their turn. Mona took each one of them separately into a dark and very small room without any windows; it almost resembled a prison cell.

It was an interrogation room used primarily for adults. Mona was large in stature and abrasive in her mannerisms, and these interviews with my children went on for several weeks. Sometimes they would admit "yes," something had happened, other times they would say absolutely nothing. Each time they came out of the interrogation room, I could see how traumatized they were. I was furious with Mona.

"You can't interview these little children like they are adult criminals."

She wouldn't listen, instead she said, "Well, I don't think anything has even happened to your boys, because they won't talk. As for Alex, it was nothing more than innocent play between two curious boys."

Knowing she was wrong, I sought out a reputable counselor who specialized in sexual abuse. Adele was wonderful with the boys. She took her time and brought them into her center where she had toys, colorful wallpaper, games, and small child-size chairs and tables. She also had anatomically correct dolls to help the boys explain what happened to them. The other mothers brought their children to Adele and she concluded that, in her professional opinion, the alleged perpetrators had sexually abused these boys.

Mona re-opened the case when, completely unexpectedly, Robby told her that Craig also put things in his bottom.

When Robby was asked to describe what "things," Robby innocently said, "I don't know, but it felt like a telephone."

That did it with Mona. She laughed when she said, "Janice, a man doesn't put a telephone inside bottoms."

"You're right, Mona," I answered sarcastically, "but a child this age doesn't know how to describe a penis."

Any fool would know that Robby didn't actually mean a "telephone." Mona was offended by what I said, and from that moment on we really didn't get along. Later, the county attorney referred to her report as being "inept." Because of her sloppy investigation, too many mistakes had been made and it would be difficult at best to prosecute anyone.

Adele continued working with my boys. We were heartsick when the final outcome revealed this entire family had systematically abused Robby and Darinn for nearly a year. My children's allegations painted a picture of an extremely dangerous family. The mother and father engaged in sexual activity with my two children along with the son and two daughters.

Armed with new evidence, Bobby and I demanded the police fully investigate the allegations. Mona requested that my children have a medical exam. We took them to a doctor who had worked in the emergency room back east and had experience with sexual abuse cases. A rectal exam revealed extensive scar tissue, a result from an object large enough to penetrate their rectum repeatedly.

Craig had been a minister at one time and his family was highly regarded in the neighborhood. As a family, they went door to door explaining what Bobby and I had accused them of. The neighborhood took sides and the majority of them could not believe this nice family could do such a thing. It wasn't just a police matter; it became a neighborhood nightmare. My children were ridiculed, teased by other adults and children in the neighborhood and Craig was brave enough to openly threaten my boys if they said another word.

The investigation was a complete travesty, and the police department knew it. Mona waited too long and let things get out of hand. Infuriated, Adele agreed to go with me to pay a visit to Mesa's Mayor. Somehow, a local television station got wind of it and showed up on the front steps of the City Building. The Mayor promised his full cooperation, what else could he say with a camera in his face?

The alleged perpetrators were never prosecuted. Charges were never filed. Mona turned the situation around one afternoon when she took me aside and told me I was the real fool. "Your children are accusing the wrong man," she said.

As a result of the medical exam and since my two children were the only ones that underwent the exam; it was her opinion that the sexual abuse happened inside our home. It was her opinion that it just wasn't possible for someone else to have this kind of access to children, even though she knew they were in Sara's care at least six hours every day for one year.

Did Mona scare me? You bet she did. I didn't know who to believe. I never had a problem believing my children, but it is easy to feel overwhelmed with so many questions being asked, and my boys would sometimes admit and sometimes deny and at times refuse to say anything at all. I took them both aside and asked questions about their father, and without hesitation they continued to accuse Craig and his family for the sexual abuse, to this day they have yet to refute what they said as children.

I will say that one good thing came out of what happened. A supervisor at the police department put in a request to have a special room made for small children to be interviewed in alleged sexual abuse cases. Of course, she said one was already in the works; it had nothing to do with the injustice done to my children and my own outcry for a better system to be put in place for small children.

Our local television station aired the story along with personal interviews involving all three mothers, Heidi, Donna and myself. They are courageous women who didn't give up and helped fight for justice against a system which greatly failed this particular group of small children, not to mention protecting others from the same fate.

The legal system failed me also. I didn't trust them from the beginning, because of their failure to help me when I was raped. But after this I wouldn't be surprised at anything. We had the support of an expert therapist, a medical doctor and I knew my children were telling the truth as well as the other children, but it wasn't enough for the victims to see justice.

This period in my life became one of the darkest and most difficult I ever faced. For days, I couldn't move from my living room couch. I was living a nightmare and it never seemed to end. I felt as though heartache had followed me everyday of my life and this was all I would ever know. Even though I had failed as a wife, I never wanted to fail my children, and I felt responsible for their pain.

Looking back, there were many times my children tried to tell me. I could see their little faces looking up at me pleading and begging to stay home. But, instead, I would pry their little fingers away from me and force them to stay telling them to "be good and obey" Sara. There were warning signs of sexual abuse from the beginning, but I really didn't know what to look for.

At night I would weep as I tried to hold my two little ones and they wouldn't let me. Instead, they would scream at me and destroy their toys. One afternoon, I was desperate. I thought it would be better if I took my children and went to my mother's. My mind was running wild, and I was confused. Was Mona right? Did Bobby sexually abuse his own children? When I asked them they said no, but I didn't know what to believe.

I packed our clothes while my husband was gone, feeling that I really should leave and stay with my mother for a while, when suddenly I thought, *"Take all you can and don't come back."*

Before I could talk myself out of it, I packed the car with everything I could possibly fit into the back seat. Running from room to room, throwing clothes in plastic bags, I was begging my kids to hurry and get in the car. My children were bewildered and confused.

We drove around town while I tried to make up my mind. The Arizona sun was scorching that day and I didn't have air-conditioning. Hot and tired my kids were fighting and complaining.

I stopped at a convenience store and bought us all drinks but I was frightened. I didn't know what to do. It had been a long time since I had made any decision on my own.

My thoughts were jumbled *"Do I dare?"* and then, *"I can't believe I'm doing this."* Finally, I felt guilty. As a family, we were being torn apart by the repercussions of the abuse the children had suffered, and I felt sorry for Bobby knowing I was taking his children away from him. With a heavy heart, I turned my car around and headed for home.

In the meantime, my husband came home and found I had packed up the kids and taken them away from him. As I drove into the driveway, I saw him standing by the front door and a sinking feeling came over me. He didn't say anything in front of the kids; he waited until he had all of us behind closed doors.

He grabbed me by the arm, and as he twisted it, he wanted to know what I was trying to pull. I told him I was just trying to do what was best for our boys, but he continued twisting my arm until I thought he would break it. He yelled at the kids to get in their room and then forced me into our bedroom, locking the door behind him. Then he began throwing me around the room like a rag doll.

"Where in the hell did you think you were going?" he screamed.

I tried answering him, but every time I opened my mouth, he slapped me.

"I'll kill you this time," he swore as he knocked me to the floor.

I felt one blow after another as he continued screaming, "Fucking bitch…"

Everything happened so fast. Fending off each blow, I was terrified.

I could hear the boys screaming in the other room, but I didn't have time to think. In a heartbeat, Bobby was on top of me, hitting me like a punching bag in the ribs.

I struggled against him, screaming in bloody terror, I fought against him.

For a split second, I felt enough space to pull away from him. I scrambled to my knees, he tried grabbing hold of me but I ran, jumping over the bed as he chased after me.

Desperately, I wanted to reach the bathroom, but he was faster than I was. He grabbed me by the neck, throwing me up against the wall. Screaming for help, I knew no one would hear me locked inside my bedroom, and I was terrified that this time I would be dead.

"Please let me go," I begged.

Shut the fuck up," he yelled while punching me in the stomach. I doubled over in pain.

Crumpled in a heap on my bedroom floor, no longer able to fight back, he stopped beating me. Then calmly, as he had done so many times before, he walked away from me.

"Don't you ever leave again with my boys," he yelled. "Get the hell out, Janice, I don't care if I ever see you again, but don't ever take my boys. If you do, I swear I'll kill you," just before he opened the door and left.

As soon as my children heard the closing of the front door, they came out of their rooms obviously frightened.

"Mommy, Mommy are you hurt?" they screamed as they ran into my room.

I didn't want them to see me. I just wanted them to leave me alone.

"Go away, kids, I'm okay. Find some toys, or go out and play. Just let me rest." My head ached. My body was bruised and it was hard to breath. Touching myself, I tried to see if any bones were broken.

I cried, but soon the sobbing stopped. Deepening despair settled in the pit of my stomach. He could have killed me.

Why did he stop?

Runaway thoughts tormented me. How long could I go on?

That afternoon, he beat me worse than ever before, and for nearly a week, I could hardly get out of bed, not just from physical pain or wanting to hide my bruises—I just didn't have the will to face another day.

For weeks to come, my world was dark, darker than it had been before. I managed to get through each day as long as nothing else happened. It was enough to keep myself safe away from an angry husband.

Caring for my children, as they grew older, seemed impossible but how could this have happened to them? How could I have failed them? Why was God doing this to me?

I turned to my Bishop in my hour of most desperate help and he only said, "the sun will shine again tomorrow."

What in the hell did he know? Why did I waste my time turning to those who never once had an answer for me?

Maybe the sun always shined brightly in his life, but I never felt the warmth of sunlight. I lived in a world of darkness—its called paralyzing fear.

Now, I was really angry with God. He had never answered my prayers and I lived with that. I had been violated and stripped of dignity with the rape and I lived with that.

I had been beaten and humiliated by my husband and I lived with that.

But I could not believe in a God who allowed terrible things to happen children—my children. I didn't know how to live with my children's pain, but I wasn't able to make it go away. My heart didn't have the room to carry such inner pain—betrayed by those I trusted.

I felt alone in a house I could not clean, dirty clothes and dishes everywhere, living with hurting children and an angry husband. It didn't seem to matter how I felt; my feelings were never important.

In my eyes, I was everything my husband accused me of being, a negligent mother, miserable housekeeper, an undesirable wife.

With a heavy heart, I tried getting back into life again. I had a job that was important to me, but from the beginning, Bobby continuously showed up at my office creating scenes by fighting with me. The builder for whom I worked asked me to keep my husband away or he said he would get a restraining order. I wasn't able to keep Bobby away from me at the office any more than I could control his behavior at home.

One day, the owner of the subdivision handed me a piece of paper. It was a list of every broker Bobby had ever worked for, and the list was quite lengthy.

My boss had also been my Bishop at one time. He knew of the abuse and our welfare dependency, but that afternoon he embarrassed me in front of co-workers by saying, "Do you know what kind of man your husband is?"

Humiliated, I answered, "I don't want to answer that here in the office."

He snatched the paper from my hand and said, "Keep him away from here or I'll have him arrested."

From that day on, I felt hostility from my two co-workers. To say the least, I felt inferior and shamed by what they knew of me. It seemed as though I was assigned floor duty on every holiday and that angered Bobby.

Then one Sunday, which happened to be Mother's Day, Bobby refused to let me go to work.

That was the last straw. Everyone was really angry with me; consequently, I let Bobby convince me I was better off quitting.

Even though I was promised I would be paid my commission on prior sales, the owner refused to honor that commitment.

Eight

A lull in the Storm

Even during stormy weather there is a moment of calmness, but when you are a battered woman the lull ends only too soon.

Memories of cool desert air, a breeze dancing with soft, flowing curtains and doves cooing in our back yard, momentarily reflect peaceful memories—we were in another home and it still smelled of fresh paint.

Our old neighborhood was on the other side of town. Unfriendly neighbors, who talked behind our backs and taunted my children, were fading into forgotten memories.

I was a mother with a mission. I was doing something positive to help my children recover and I also agreed to another television interview about the scandal in our old neighborhood—charges would never be filed against the alleged sex offenders, but I still wanted people to know that this sort of thing happens in well-kept, middle class neighborhoods.

The founder of the clinic, where my children received counseling, was a kind and loving older woman. She insisted that both Bobby and I were victims of sexual abuse—I denied it. I didn't want Bobby to know what happened to me as a child. She explained to me the reasons why I was unable to cope with my children's abuse. I wasn't experiencing their pain, I was reliving my own.

Adele, impressed with my natural ability to work with victims, asked me to help her. Several hours each week I spent time in her small clinic for sexually abused children.

A young woman, in her early 20's came in each week for a group therapy session. I will always remember her. She was also Mormon and a victim of incest. My heart ached for her. She was lost in a world of pain.

She blamed herself—hostility, guilt and extreme self-loathing consumed her and she couldn't stop running long enough to let healing begin. She was terrified of what was inside her. Everything she had been taught in church about purity only deepened her wounds. I did my best to love her and help her to see her inner beauty—she saw nothing other than the bad little girl she had been having sex with her older brother.

I seemed more in control of my life during this time—not that Bobby had changed but something inside me had changed. I found purpose and meaning in my life even though it came to me as a gift in bitter wrappings from my children's pain, I was helping others—I was giving of myself. Even then I knew this was my mission.

My husband also found someone else to apply for another loan for us to build a home. We found a set of plans that we both fell in love with. It was our dream home, a beautiful Victorian house with stained glass windows and a porch that wrapped around the house.

You may be wondering, as did many others, how we managed to get into homes without a penny to our name. I don't know that I can explain it since it gets a little complicated, but Bobby was very clever.

What he did was not always legal, but he could put real estate deals together when he needed to, and this is how we were able to always find a home to live in. We didn't make the payments for very long, but another house always seemed to be there for us. While our home was under construction, Bobby found another job, one that made him money. He found owners that needed to dump their investment properties.

During this time, lending institutions made it easy for people to assume a loan without qualifying for it. Bobby took over several loans on different apartment complexes and duplexes. He scammed the money that came in from the rent and put it in his pocket. As soon as one loan was foreclosed, he found another one to assume.

Bobby was gone most of the time, collecting rent, and making repairs or whatever else needed to be done. Even though I didn't approve of what he was doing, I kept it to myself but I was bothered by my husband's deceit.

Once, I did confess to our Bishop in an interview for a temple recommend, which happened once a year. I didn't feel right about lying to the Bishop, so when he asked me if I paid a full tithing, I said no.

I told him that Bobby stole the money we had, and I didn't think the Lord wanted dirty money.

I didn't walk out of the Bishop's office with a signed temple recommend, but Bobby did. He went in right after I did and whatever he said seemed to be enough—Bobby was a worthy member; he even had a signed temple recommend proving it.

Driving home that evening, Bobby nearly wrecked his pick-up because he was so angry with me. He couldn't believe I told the Bishop what I did. He accused me of ruining his reputation.

I felt like saying, "If the shoe fits, Bobby, wear it." Of course, I didn't. I agreed with him that I made an awful mistake, and I promised that in our next interview with the Bishop, I wouldn't be so dumb.

Bobby and I were both active in the ward. I was the music director and I enjoyed my calling. I was making new friends and so were my children. I gave thanks for each day when no one got hurt.

Then the lull ended. Bobby was angry with the kids all the time. One night Rob and Darinn were quietly playing in their room. They had taken a box of finger paints and spread paper out on their bedroom floor. Bobby went in to check on them. The next minute I heard him screaming at them. I ran to the door and found him standing them against the wall interrogating each one.

"Who got the fucking paint on the floor?" he yelled.

"Bobby, please for Heaven's sake, it's a smear. I can clean it up."

"Shut up, bitch," he yelled back at me. "I'm not going to ask you dumb little shits one more time who in the hell got paint on the floor."

Of course, they both denied it. They were afraid of what he would do to them.

I begged the boys, "Just tell your Daddy who did it, and he won't be mad at you." I was lying and I knew it, but if they confessed earlier on, their punishment would be less severe.

It didn't matter what I said, they weren't about to accept the blame. Perhaps, neither one of them really knew who spilled the paint. I ran into the kitchen to grab some cleaning supplies while Bobby was still screaming at the kids. I was on the floor scrubbing and they were up against the wall being yelled at. Disgusted that neither one would answer him, he took off his belt.

I knew they were in for it. Bobby started whipping them repeatedly because now he had a liar to punish as well as the perpetrator of the initial crime. As I said before, Bobby hated liars, and everyone except him was always a liar.

My two little boys were jumping around the room screaming as the belt hit their legs, and I was screaming at Bobby to stop. Darinn was completely knocked off his feet; the belt hit him so hard. Then he screamed, "I did it, Daddy, I was the one that did it."

"Fucking liar," Bobby screamed at him. "You both are fucking liars."

The more I begged him to stop, the angrier he became. I ran in front of his belt to stop him, but he turned the belt on me. I was hysterical trying to protect them while at the same time trying to fend off that vicious belt from me.

I screamed at the kids to stop running. "Stand still," I screamed, "and then he won't hit you as hard." But they wouldn't stop running, and Bobby hit them across their backs and alongside their faces ripping welts into their legs until he was exhausted. He whipped them until neither one could stand.

Once the crisis was over, my two little boys and I huddled together on the floor crying and comforting each other.

Over and over my children said, "I'm sorry for lying, Mommy,"

As if that would ease their pain. They sobbed as I held them in my arms. I guess because I was able to scream at Bobby after he was done to get the hell out of the room and leave us alone that somehow made me feel I was in control, or perhaps our home was so out of control no one was controlling anything. Pain bounced off the walls as much as anger.

The boys were afraid of their Dad, even before he beat them. If he played too rough and they complained, he got angry. They had to tiptoe around him and stay out of his way so as not to make him angry. Not only did I have to learn how to obey the rules of the house, now I had to teach my children. They never learned to play by his rules any better than I had.

Long before this happened, I stopped looking for ways to escape. I stopped believing I could escape. This was my life. Bobby had beaten me, not only physically but mentally as well—I was his prisoner even if I didn't consciously see it that way. I just didn't believe in myself. I had left enough times only to return that I didn't trust myself. And I certainly wasn't going to put myself through hell upon returning. Those beatings were of the worst kind.

Several years after filing suit against our insurance company for breech of contract, our long awaited court date finally arrived. The trial lasted about two weeks. Once it was over and the jury was in deliberation, we waited.

The following day we received word that they had received a decision, I was apprehensive. What if we lost? I just knew Bobby would fly off the handle and scream at everyone inside the courthouse and I didn't want to be there. So I faked an excruciating headache. I regretted that once Bobby returned home and said that the jury awarded us a large settlement, of course, our insurance company appealed but at least it was over.

Several months later we reached an agreement with our insurance company and with the small amount we received, Bobby bought himself a pick-up. I put what was left aside to open a small business. Knowing that if I didn't invest what money we had into some kind of income for the future, I would never see that kind of stability in my marriage. I couldn't imagine living on welfare the rest of my married life. But I also knew that was a real possibility.

Nathan, my fourth son was born on July 20, 1987; he was to have been my girl. As soon as I learned I was pregnant, I felt sure I would give birth to the daughter I longed for. In no time I had drawers filled with pink outfits, but I had a sonogram just before he was born, and so I knew I was having another boy.

My heart was so set on a little girl that at first, I was disappointed. But I don't know how any mother feels the least bit of disappointment when the baby is born and she holds him in her arms. No matter what Bobby had done to me, there was still a mother's love he could never touch.

Robby and Darinn were in school, and Justin spent most of his time with his father. Bobby would bring him home, after being gone all day, loaded with toys. The other boys were so jealous. I asked Bobby to treat them equally, but he never listened. First, he spoiled Robby, ignored Darinn, and took up with Justin where he left off with Robby.

Bobby and I decided to open a country store. We went on buying trips. Our life together seemed to change for a while and one of my most memorable experiences with Bobby was the week we spent in Pennsylvania.

We were there during the fall. Never had I seen such brilliant autumn colors—leaves falling in brisk air covering the ground with a blanket of orange, red and yellow hues. Candles shining in neighborhood windows welcomed passing strangers, and seas of green covering rolling hills painted an intriguing scene.

The countryside was breathtaking, and each row of clotheslines with hanging Amish Quilts captivated the eye as far as you could see—they were unending from farm to farm. Renewed by wisps of flickering hope, I fervently prayed for lasting memories of happier days.

Over the following months, I was so involved with the business; it became part of my life. Wholesale gift shows were held in California and we would drive there, stay the night, attend the show and come home. I was creative, and what I didn't purchase, I made.

Bobby was a skilled craftsman. He made beautiful furniture, mostly primitive or Amish style, and we added that to our shop. I found a part of myself that was missing in the midst of painting walls, putting up wallpaper and creating wreaths, dolls and other homemade items.

My store was more than just a part of me; it was almost like a child that slipped quietly into my life. A rare gift from Heaven renewing my faith in the goodness life has to offer.

Mornings were different. I didn't dread facing the day. Instead, I looked forward to unlocking the front door, smelling fragrant spices and becoming lost in another world.

My store was as much a part of me as each breath I took. I saw it as my last resort; it would either be a success or a complete failure that would destroy my life.

Every morning I went to work and stayed long after closing hours painting, sewing or creating floral arrangements. I did everything I could, not only for my business, but to keep me away from home.

I would close my shop long enough to pick the kids up from school and return to the shop to finish working. Even today, somewhere in faded yellow memories my little blue house on Main Street still exists and I'm heavy with child rocking back and forth in an old chair greeting my customers and loving the smells.

On Saturdays, Rob, Darinn and Justin worked with me. They mowed the lawn, cleaned out my craft room, they even loved to sit at the counter and help me make sales.

At the end of the week, I would pay them and out the front door they ran heading straight for Dairy Queen. Before they returned most their money had been spent.

This was living. This was joy. Watching my children laugh and work together filled my soul with thanksgiving and then I softly whispered, *"Thank you God for giving me another chance."*

I knew this was my last chance to make something out of my life that I could share with my children. I was tired of seeing my children in shabby shoes and faded jeans and cared for by a worn out mother.

One afternoon, I was at the doctor's office and the nurse did an ultrasound. My doctor's staff knew how badly I wanted a girl. That afternoon, she jubilantly exclaimed that this baby was indeed a girl. Quickly, she showed me on the monitor just what she was seeing.

I was elated. There on the screen was proof I was carrying a girl. After four boys, I had almost given up hope. Rapidly, that very afternoon I was planning my daughter's life—she would never grow up to be like me!

Lynsey was breach just before she was born, so my doctor sent me to the hospital where a team of doctors and nurses turned her while she was still inside. That's an experience I wouldn't opt for again.

I was ready to slap the doctor upside the head when he said, "Now this will just hurt a little bit," as he used his hands to slowly inch her half way around inside my stomach. I felt like I could have walked to China before he was finished.

Why do male doctors think they know what it feels like moving a baby around inside the womb enough to say, "It's only going to hurt a little bit?"

A kind sister in our ward, Judy Kelly, often cared for Nathan. When I was emotionally exhausted, this sweet lady came over and took Nathan home with her. She was a mother to me and an angel to my baby son. Inside her safe home, she held him and loved him as though he was one of her own. Even though my life is not one I would wish on anyone, I have been blessed with Earth-angels who came into my life when I needed them—God bless them wherever they are today.

Then things began to change. We weren't doing as well. Several of the duplexes Bobby owned were foreclosed. Our business struggled to keep up with its expenses. Bobby returned the brand new Lincoln Continental I was driving. A friend wasn't able to make his payments so Bobby offered to make them for him if we had use of the car. We kept the car for nearly six months before I had to give it back—I wasn't disappointed because I knew sooner or later that would happen.

It wasn't long before our telephone service was disconnected, then it was our lights. Fighting with Bobby seemed endless. I sold what I could at flea markets on Saturdays. I would take merchandise from my store and sell whatever I could at a discount just to make enough money for things such as food and gas.

I faced each day with dread and despair. But I was also anxiously awaiting the birth of my daughter.

On February 28, 1988, I brought Lynsey home from the hospital and carried her up the staircase leading into her bedroom. White lacy curtains kept the sun away. Pink wallpaper, with tiny teddy bears, lined her walls giving the room a delicate baby touch. Her days, as well as mine, were limited in my beloved home.

My baby girl was the center of my life. I dressed her in everything pink, from socks to diapers to warm comfy blankets, including the little bows stuck in her hair with honey (maybe this is why even to this day Lynsey detests anything pink).

She was beautiful as a baby, and she still is.

Lynsey has a mind of her own and always has. Sometimes I feel cursed because of this, and then I remember how I used to be, that's when I encourage her to be herself. I don't ever want to take away her individuality and right to be loved and treated with respect.

Nine

Fading Dreams

I didn't listen to my heart, but I couldn't deny dreams fading as they are washed away along the shores of anguish.

It wasn't long before Bobby no longer had any one of his apartment complexes—they had all been foreclosed, and I wasn't even disappointed. It bothered me that many of his renters couldn't afford to find another place to live once the bank gave them an eviction notice without refunding their deposits.

The day came all too soon when we had to pack everything that belonged to us; it was time to say goodbye to another place I had called home. I remember those days all too well, because I remember packing a zillion boxes and hating the life I had been living. I threw stuff into boxes so unorganized that many things were broken, but I didn't care. I didn't even want to take them with me. I was angry, tired and resentful—not enough to divorce my husband, but I hated him enough to wish he were dead.

Once I had enough boxes packed, I brought them to the garage and loaded them into the old blue station wagon that my mother had purchased for me. Where was Bobby? I didn't know and I didn't care. He wasn't much help when I was crying and I needed this time to be alone.

I had to say goodbye to my home—each tear that fell washed away another hope and another dream. I had a right to cry, and I didn't want him to see my tears. They were sacred to me and they gave meaning to something I had forgotten—to honor my feelings.

Slowly, I made my way back into the house, mesmerized by the flowers I had just planted. They were blooming and my vines were sprouting new growth. Old orange trees shaded the front porch; they were always my favorite, and that day fragrant breezes danced with my pink ruffled curtains. Breathing in the air around me, I stumbled against the stairs, unable to see past an ocean of tears. I stayed there for a moment, and then I slowly entered the house making my way into my bathroom with another box that needed to be filled.

I paused from packing to gaze out my bathroom window. Watching the birds gather around a feeder I had hanging, I envied those little feathery friends; they never had to worry about someone taking their home away from them.

As for me, this was my life story. Sadness, deeper than I had ever felt before, seeped into my heart, like warm running water, threatening to drown me in sorrow.

Bobby had made arrangements with an owner to purchase a house that was just around the corner from our beautiful home that was in foreclosure. He gave him a small deposit and they both signed the contract. I hated deceiving others, I knew that Bobby wouldn't pay the owner when the first payment was due, but Bobby knew, because of the purchase agreement, we would have several months before the owner could have us evicted.

Later, I spoke to our Bishop concerning our need for welfare assistance. In his office I cried. I said I couldn't do it anymore; I was tired of being a wife that felt like she needed to "endure to the end."

I tried to make him understand the dire circumstances in our home, not only financially but also emotionally. In desperation, I entrusted him with my soul, praying he would have the answer I needed when I told him, "My husband is abusive, and he is destroying our family."

The only answer he had was a two-part question.

Was I conducting family home-evenings every Monday night, and was I paying my tithing? Because, he said, if I would always remember to do that, our family would receive the blessings from our obedience.

He also knew that Bobby and I had not been attending the temple like we should.

"Go home," he said, "and think about the things you should be doing and maybe you will realize a greater need to be faithful to those instructions received from the First Presidency of the Church."

I left his office feeling more burdened than ever. I had gone to him in hopes that he would chastise my husband, call him to repentance or force him into counseling, instead I felt more burdened with guilt. What more could I possibly do?

Everything around me appeared to be dark and gloomy and hopeless. I didn't want to get out of bed. But my children needed me and so did my store—somehow I made myself do what my heart no longer believed in doing, even though I desperately wanted to give up and say, "I surrender to all the mistakes I have ever made, just don't make me face another day."

Bobby wasn't working in real estate or any other type of job. My store barely kept up with its own financial obligations. It just wasn't possible to support our needs at home also. I begged Bobby to find a job, until we built the business up. He wouldn't hear of it. The store, he said, was his.

It was paid for with his money (I never figured that one out) and I was running it into the ground. Since there wasn't enough money to support our household expenses and the store's expenses, I had to be doing something wrong. Bobby decided I had to stay home, where I couldn't mess things up any worse than I already had, and he would run the business.

At home, the days were long and I felt lifeless. Some days I hardly left my bed. Sometimes I fixed breakfast for the kids and sometimes I didn't. I longed to be back at my store; it was all I had left.

Then I found out I was pregnant. What was I thinking? Or was I thinking at all? How could I possibly bring another baby into my home? My life felt like a runaway train and I didn't know how to stop it.

Lynsey wasn't even a year old when I found out I would be having another baby. I don't remember caring for her. Perhaps she stayed covered up in bed with me.

Where was Nathan? Maybe he quietly played in his bedroom afraid to make any noise, fearing that he might wake the mean and nasty dragon that I had become. I didn't have the strength to care for my children, instead I wanted to stop breathing and softly fade away, just like nighttime shadows dancing on the wall disappear in early morning light—they aren't real and neither was my life.

Bobby arrived home late one evening and walked into a dirty kitchen. The sink was filled with every dish we owned. The laundry room floor was covered with dirty clothes. I waited for him to start yelling—this time I don't know that I even cared. That is, until Bobby started throwing things around in the kitchen, yelling loud enough for the neighborhood to hear.

His frustration was all about me. He said out loud to himself that since the bitch he had for a wife couldn't clean house or fix a decent meal, he was going to Kentucky Fried Chicken to get something for the kids to eat.

He returned with an armful of boxes. He opened each one and put food on their plates. I came into the kitchen to make sure the kids were okay. The minute I saw him open up a container with coleslaw I started to say, "Don't give that to Darinn," but I was too late. Bobby had already heaped a ton of coleslaw onto his plate. Darinn hated coleslaw and I knew that a war was about to start.

Silently, I prayed, *"Darinn, just eat it."*

Instead, the first thing Darinn said was, "Dad, why did you give me coleslaw, when you know I hate it?"

Oh boy, lightning was about to hit.

"You ungrateful son of a bitch," he yelled at Darinn. "After all the money I've spent just to feed you when your fucking mother won't get her damn ass out of bed to do it and you tell me you won't eat it?"

My boys never learned. They were supposed to do things they didn't want to do and say things they didn't want to say to save the family peace. But Darinn wasn't about to cooperate; he never did when he felt that he was in the right.

Bobby lost his patience, and grabbed the spoon and started shoving the coleslaw into Darinn's mouth. Darinn was gagging with each spoonful, and Bobby only shoveled it in faster.

I begged Bobby to slow down and let Darinn do it himself. He warned me to stay out of it.

Then Darinn started crying. Between sniffling and tears, his Dad forced one spoonful after another until suddenly Darinn vomited all over his plate.

Without missing a beat, Bobby scooped up the coleslaw mixed with vomit and continued forcing it down Darinn's mouth.

I grabbed Bobby by the hand and told him to stop his madness. Bobby threw me against the kitchen wall. Pictures and glass plates came crashing to the floor as Bobby smashed my head against the wall.

He was wildly screaming, "Keep your fucking mouth shut, bitch."

The kids were screaming, "Dad, stop it, you're going to kill Mom."

This bitch needs to die," he screamed back. Each time he hit my head against the wall, I saw stars. My head was pounding. I tried to push him off but he kneed me in the stomach knocking the breath out of me. Darinn got up from the table trying to pull Bobby off me, screaming, "I'll eat it, Dad. I promise, I'll eat it. Just let go of Mom."

Bobby let me drop to the floor as he said, "Get the hell out of here, I can't stand to see your face."

He ordered the kids to get back to the table and for everyone to shut up. Then he told the kids, "See what your Mom causes every time? All she had to do was clean up this fucking house and take care of you kids like she is supposed to."

Clothes were piled everywhere, even in my bedroom and I could hardly find my way to bed. Bobby came inside the doorway and said that if I didn't straighten up he was going to call Child Protective Services and have the children taken away from me. I had ruined him financially and I was nothing more than a burden to him.

I couldn't stop sobbing. I hated myself when I did that. Why couldn't I act like someone strong enough to leave him? Instead, I whimpered like a fool. I begged Bobby to leave me alone. I was sick, I told him.

"You're sick all right, bitch," he screamed back at me "And I'm sick of putting up with you."

"You don't understand, Bobby. I really need help. I'm afraid that I'm going to die."

"Good," he said, "save me from doing it for you."

We were forced to move again after six months because we failed to make any payments to the owner. Bobby found a house across town. He took money from the business to pay the rent so, consequently, we were behind on our business lease.

Bobby and I packed all our belongings again and I think the only lesson I had learned was that I should have kept everything in boxes from the last move. We never stayed in any house long enough to make unpacking worthwhile.

My boys enrolled in yet another school. This time Robby's teacher called me in for a parent/teacher conference. She said Robby had difficulties in class, and she wanted him tested. He was eight years old and in the third grade. He had struggled since kindergarten and even though other teachers had mentioned a learning disability, nothing was ever really done about it. I had taken Robby for tutoring, but he wasn't able to keep up with his class.

Over the following year, I felt extremely frustrated with the education system. Robby didn't qualify for any educational program. In time I felt pressured into placing him in the educable mentally handicapped children's program. Since he really didn't fit the requirements for that program, I refused to enroll him. Consequently Rob stayed within the mainstream while completely unable to keep up with the other kids.

As Robby grew older, he shut out the world. He had moved from too many neighborhoods and grade schools. Robby had a tender heart that had been shattered, and he would never let anyone get close to him. Then a woman in our ward told me about someone that had a private school.

When I met Belle, she was an angel who left her wings in heaven. Spiritually gifted in healing, Belle diligently worked with Robby. She had a way with broken hearts, and she knew how to reach those who had emotionally shut down. She had devoted her life to helping students achieve to the best of their own ability and I know she made a difference in my son's life. Even though our resources were limited, Belle never turned anyone away because they couldn't pay for her services.

Small, healthy changes were taking place within Rob. He spent his days at Belle's learning center and he played baseball in the evenings. He was also naturally gifted as the team pitcher. Bobby volunteered to coach his team one year and this is how he knew that a team of professional ballplayers was touring the country looking for talented young players for the "Young American Ambassadors." Those who made the team would have the opportunity to play against teams in foreign countries. Bobby told Robby he had to try out.

I remember the day I took him to the ballpark for try-outs. "Mom," he said, "I'll never be good enough to make the team."

I promised him that if he did his very best he would be proud of his courage, and that would be enough. Gallantly, he held on to his glove as he walked toward a group of people he had never met before. My heart ached seeing this small young boy who, at ten years of age had faced more challenges in his life than I ever knew existed, walk across the field, but I was also extremely proud of him.

A few weeks later, he received an official letter in the mail from the "American Ambassadors." He ripped open the envelope. The instant he read it, he started jumping up and down shouting, "I made the team, Mom." He kept repeating those words; unable to believe something good had actually happened in his life. I was as excited and happy for him as he was.

As I read the letter, my heart sank. He would need several thousand dollars, and we just didn't have it. I had to wonder if Bobby had known it would take money before he encouraged Rob to try out. I asked my husband why he didn't tell us about the cost.

He answered me saying, "I just wanted to see if he could make the team."

Bobby wouldn't tell Robby so I had to tell him that he couldn't go. The disappointment on his face transcends any word in my vocabulary, but my heart still felt his pain. To this day Rob has never forgotten that he made the team; he talks about it often wishing that if his life had been different he could have realized his dreams. It was a cruel joke on Bobby's part, perhaps unintentionally played, but I will add it to the list of his many unforgivable deeds.

Bobby had been working at the shop for quite some time while I stayed at home. One day, a delivery truck showed up at my door. The driver told me my husband had sent him to pick up a check for a delivery he had made at the store. Quickly, I called Bobby and he instructed me that I was to make out two post-dated checks, explaining that he knew what he was doing.

"Why do you want me to sign the checks?" I asked.

He said he had run out of checks at the store and knew I had extra business checks at home.

Just to make sure, I called the company long distance and talked to their bookkeeper. She said Bobby had made prior arrangements with the owner and the owner would accept two post-dated checks exactly fifteen days apart.

I called Bobby and said, "I can't do this. We can't afford to carry inventory like that and pay for it in less than 30 days."

Bobby assured me he had a customer that had placed an order for the furniture and he would deposit the money as soon as he made the delivery.

Reluctantly, I signed the checks, gave them to the driver and he left. I walked back inside the kitchen with a sinking feeling that I had just done something I would regret.

Bobby didn't deliver the furniture like he said he would. When I questioned him about it, he was irritated and told me, "The furniture isn't worth a dime, and I can't sell it." He went on to say that he had never seen such sloppy craftsmanship and I was to send the furniture back.

I was furious. I couldn't just send back an entire truckload of furniture. Knowing Bobby had lied about having the furniture previously sold, I called the owner and explained that we weren't satisfied with the furniture he had shipped. The owner was polite and said he would send a truck within a few weeks from California. I explained that I would have to place a stop payment on the checks since I didn't have sufficient funds to cover the amounts. He said okay.

On the day the truck was to arrive, Bobby said he would open the store and help the driver load the furniture. So I stayed home.

Within a few hours I received a call from Bobby. He said the police were at the shop.

"Why?" I asked.

He told me he didn't like the attitude of the truck driver and wasn't about to let him on the property. The truck driver called the police for assistance, but they, without a court order, could not force Bobby to open the doors.

Panicked, I begged Bobby, "For Heaven's sake, please let the driver take the furniture. I gave the owner my word. I've already put a stop payment on the checks. You can't do this."

He hung up the phone on me and I didn't have a way to get to the store to do anything about it. I had the owner's phone number, so I called him and apologized. I said it was a misunderstanding and to please send the driver back and I would see to it he received his furniture.

The truck driver returned. Again, Bobby refused to let him on the property. The truck driver left and when I called the owner several days later, he was furious. He said they didn't make deliveries in Arizona and California except several times a year. It would take him a while before his driver would be in our area.

I stayed at the store full time from then on, and Bobby stayed at home. He built country pine furniture. There was a demand for what he made, he just couldn't keep up with the orders.

My life as I had known it with Bobby, was slowly coming to end. As I look back, it was as though a fairy Godmother, determined to change my life once and for all, was causing things to really fall apart.

Mesa is infamous for having holiday boutiques. Mormon women who got together to sell their handmade crafts held these boutiques in homes. First, it started out as something small and insignificant. Later, they had created a booming business, especially during peak seasons for business owners. Consequently, gift shops like mine suffered.

It wasn't long before the doors to my shop closed, and so did my elusive dreams. I had a "going out of business sale," and each day spent in my store brought heartache deeper than any other.

That same year, I gave birth to another son, Westin. In twelve years, I had given birth to six children, and I loved them dearly, but this was not the way I had planned my life or theirs. This time, I stayed at my mother's in Mexico until Westin was born. Several weeks later, I took him home. Severely depressed, I felt more like a zombie getting up at night, fixing his bottle, feeding him and waiting until he went back to sleep.

One night, I placed him on the kitchen counter, right next to me, while I mixed his formula. I had been without sleep for days and I wasn't thinking. Everything seemed to be in slow motion. I turned for just a second and the baby fell. He landed on the hard tile floor. It sounded like a tomato had been smashed against the wall. I grabbed him and picked him up from the floor. The baby was screaming and I could hear my husband yelling form the bedroom, "Shut that damn baby up."

Running into the bathroom, I quickly closed the door. Sobbing, I held my baby and I stayed in the bathroom most of the night—praying that he would be okay. The moment he closed his eyes I would wake him, fearing what I might have done.

I wasn't thinking rationally. *What if I called someone? What if I rushed my baby to the ER? Would my husband yell at me? Would he curse me until he used his hands? Would he threaten to kill me if I exploited our family secret?* Sobbing, I couldn't think. I wanted to silence the demons; they said I was a bad mother.

A sense of complete helplessness took over and I couldn't think for myself. If only I had some sleep, then I maybe could think more clearly. Panic swelled inside my stomach, my baby was going to die. My thoughts were running wild, and all I wanted to do was sleep and never wake up.

I felt the arms of all my children reaching out to me at the same time, crying, and begging for me to save them. Panicked, I wanted to run. They needed something more than I could offer them. Too many years without a moment of peace, I was so sick of living.

Then one morning my sisters appeared at my doorstep. One of them had on a pair of cleaning gloves; the other had a bucket full of cleaning supplies. They told me to go in my bedroom and rest—they would take care of the kids and clean my house.

Somehow, I made it through the first few months after giving birth to Westin but then late one night as I held my newborn baby, a memory of long ago filled my heart.

I was in a cold room staring up at the lights.

Someone was saying, "It will soon be over." I was ending my unborn baby's life. I could not stop the hands of time from taking me back. Grief washed over me as though I had suddenly suffered a profound death—a loss so great I could not bear the pain.

Back and forth I rocked Westin, unable to stop the tears. The life I had once ended by having an abortion still remained with me after all the years that had passed. Is this how a mother is to be punished when she takes away the life of her unborn child? I hurt so deeply I felt grief fill every pore of my body as though I was bleeding.

The choices I had made, first as a young woman, then as a mother, filled my heart with sorrow. I knew that every child to whom I gave birth was to have made up for the one I did not. Was I ever to be forgiven? As I watched my sleeping baby, I wanted to turn back the hands of time. Life would have been so different had I made different choices.

I felt suffocated in the life l had created; I could feel my time was running out. I didn't have the emotional stability to care for this baby, and I knew it. My other children struggled in school, and I felt drained of the strength I needed to function as a mother.

Bobby and I were forced to move again. We couldn't pay our rent. We stayed beyond our 30 days, but that gave us time to come up with enough money to move into something else. Bobby found a house just around the corner. It was an older house, one that had a barn and a huge back yard. To the side was a garden filled with grapevines.

Yes, I thought to myself, I can turn this one into a home.

Bobby told me he had worked out another deal with the owner—the house didn't have a mortgage. We could live there and pay the owners rent until we found suitable financing.

Once again, my family packed their belongings. This time, my children were old enough to help. I felt like we were a family of tiny waifs, ungrounded and wounded. But they were also excited; no one liked the house we were living in. It didn't have enough windows to let the sunshine in. It was old and needed repairs, and it never felt like home.

We moved in the fall, and leaves had covered the yard. For a while, I remember laughter as Nate and Lynsey played in piles of leaves.

We hadn't been in our home more than several months before we were behind on our payments. I went to our Bishop and asked for help. Our Bishop, being concerned, agreed to help us with rent, utilities and food. After paying our bills for six months, the Bishop insisted Bobby find suitable employment. Selling real estate wasn't enough. Of course, Bobby refused.

"With my education," he adamantly said, "I will never lower myself to work for minimum wages."

"But you aren't making any money at what you are doing," was the Bishop's reply.

Bobby was insulted and his relationship with the Bishop was severely strained.

The Bishop called me one morning to suggest I convince Bobby he should take any job he could find.

"He has an awful temper, and I'm afraid to talk to him," he said. Tears quickly sprang to my eyes, and it was all I could do to choke back the tears.

"I know, Bishop," I said. "This is what I've been trying to tell you.

"Well," he said, "I don't know how I can help you, but I can't allow you to receive welfare assistance under the circumstances…"

Placing the receiver into its cradle, I fell into a heap on the floor. Sobbing, never had I felt such distress. I had always been trained to ask my church leaders for help. I wasn't to go outside my faith for anything. The outside world would only lead me astray because they didn't understand our family values. Paralyzing fear raced through me. I knew that I would die before I would ever find a way out.

Frantically, Bobby tried to find a way out of the mess we were in. He found that solution one morning when my mother called to see how I was doing. Bobby told her I was really depressed because we were losing our home. I would have never gone to my mother to ask her for a dime, but Bobby did and my mother sent us the money to catch up our house payments.

One day, Bobby had another idea. Years before we met, he mentioned he had graduated from Arizona State University. His certificate was hanging on our wall. He wanted to go back to ASU and get his teaching certificate. He said it would only take him two semesters, as he had already graduated from ASU, and I was desperate enough to believe him. He also asked my mother to continue helping us while he got through one year of school.

For the first time, I felt a glimmer of hope. A teaching job would offer consistent income, one I had never had with Bobby.

That fall, Bobby enrolled in classes at Arizona State University, and school had also started for my children. But even with hope for a better way of living, I didn't want to get out of bed each morning. I couldn't put one foot in front of the other without falling a part, but fear was the only motivator that forced me to do it. Bobby couldn't tolerate it when I was sick and needed to stay in bed. Terrified of his temper, each morning I forced myself to get up and fix breakfast, but I didn't do it without crying and I don't remember taking a shower before I dressed or fixing my hair.

The boys were older now and they had friends over. One evening, they built a skate ramp in front of our house. They made a mess with boards lying in the street. Bobby drove up, jumped out of his pick-up and started swearing at the boys. Hearing Bobby yell, I ran outside to the carport. Helplessly, I listened, as he demanded they clean it up. "Fucking assholes," he shouted as he threw boards at all of them, but in throwing boards, nails and tools he only fueled his rage until he had completely broken a part their skate ramp.

I felt my heart twist in agony for my boys. They were so embarrassed and humiliated in front of their friends. I tried to stop him, but he yelled at me for allowing them to make our street look like a place "where white trash lived."

I felt like saying that's exactly what we are, white trash, because you've made us look like that. Rob and Darinn's friends ran from our house that day and didn't come over again.

Rob and Darinn would use Bobby's tools and not put them back. Bobby would drive into the driveway, see their bikes torn a part with his tools and then start yelling at everyone. Often bikes would be flying as he threw them at the boys.

Once they took his hunting knife and lost it in the back yard. It was a knife he claimed to have carried with him while in the Navy Seals. This knife meant the world to him and the boys knew better than to even touch it.

A few days went by before Bobby noticed his knife was missing. Then, late one afternoon I watched Bobby storm across the yard to where they were both playing. Just by his demeanor I knew the boys had done something.

My stomach knotted.

I watched from the bedroom window. Unable to hear what he was saying, still, I knew he was angry as the boys tried to back away from him.

Suddenly, he grabbed Darinn by the neck and swiftly kicked him just before he threw him against the ground. Robby started running, but Bobby caught up with him. Knocking him across the face, Robby fell backwards. Hysterically, I ran for the door.

Bobby and I met by the back door. He shoved me out of his way and said, "Stay out of this, Janice." His threat didn't stop me.

Running toward the boys I yelled, "What's wrong?"

Darinn said, "Mom, we lost Dad's army knife and if we don't find it he is going to kill us."

Frantically, they were searching underneath brush and dried leaves. Helplessly, I wanted to protect them from their Dad.

I ran back to the house. "Leave them alone," I screamed at Bobby. "Just let them look for it before you go out there."

Bobby struck my face. "Keep the fuck out of this, Janice, or I'll hurt them even worse."

I knew that if I went outside their fate *would* be much worse. Terrified for their safety, I stayed inside the living room. Then I heard the boys screaming. Running to the window, I watched as Bobby towered over them. He would wait for a few seconds before he struck them again with his belt. Scampering everywhere, I watched as they frantically searched for a knife that had mysteriously vanished.

It was nearly sundown when Bobby forced them inside the house ordering them into their bedroom. He locked the door behind them. As they screamed for help, I pounded on the door begging Bobby to stop. Finally, when Bobby opened the door he walked right passed me.

Horrified, I looked inside. Huddled in a corner, Darinn seemed like an empty shell of a little boy. Robby was holding tightly to his bedpost. Tears streaming down their dirty little faces, I muffled my cry when I saw welts and blood covering their bare little legs.

Words cannot describe my pain, my guilt and the extreme hatred I felt toward their father. "I'm so sorry," I cried. Moving toward them, I wanted to comfort them until one of them said, "Mom, just get out. Don't even touch us."

Sobbing, I walked outside and into the barn. Afraid to face my husband, and terrified of what I saw in the eyes of my children, I knew without a doubt I had also destroyed my children. It was too late for any one of us—we were a shattered family—what I saw in their eyes I felt in my heart.

The following day, Rob and Darinn wore long pants instead of their customary short ones. Unbelievably brainwashed, I was terrified the school nurse would suspect something was wrong with them. I was terrified they would tell their teachers. Until they returned home from school that afternoon, without a doubt, I knew I was going to lose my children. I wasn't afraid that they would take *us* away from Bobby, but that they would take my kids away from me.

Over the following months, it seemed to be worse for my boys. Bobby wasn't using me as his whipping post. He was after his children and they were forever getting into trouble. Rob threw a baseball and it shattered the bathroom window. He ran. He hid in the barn for several hours and Bobby couldn't find him. Later on, Darinn accidentally broke Bobby's jar of precious antique marbles. He was whipped for that mistake. Even the doors and walls in our home bore the signs of Bobby's rage.

Nathan, Lynsey and Westin learned to run into their rooms and hide underneath their beds.

Early in the mornings, Bobby delivered newspapers. He would leave the house around 4 a.m. and he always forced the boys to go with him. They hated to go. Bobby yelled at them each time they did any little thing wrong, such as not fold fast enough or throw the paper in the wrong place. Every morning before they left for school, they were emotionally drained, nervous and tired.

Whenever I needed my husband to take over, he became angry. Instead of helping me, he would shame me for my mental state.

"You're really crazy," he would say, and warn the children to stay away from me.

Many times when he reduced me to a whimpering child, he would remind the kids what he had to put up with. "Look at your mother," he would say. "She's really crazy, isn't she?"

Often, he would drag me by my hair, forcing me to see clothes that were piling up, garbage that hadn't been disposed of, and dust on the furniture and fingerprints on the wall. "I can't depend on you for anything. You are as worthless as they come," he said, as he spit in my face. "I work my ass off while you sit on yours, and I'll be damned if I'm going to do your job."

Because it wasn't his job to help me clean the house, the house remained unkempt; the children had been fixing their own meals and digging through dirty piles of laundry to find a shirt or a pair of socks. Even though I tried, I just couldn't force myself out of bed.

One morning as I struggled to get out of bed, I was feeling anxious because I knew my husband was really angry with me. That morning, I walked into the living room before the children left for school, and he began cursing me for the mess our lives were in. Our home was in foreclosure, my store had closed and he blamed me for everything. He said I had ruined his life and he wanted me to acknowledge how greatly I had failed. He began by throwing dirty dishes at me as he shoved me around the kitchen.

That's when the hitting began. The kids begged him to stop, but he wouldn't listen. Instead, he grabbed a hall tree standing in the corner and began beating me over the back with it. The kids screamed as I fell to the floor and he continued to beat me.

No matter how hard my children tried, they couldn't make him stop. Finally, he shouted, "You're not even worth wasting my time."

Only then did he walk away. Once he did, I was unable to breathe or stand so my children helped me into my bedroom. The pain was so great it felt as though he had broken a rib. I had bruises all over my body and there was no way my children could leave for school. Instead, they climbed into bed with me and promised they would behave if I would only get better.

"We promise, Mommy, we won't make Daddy mad. Just stop crying," they kept repeating as they stroked my face and put their little arms around me.

Most of my life I had wanted nothing more than to be a mother, but never once did I image my life would turn out the way it did. I was severely depressed, unable to cope with anything. Unable to shut out the pain, I screamed in terror knowing my mind was slipping away into outer darkness and I would never return.

Often, I would find myself in my closet. Perhaps I found refuge in the darkness; perhaps I thought I could lie down and die; perhaps there just wasn't any other place left to go. I still remember my children begging me to stop crying and come out. They would find me huddled in a corner, sobbing uncontrollably.

One afternoon, I made my way into the living room and opened the Yellow Pages. I needed to find a doctor. I found a general practitioner whose office was close by and dialed his number. The moment his receptionist answered, I hung up.

"What will I say to them?"

I dialed several times before I stayed on the line and said, "I need help." An appointment was made for that afternoon, and I was nervous about going. Making that first call to a doctor took incredible strength.

Dr. Stevens had some blood work done, and later we talked. He explained why I felt so despondent and my inability to function. I suffered from bipolar depression. I cried a flood of tears when he said I wasn't stupid or weak, but that I had an illness. He said many people suffer from the same disorder but there was help. His voice was gentle and comforting.

He prescribed an antidepressant and said it would take several weeks before

I would feel a difference. Soon after my first appointment with Dr. Stevens there was a knock at my door. I opened it to find two policemen on the other side. I asked them what they wanted and they said they needed to talk to me. A complaint had been filed with the county attorney. I was being accused of fraud—those two checks I had placed a stop payment on were both staring me in the face. I answered questions that afternoon and I knew more were soon to follow.

Within a week or so, I was given a court order to turn over all my business records and an audit was being done on my banking transactions. This was not what I needed at the time—perhaps this was going to be the straw that broke the camel's back. I could hardly make it through interviews until finally I sought legal counsel. I explained to an attorney what my husband had done—I didn't intentionally defraud anyone. I don't think the county attorney or the owner of the furniture really cared to listen to my excuses—they were going after me.

I asked my attorney to find a way to settle the charges, and I would agree to make monthly payments until it was paid in full. I then used the money my Mom had sent to pay my attorney.

Finally, an agreement was reached. I was to make monthly payments in the amount of $600 until the debt was satisfied. I had absolutely no idea how I was going to do that. We didn't have any income. Bobby was a full-time student and I wasn't working until I felt forced into finding a part-time job. A neighbor knew that I was looking for work; he had me work in his office for five hours a day, but I couldn't handle it. Sometimes I couldn't get dressed much less leave the house.

If I thought life couldn't get any worse than that—I was wrong.

Not too long after that incident, I was in the bedroom and it was late in the evening when my son ran into the room whispering, "Mom, there are cops all over the place; they are even in the back yard."

I jumped to my feet just as the front doorbell rang. Rushing to the door I answered it. They had an arrest warrant—for me. Apparently, I had written a check for $800 on a closed account for merchandise received at my business.

I denied it. I had never written a check on a closed account. The police officers were not in possession of the check, but they said I signed it. They were to take me into custody and then extradite me to the state in which the check was received. My heart was pounding. I could hardly breathe. I kept on saying there must be some mistake

Bobby came strolling in the kitchen with a look of surprise on his face. He wanted to know what all the commotion was about. The police officer explained to him what they were about to do. My husband said since it didn't involve him he would go back and watch TV.

With tears in my eyes, and six children hanging on my waist, thank Heaven the supervisor took pity on me.

He made several phone calls and then said to me, "Since you do not appear to be a flight risk, I've been given permission to let you stay here tonight. By tomorrow you will need to contact the person whom you gave the check to and make arrangements to pay it."

He took me aside and said, "The signature on the check isn't really legible, but since only your name appears on the closed account, charges were brought against you."

The following morning my neighbor, who was also an attorney, stopped by and said he saw all the police cars at my house the night before. He wanted to know what he could do to help. I explained the situation and he said he would make the phone call for me.

Later that afternoon, he called me and said that all charges would be dropped if I had a certified check to him in the amount of $800 before 5 p.m. Once again, I took my mother's money she had sent for my house payment. The other money I owed would have to wait; I was putting out one fire at a time.

It didn't take more than several weeks before my neighbor called me from his office and said he had received the check I allegedly had written. He said, "You need to take a look at this. I think your signature has been forged all right."

I hung the phone up, and turned around to see Bobby standing in back of me. Meekly he said, "I need to tell you something." Hesitating he continued, "I've been thinking about that check they said you wrote, and I sort of remember receiving an order in that amount at the shop. I paid for it, but how was I to know that account had been closed?"

He must have thought I was brain dead—why did he forge my name at the bottom of the check? I called my neighbor at his office and told him it wouldn't be necessary to see the check—Bobby was the one that signed my name and he said, "I know."

The following day, Bobby demanded I get off my bed long enough to call the administration office at Arizona State University. He needed to know if his financial aid check had arrived so he could pick it up. I made the phone call for him. The voice on the other end said she could not give me the information I needed; it was confidential. I begged her to tell me. She must have sensed some urgency or reason to tell me what she did because she finally agreed that if I could identify myself as Bobby's wife she would release the information. She asked me questions about Bobby and I knew all the answers except one. I told her Bobby had graduated from ASU and she said I was wrong.

"How could I be," I asked her, "when I have his degree hanging on my wall?" I insisted she must be mistaken.

She quietly answered me, "I'm not mistaken. Your husband enrolled as a freshman just this semester."

As I hung up the phone I thought, *"And he will never live long enough to finish it."*

Shocked beyond belief, I waited for Bobby to walk through the front door. If I had a machine gun, even a small handgun would have worked, I would have killed him. But a good Christian woman doesn't kill her husband; therefore, I thought I would give him a chance to explain why he lied. Then I thought of my mother, my dear sweet trusting mother, doing all she could to help me because I wouldn't leave my lying, abusive husband.

Bobby returned home that afternoon. The first thing he wanted to know was if I had the information he wanted from ASU.

"I got more than I wanted from the admissions office," I said and then I asked him to explain to me how he got a bogus diploma from ASU when he had never graduated. He walked up to me as though he was going to slap my silly face for accusing him of something so ridiculous as lying. "Don't lie to me anymore, Bobby. I know the truth and there is nothing you can say that will convince me to ever believe in you again."

He mumbled something like I had no right to get into his affairs and walked out of the room.

I wasn't as angry with Bobby as much as I was devastated at the awful truth. How was I going to tell my mother? I had lied to her about everything. The money she sent for the house payment, I used to keep me out of jail and we were still losing our home. I had been such a fool. Even though Bobby had betrayed me, I had betrayed my mother's trust.

Ten

In the Still of the Night

Be a lantern unto my feet. Guide me to a place where I'll be safe. Bring comfort to a frightened heart I prayed, and in the still of the night God answered me.

My world seemed to be spinning out of control as I parked the car and walked toward the entrance of Smith's food store. The minute I entered, I felt the walls closing in on me. Silently I talked to myself, trying to calm down, but it didn't work. In the middle of the store, the lights nearly blinded me. Completely disoriented, I didn't know which direction would lead me back outside. I frantically walked up and down the same aisle, blinded by my own tears. As soon as I took a few steps in one direction, I became hysterical. I sat down on the floor and started sobbing. A clerk ran up to me and asked if she could help. I told her I wasn't feeling well, and I needed help to get outside the store. She walked with me to the front entrance and asked if I wanted her to call someone. I felt so relieved to feel the sun on my face, and knowing I was finally outside, I told her no, I was okay and could drive myself home.

From that day on, I stopped leaving the house. Although, for a short period of time I felt better because of the antidepressant, it didn't last. In time, I was unable to leave my bedroom. I cried endlessly because it took more strength than I had to put one foot in front of the other and get out of bed. Often I would feel terrified that Bobby was going to walk through the bedroom door and beat me because I was still in bed. Bobby hated to see me with my head covered up, but I literally couldn't face the awful task of getting dressed, putting on my shoes or combing my hair. It all seemed surreal except for the constant fear I had that Bobby was going to hurt me.

One afternoon, I remember hearing the front door open, and I panicked. I grabbed my blanket and hid in the closet. It was dark inside as I huddled against the corner. I heard footsteps coming closer and I began to scream many times, "Please don't hurt me, Bobby."

The closet door opened and through streams of sunlight Bobby was standing there, then he began to laugh. He told me I really was crazy and he slammed the door shut again. He yelled at the kids to come and see what he had found hiding inside his closet—a demented fool.

He made fun of me as the kids were forced to watch. "This is your mother, kids," he laughed. "She is the one who is crazy. Look at her curled up like a baby crying her heart out, doesn't she make you sick? It's because of her we are losing our home." He slammed the door shut once again as I sobbed, knowing I really was crazy. I could hear him tell the kids about all the medication I was taking and how it was only making me worse. Stay away from her was the last thing I heard him say.

At night I would write letters to my children begging their forgiveness, and then I would seal each one and print their names on each envelope. I wrote a letter to my mother, begging her to take care of my children if something happened to me and to take them away from their father.

A few days later, Darinn came into the living room where I was sleeping. He woke me up and said, "Mom, I need to talk to you." It seemed overnight that this little boy had grown like a weed. He was eleven and seemed to grow out of his clothes before he wore them. For days he had been complaining about not having anything to wear. Even though he was younger than Robby, he was much taller so he couldn't share clothes with his brother. I knew what Darinn wanted before he asked, but unable to cope with anything, I answered, "Not now, Darinn, ask me later."

Darinn said, "You always say later, Mom, but you never listen to me." With tears in his eyes he said, "My tennis shoes have holes in them. I'm embarrassed to wear them to school. Can't I please get a new pair?"

My mind flew into a panic—he was asking something of me and I couldn't think. I didn't have any money and I didn't have an answer for him, then I started to cry. Sobbing with my head in my hands, I screamed without stopping. Bobby came running into the room holding his weight belt demanding to know what in the hell was going on. Darinn ran into his room and tried to lock his door. Bobby beat him to it.

I stopped crying when the sounds coming from the bedroom terrified me.

I could hear both my sons screaming bloody murder as Bobby hit them with his weight belt. Over and over, he whipped them. Darinn jumped on top of their bunk beds, Robby wouldn't move. He stood there while Bobby ripped welts into his skin. Tears were running down his face while he held his fists tightly against his sides.

"For God's sake, Bobby, you're going to kill him," I screamed as I put my hands up to my mouth. Bobby wouldn't stop. He grabbed Darinn from the bed, threw him to the ground and beat him with that horrid belt.

Knowing I had to do something, I ran in front of the belt to stop him. He threw me back and told me to get the hell out of the room. I ran toward him again and screamed, "Beat me, Bobby, but leave my boys alone."

Bobby whirled around and let me have it. I have never felt anything burn like the sting of that belt. I thought I had experienced physical pain before, but nothing hurt like that did. He raised his hand to swing one more time and the boys tried to stop him—I ran from the room screaming into the kitchen. I ripped the buttons from my nightgown and dug my nails into my skin.

"I want to die!" I screamed. I don't know that I felt coherent. I don't know that my mind didn't snap but I was at the end of my rope.

Bobby stopped beating his wounded boys, leaving them in their room crying, then pushed me aside yelling that this was my fault.

"You're a pathetic bitch," he said as he stormed down the hallway ranting, "You have done this to your kids," and slammed his bedroom door.

That night, in my wild and crazy head, I felt the attic doors swing open. The woman I hated, the one who hid upstairs and ruined everything suddenly stomped down the stairs. With one wave of her hands, the walls of denial shattered releasing my anguished pain—there was nothing left to live for.

I emptied my cupboard, took out pills of every kind and swallowed a handful at a time.

I made my way to the living room, lay down on the couch and pulled a quilt over me—peace filling my being, I believed the pain would now stop.

I wouldn't hurt anymore.

I listened to my boys crying and my heart shattered into a million tiny pieces then my world fell silent.

I don't know when, but Darinn found the empty pill containers spread all over the kitchen counter and the next thing I remember was my son screaming at me and trying to make me get up. I knew he was there, but I couldn't respond to him.

He ran to get Bobby, but came back into the room with tears streaming down his face. He later told me that his father said, "If your mother is that stupid, then let her die." Instead, Darinn ran across the yard and pounded on my neighbor's door.

My friend and her husband rushed me to the emergency room. What I remember from that horrible night was my arms and ankles strapped to a hospital bed with tubes forced down my throat. I knew for sure I was going to die that night, but not from the pills I took. The nurses were going to be the ones to kill me.

My next door neighbor, Rowena, stayed by my side throughout the night tightly holding my hand as water was pumped through one tube and my stomach contents flowed through the other. I tried to break free from the bands that held my wrists in place.

I gagged and arched my body trying to stop their madness. But no one stopped until they were finished. For a while I was left alone. Tears stained my pillow. Was I crying because I still lived? Or did I feel shame from the darkest portion of my heart?

Later a doctor came in the room asking me questions. He wanted to know if I had tried committing suicide before, I answered him, "No," this is my first time.

He said they were going to admit me and I knew what that meant. They were going to lock me in a room and throw away the key. I grabbed hold of his arm and said that I would never do this again; my children needed me at home. Reality struck me and I felt heart-wrenching guilt.

He patted me on my hand, and said, "I understand." Then he walked away.

I tried to listen to whispered voices between the nurse and doctors, and then Rowena left her chair.

I kept saying, "I promise never to do this again, if you will just let me go home."

I had been there all night. I was exhausted and mentally drained, but I desperately wanted to go home. Perhaps the doctor came back in and talked to me, I don't remember but he did finally allow my friend to take me home.

I don't even remember the ride home. When we drove into our driveway, Rowena helped me from the car and walked with me to my front door. The door was locked. She rang the doorbell quite a few times.

She looked at me strangely and said, "Where is your husband? This was the first time Bobby's name was even mentioned.

Bobby finally came to the door opening it just a crack. He took one look at me and slammed the door in my face. Rowena twisted the doorknob and it was open.

"It's okay, Rowena," I said. "I'll be okay."

She hesitated and didn't want to leave me there, but I told her that she was only next-door and if I needed her I would call.

Rowena hugged me and for a moment I almost said, "Help me get away from here," but I didn't.

She didn't say anything either, slowly she just walked away. A friend, unlike any other, stayed by my side and never once judged me—her love was sweet and tender and her eyes said, "I understand, my friend."

But I couldn't tell her—I was so ashamed of me.

I called Belle within a few days. We had become friends and I trusted her more than anyone else.

For days afterward I would call her late into the night and we talked for hours. I was still afraid to tell her that Bobby was physically abusive but I sensed that she knew. Belle gave me the name of a therapist and made me promise to make an appointment.

Finally, I made an appointment with the therapist. I met with Jori several times before Bobby insisted on going with me.

Bobby complained about my emotional instability and how difficult it was for him to live with me. He wanted Jori to cure me so we could repair our relationship.

Then Jori asked Bobby some personal questions and he blew up at her. Flying from his chair, he leapt into her face and said she was a "bitch that hated men." Bobby exposed his true colors to Jori without me doing it for him, but Jori needed me to tell her and I couldn't do it.

During the week that followed, I became even more despondent. Unable to get dressed or tie my shoes, a shower was completely out of the question. Waves and waves of anger thrashed inside me. I was angry with God. I was angry with Bobby, but most of all I hated the sight of myself.

I thought constantly about dying. It seemed to be the only answer for me. I was too angry to live and too wounded to leave. Dr. Stevens gave me all the help he could, but medication wasn't enough. Jori was there for me, but I was too afraid to open up to her. Even though I wanted to get well, reality had completely disappeared and depression had its fearsome hold on me.

Perhaps God really does works in mysterious ways. Even though I was silently wasting away, looking back I believe God's angels were busy at work. I had been praying for a miracle and if miracles still happened, I was in desperate need of one.

Over the years, I had created my own Gethsemane and I could no longer bear to carry the weight of my pain. My will to live had completely faded as surely as the flame on a candle fades in pouring rain, and once again I welcomed the thought of death.

In the still of the night, as I struggled with despair, the answer seemed so clear: it would be okay to end my life since my children would be better off without a mother who had destroyed herself and failed to protect them against their violently abusive father.

I waited until everyone was asleep, then made my way into the kitchen and reached for the sleeping pills I had carefully stashed away. I knew exactly what needed to be done and this time no one would find me.

With the pill bottle in my hand, I gently kissed my sleeping children goodbye.

Then I went into a spare bedroom and knelt by the bed. Somehow I wanted to make peace with God before I took the pills. My heart was heavy as I prayed, *"Father in Heaven, why have you deserted me?"*

Tears covered my face, soaking my sheets and blanket.

"I need you, God, I don't want to live, but I just need to know why. Why would you abandon my children and me?"

I was so angry with God, yet in my most desperate hour I needed him more than ever before.

I begged him to answer me, *"Why, God, why have you done this to me?"*

I stayed on my knees what seemed to be forever, but I felt nothing. Foreboding silence claimed any hope I may have had.

My room was dark, cold, and empty—just as the life I lived was void of light. Shivering from the cold in the air, or perhaps from fear, I slowly climbed into bed, knowing God would never answer me.

I wrapped my arms tightly around myself, as if to say goodbye, and then I reached for the pills.

Suddenly, a glowing light appeared. Soft and subtle, yet beautifully iridescent, it seemed to fill the space surrounding me with an answer I had been begging to hear.

A calm feeling came over me, silencing the sounds coming from my broken heart; shimmering light flowed as a gentle stream into my body.

A tender love cradled me like a mother holding her newborn babe, and a voice I believed to be that of God gently whispered: *"My dear child, I am with you; I have always been with you."*

The radiant light that flooded my bedroom filled me with incredible strength. With sudden, inexplicable clarity, I felt separated, as though I was floating somewhere above my own body.

As I gazed down upon her face, her appearance was that of a heartbroken child.

In my heart I felt compassion for her, and even though it was my face I looked down upon, I seemed separate from and undamaged by her pain.

Then, just as quickly as I felt myself above my body, I returned.

I felt the presence of angel wings fluttering above my pillow as tiny threads of fine light flowed throughout my body. The power of this light was dramatically healing my emotional body. As if in fast motion, I felt emotional healing taking place—the same as you would physically if you had an open flesh wound. Then all during the night, incredible love comforted me.

I felt courage, hope, and a sense of power swell into the birthing of new life.

Surrounded by love, I felt an infusion of knowledge that I hadn't understood before.

For many years, I had been mistaken. God had never abandoned me; it was I that had forsaken God.

Sleep did not come for many hours and long into the first rays of early morning light, a soft whispering voice let me know that soon my mission would unfold. For the time being, I was to leave my husband.

Many things I had yet to understand, but I was also promised that I would have the guidance that I needed and many doors would open for me with opportunities to live the life I was meant to live.

Without a doubt, I believe God and His angels intervened. Without this divine intervention I don't know that I would have ever found the courage and the strength to get away from my abusive husband.

Years of violence, the police at my door, fraud charges and Bobby's true exposure were finally enough to give me permission to break the vows of silence. The power was mine to do what should have been done fifteen years ago.

In the past, I had stayed away from family as much as I could, but I now realized they couldn't help as long as I wouldn't let them know how. Later that afternoon, I called my sister, Marsha, and told her I was leaving my husband and she said, "Oh, Janice, it's about time."

When I finally confided in my sister, it felt as though the weight of the world was lifted. I begged her not to tell my mother and she promised she wouldn't.

Ten minutes after I hung up the phone, I received a call from my mother and she said, "Marsha just called me, how can I help?"

From that minute on, my mother became my strength.

"We'll get through this together," she promised.

My mother offered to help me move into another home. Since I didn't have a car, she told me to look for a used car and she would send me the money to pay for it.

I convinced my husband I needed time to be alone to get well. Since we were losing yet another home in foreclosure, it was mutually agreed that my husband would stay where we were until the foreclosure sale.

I allowed him to believe he would move in with the children and me when that was finished.

During the week, my husband helped me move furniture into the home I had rented, believing he would soon follow. Once I actually set my plan into motion there was no turning back; I knew my life depended upon it.

I had to get away from his abuse if I were to survive.

Eleven

Facing Reality

*Sometime in your life you will go on a journey. It will be the longest journey
you have ever taken; it is the journey to find yourself.*
- Kathleen Sharp

An emotional breakdown can be a blessing in disguise. It's as
though an unseen wrecking ball smashes the house you lived in,
the one fear built, and nothing is left but the angry woman that
lived inside.

I was scared, or perhaps in a state of shock realizing I had finally taken
that terrifying *first* step—the one I had been unable to make for so many
years. At first, life seemed surreal. While those around me seemed to be
going about their lives the way they always had, my world had turned upside
down.

It wasn't that my world hadn't already been turned upside down, but
this time, I was facing reality.

There was constant fighting in our home. Just dressing and combing my
hair each day was accomplishing a difficult task. Many times, the only place
I felt safe enough to cry was my bathroom. I still remember sitting in my tub
with the water running and sobbing as though my heart would break. I
didn't want my children to see me so distraught when they needed me most,
yet I couldn't hide it from them either.

I may have been getting up each day, but my heart had shriveled into
this dried pitiful prune pit. I was consumed with anger and frightened that

I couldn't feel anything else. I don't know if this is a reason, but I also I did many things of which I am ashamed.

I can remember walking into a store and stuffing merchandise into my purse and brazenly walking out of the store as if it didn't matter. I hated what I was doing, but at least I felt in control. Stealing released a sudden rush of adrenaline and from my racing pulse to a heart frantically beating, I felt alive and in control. Admitting this sounds like a poor excuse for intolerable behavior, but I was in a poor state of thinking.

This was a terrible time. I had to rely on State Welfare Assistance as well as my mother's help.

Even though it was difficult to accept help from my mother, she was the only stabilizing force in my life, and without her I couldn't have survived.

Having been fired from several jobs while still living with Bobby, I was now unable to hold a job. I knew I had finally done the right thing by leaving, but doing it after I was so emotionally destroyed seems like a bad dream.

One morning, I took a long, hard look into my bathroom mirror. The face of the woman staring back at me frightened me so much that reality finally started to sink in. I couldn't believe the reflection was me, but the freedom I felt as I saw my own reflection gave me the courage to gently touch my face and feel the emptiness in my heart. I wept that morning, knowing how much of me the abuse had destroyed.

Jori and I met twice a week. I was terrified I was going to hurt myself or even my children. For years, I had stuffed my pain and I was terrified of the rage I felt.

My children were also afraid of me and Bobby fueled their fear. He used every chance he had to turn them against me.

"She is sick," Bobby would say. "How could anyone expect me to live with that?" He spent his time convincing my three older children that I was to blame for the pain in their lives and what my children saw reinforced the awful things he said.

I *was* sick. Emotionally I had been destroyed. My mother did the best she could under the circumstances, but I don't think anyone realized the severity of my depression. I wasn't capable of taking care of six children. They needed stability in their life and I couldn't offer that to them emotionally. I know I further traumatized them by my own behavior. What they saw in me was frightening. One moment I would be okay, but the next they would find me huddled in a corner sobbing because I couldn't face cleaning the kitchen or fixing them breakfast. I would scream at them for just about anything. I guess I really expected too much from them. I wanted my children to work together and I also wanted them to help take care of me, but they were only children.

Perhaps entering a shelter would have been more appropriate for the kids and me at that time, but I didn't do it. Instead, I found a way to leave Bobby without facing the reality that I couldn't take care of my children or myself, and that my life was still in danger.

Even though Bobby and I were living in separate houses, he still felt he owned me. I was his wife, or better, his possession. He didn't want me making any decisions without him. Actually, I was dependent upon him for everything. It didn't take long before I realized how much Bobby did of my thinking and decision-making. I needed to ask him if it was okay for me to do just about anything. At first, I couldn't make even the most insignificant decision without running to the phone to call him. I hated him and I wanted him out of my life and yet I called him over silly things. At one time, I relied on Bobby believing he was the support I needed. Once I faced the truth, I realized that Bobby was incapable of taking care of anyone least of all himself.

Soon Bobby began to pressure me, it was time for him to be together with his family, he said. I wasn't emotionally competent to live on my own. I needed him to help me recover from depression and control the older boys' behavior. One afternoon, he began moving his personal belongings into my bedroom, and I knew it was time to tell him he wasn't welcome.

I was as prepared as I could be when I told him I was filing for divorce, and I wanted him to stay away from the children and me. First, he didn't believe me, and then he went ballistic. He grabbed me, and I struggled until I got away. With only the bed between us, he screamed, "Bitch, you will find yourself in fucking hell if you ever try leaving me."

Frightened, I tried to grab the phone but he ripped it out of the wall. We screamed at each other. I yelled at him to leave and he shouted that I still belonged to him, and I had ruined his life so I had to stay and pay for the years he put up living with me.

Before I knew it, Bobby had a hold of me, throwing me onto my bed with his hands around my neck. But this was a woman he had never reckoned with before, because this time I fought back.

A raging force built inside of me, and with all my might I drew my knees into my abdomen, and then with a powerful force I kicked him.

He was startled as he fell backward. Scrambling to my feet, I grabbed a clothes hamper (it was the only thing close enough to me) and began swinging it.

Before he had a chance to react, I was wildly screaming and beating him with unbelievable strength. Over and over I beat him with the empty clothes hamper—he didn't have a chance to hit me back.

Years of imprisoned rage wanted to see him dead as I screamed, "It is your turn to live in hell. If you ever touch me again, I will have you thrown in jail!"

I don't know that I was physically hurting him, but I was wild with fury, screaming uncontrollably that I would kill him. Completely thrown off guard, Bobby backed away from me. Once he did, I threw down my only weapon, and told him the house was in my name, the car was in my name, and I would file for a restraining order against him if I had to.

Triumphant that I had finally stood up to him, I yelled in his face, "Get the hell out of my house."

He grabbed some of his personal belongings and turned around to leave, but not before he said, "I'll be back, I promise you that."

For the first time, I didn't feel sorry for him. I didn't feel guilty for hurting him or taking anything away from him like I had in the past. Many times in the past, I didn't call the police because I didn't want my children see their father handcuffed and taken off to jail. I also didn't want to see him suffer, even though it was okay for me to suffer for him. Thinking about how *he* felt had been my life story, but today I was thinking about me.

I wasn't really that brave though. After Bobby left, I sat in the middle of the floor shaking, unable to believe this day had finally come. Every second that I stood up to him, I was terrified it would be my last, but once I started there was no turning back. Without a doubt, I knew that should I waiver in my decision to leave, I wouldn't survive another harsh beating.

For weeks, he watched every move I made. I could see him following me, and I saw him drive slowly by my house every evening to make sure I was still there. He would telephone me late into the night and beg me to forgive him; he even said he would go to counseling.

I told him he was about fifteen years too late; I would never take him back. Then he threatened to kill himself, but I didn't care.

I told him he deserved to die for what he had done to me and his own children. I told him hell was too good for him.

Unable to control my anger, I wanted him to hurt as much as he had hurt me. He may have been remorseful for a few minutes, but as soon as I said, " People like you don't deserve to live and I promise you this, I will *never* come back to you," Bobby was no longer repentant. Instead, he was just as vile and dangerous as before.

"You're a sick bitch," he said. "I'll ruin your life if you destroy mine by leaving me."

I knew Bobby meant every word. He swore he would take away the kids, and I would never see them again. He promised to shout to the whole world each and every one of my dark secrets and I knew exactly what he meant by that.

"Everyone," he said, "will know the whole truth about you." The war was on. Bobby wasn't going to let me walk away without a fight, and I was frantic.

Early in the morning, he would ring my doorbell and often past midnight he would pound on the door forcing me to open it.

"This is my house," he said. "You're my wife and I have a right to be here."

As soon as I locked the door with him on the other side, he would yell loud enough so all the neighbors could hear that I was a whore and a tramp that was destroying his kids and turning them against him.

Often, he would enter when I wasn't home. He snooped through my drawers and spilled the contents on the floor just to let me know he had been there.

It didn't take long before I realized Bobby somehow had an extra key to my house. I called a locksmith and had all my locks changed, but Bobby always found a way to get in even when I knew I had secured the doors and windows.

He fought with the kids, constantly accusing them of betraying him and he begged them to move back with him. One day, Darinn told him he was staying with his Mom and Bobby tore into him.

Bobby ridiculed him by saying "You're stupid, just like your mother." Then laughing, he said, "You'll never amount to anything."

Darinn stood up to him and told him what he said wasn't true. Bobby hit him across the face while shoving him across the room. They were yelling at each other and I was screaming at Bobby to stop.

Bobby continued shoving and hitting Darinn until they reached the top of the stairs. Then, with one swift kick, Bobby sent Darinn flying.

I ran to help Darinn. Screaming uncontrollably, Darinn was angry.

He'd hurt his ankle and couldn't stand on it—but he was also terrified. While Bobby watched from the upstairs, I grabbed Darinn and pulled him outside. Then I went back in, staying close to the open door, and told Bobby to get out before I went next door and called the police.

When was the madness going to stop? I couldn't take it. Every time Bobby drove by my house my heart leapt into my throat, and I panicked.

Between locking all the doors and watching out the window, I didn't know what else to do—I was still afraid to involve the police. I was tired of living that way and I couldn't take anymore, but truthfully, I was terrified of involving the police.

Friends in my ward listened to Bobby's side of the story. Rumors spread. Stories of my attempted suicide reached every ear willing to listen. Many sided with my estranged husband, feeling sorry for him that I wrecked his life by spending all his money then leaving him destitute and taking his children away from him.

How could people listen to his lies? Why were they so quick to judge me?

An older man, who had known me since birth, had recently moved into our ward.

His comment was, "I never see Janice at church and yet her husband attends faithfully, so, just who are we to believe?"

To make matters worse, the Bishop in my new ward didn't want to help me. He was more concerned about contributing to the break-up of a family than he was about protecting victims of violence.

And besides, according to him, what proof did he have that my husband beat me? Infuriated, my dear friend Belle told him, "Do you want to be responsible for this woman's death?"

After Belle made that comment, he agreed to help.

Finally, I made an appointment with a divorce attorney. He was aggressive and he also knew Bobby. He was ready to fight fire with fire.

But I was afraid to cross Bobby. I didn't want Bobby served with divorce papers, and so I thought I could work with him amicably once he knew I was not going to reconcile.

Bobby was irritated and would complain whenever he stopped by my house and I wasn't there. One afternoon, he waited until I returned. Immediately after got out of my car, he accused me of sleeping with someone else. Grabbing hold of me, he refused to let me go and demanded to know where I had been.

I begged him to shut up and leave me alone.

He laughed and said, "Why? I own you. You're my wife and it's my right to know who you're fucking."

Shaking my head in complete disgust, I told him to leave.

He shouted, "Answer me!"

He was hurting my arm and we were yelling at each other loud enough to bring a neighbor to her front door. She ran outside yelling at Bobby to leave me alone. As soon as Bobby saw her, he let me go, jumped in his pick-up and raced off.

Later that night, Bobby disconnected every wire and hose inside my car then slashed my tires. I couldn't prove it, but I knew he was the guilty one.

A few days later, I was in my front yard watering flowers when he drove by. Opening his door, he jumped out and told me he was sick of playing my games he wanted me back.

He grabbed me, trying to hold me close to him, kissing me up and down my neck. I struggled against him with the hose still in my hand. When he wouldn't release me, I sprayed him with water. He jumped back and I raced into the house, locking the door behind me.

With the force of his weight, he broke the door open. I ran toward the glass sliding door leading to the back patio. Then I saw Westin playing with his toys out in the backyard. I tried to reach him before Bobby had a chance, but he grabbed my three-year old.

Screaming for help, I begged Bobby to put him down; instead he ran through the back gate and jumped into his pick-up. He drove off leaving me screaming in the middle of the street at him to stop.

I called Bobby, begging him to bring Westin home. I could hear Westin screaming.

"You'll never see this baby again," he hollered before he hung up. I threatened to call the police but he only reassured me that everyone would get hurt. Scared witless, I was furious with Bobby.

He wanted me to suffer, but I wasn't about to fall into his trap. He wanted me to submit to his threats and go back to him so I quit calling him knowing it wouldn't do any good. I had to be patient and pray that he would bring Westin home on his own. Several days later, he drove up with Westin and dropped him off in the front yard.

One night, I awakened from a sound sleep at 3 a.m. to find Bobby sitting on the floor next to my bed.

I had no idea how long he had been sitting there, but as I was waking up he kept mumbling that he had put up with me for all these years and would never let me leave.

Panicked, I didn't know what to do. My phone was by the bed, but if I made the wrong move I knew Bobby would react violently. So I pretended to still be asleep.

Bobby was rocking back and forth, telling me how much he loved me and that his life was not worth living without me.

My heart was pounding, and I was afraid he would try and get into bed with me. Silently, I prayed, begging God to protect me, *"Please just make him go."*

Then Bobby started chanting, "You will have to die," over and over. Then he stopped rocking and stood up.

I knew my life was over as he slowly walked toward my bed.

Leaning down into my face he whispered, "I'll never let anyone else have you because you belong to me." My heart nearly stopped. I wasn't breathing, but I could hardly keep from screaming.

I could feel Bobby's heavy breathing, and I knew he was staring at me, but I kept my eyes tightly closed, then Bobby turned around and walked out of my room.

Relief swept through me, and I started sobbing. I felt God had somehow protected me, but I wasn't going to give Bobby another chance to test my faith in God or in the legal system.

The next morning, I made new plans.

I called a friend asking her if she would be interested in buying my furniture. Margie bought and sold used furniture as a business. I explained that I was divorcing Bobby and I needed to get out of town as soon as possible.

Later that day, Margie came over and agreed to buy most of what I had. She left me a check, along with an invoice listing each piece of furniture she had purchased. Margie knew she was to pick up the furniture after I vacated the house without letting Bobby know anything about it.

That afternoon, I made the mistake of leaving the invoice on the kitchen table. Bobby walked into my house, uninvited, and made his way into the kitchen before I knew he was there. Running down the stairs, I demanded that he leave immediately. He must have a suspicious nose letting him know when I was up to something because he was certainly suspicious that afternoon.

"What are you trying to hide from me?" he demanded to know.

I wouldn't answer him, except to tell him he was trespassing and I wanted him out. Then he saw the invoice. He grabbed it from the kitchen table and read it. I panicked and started moving toward the sliding glass door.

He jumped in front of me, waving the invoice in my face. He first grabbed me by the arm while dragging me through the house forcing me to show him exactly what I had sold.

"Fucking bitch, you don't own anything," he said as I pointed out what now belonged to Margie. Twisting my arm, he demanded I give him the money she had given me. Lying through my teeth, I swore Margie hadn't paid me yet.

Bobby shoved me against the wall yelling, "You're a fucking liar, bitch; give me the money because it doesn't belong to you."

Each time I denied having any money, he would shove me. Then Bobby's fist hit me in the stomach, and I doubled over. He threw another punch, knocking me to the floor.

Each time Bobby kicked me with his boot, he called me a "fucking bitch."

Screaming for help, I tried to protect myself. Robby heard me and came running. Once he saw his Dad, he yelled at him to stop. Robby tried getting in between Bobby and me, but Bobby threw him against the wall.

Robby ran from the room and seconds later he returned furiously trying to stop Bobby as he frantically screamed, "I've called the police, leave my Mom alone." Bobby kicked me again swearing he wasn't through with me. He ran, slammed the door and raced off in his pick-up.

Rob was bluffing and for a moment I was amazed and shocked at what just happened. Perhaps when I took the first step to own my power, my son had the courage to act on his.

For the first time, I wasn't submitting to his threats and he was losing the ultimate weapon he had over me because I was no longer feeling sorry for him. He was losing and that was something he would never let happen. Not only had I refused to let him move in with me, threatening to divorce him, but I had sold his furniture. Bobby had once beaten his boys senseless because they broke a jar containing old marbles that belonged to him, what I did was worse. If I didn't give the money to Bobby, my very life was in danger, and I knew Bobby would soon return again.

He called me later that afternoon just to remind me that he would be there the following day to pick up his money, and I damn sure better have it for him. I reassured him that I would.

Bobby had started delivering newspapers in the afternoon just before I left him and before he had to be at work he would drive by my house checking up on me. Then as soon as he was through delivering papers, he would drive by my house again before going home. But on weekends, he had to start his delivery route just before midnight.

I knew Bobby would be gone for two or three hours and that would give me enough time. I arranged with friends from my church to arrive at my house just after Bobby left for his paper route to help me pack my things into a U-Haul trailer.

I waited until I saw Bobby drive by my house and then I made the phone call. The men were waiting at Belle's house, not too far from where I lived. I was frantic. I was so afraid something would go awry, and Bobby would drive up before we were finished.

Everyone was madly dashing around the house grabbing whatever they could and throwing it inside the van. As soon as we had packed all we could, the men left and I ran to get the kids who were sleeping on the floor in an empty bedroom. I needed to get them into my Suburban before it was too late.

Afraid to say anything to my kids, I didn't tell them my plans. Rob and Darinn woke up when the men arrived at the house and they helped with the packing, but my three younger ones cried as soon as I told them we had to hurry and leave. Once it dawned on them what we were doing, they didn't' want to go.

Each minute that was wasted was precious time—I didn't have time to be gentle or reassuring and they resisted getting their clothes on complaining that they didn't want to leave their friends. They didn't want to leave their bikes and toys that we didn't have room to take. My five-year-old wanted to say goodbye to his Dad; my three-year-old just wanted to go back to sleep.

I wanted to yell at all of them, "Just shut up and get in the damn car," but I didn't because we were all extremely stressed—I just wanted to get out of there.

Finally, I had my kids settled in. They had blankets and pillows and I strapped them in best I could. Then I had to open the garage door. Shadows seemed to lurk behind the bushes and I was shaking as I cautiously opened the garage door. A soft wind rustled dried leaves causing my heart to skip a beat, and I expected Bobby to jump out of the dark at any moment.

Nighttime always intensified my fear, and if Bobby caught me he would beat the life out of me. But I didn't see anyone on the streets.

The night air was deadly still. Hurriedly, I jumped into the car and turned on the ignition. My heart was pounding as I pulled out of the driveway and began to drive away from the house, I glanced at the time and it was 1:30 in the morning—Bobby would be on his way home. I didn't know which street he would be taking but I was terrified that he would see me by the time I reached Country Club Drive.

Quivering, I wasn't thinking straight. Once I made it out of the subdivision, I headed in the wrong direction, and I didn't dare go back in fear that Bobby would be looking for me. I parked my car in back of a grocery store and waited for nearly an hour but the longer I waited the closer I felt to having a heart attack.

A friend was driving the U-Haul to a town close to the border, but she wasn't going to leave for several more hours. Finally, I decided to get out of Mesa as fast as I could. Once back out on the street, I prayed, and I drove as fast as I dared. We made it to the freeway with no sight of Bobby. Relieved, I felt the worse was over.

There were times during my drive from Arizona to Mexico that I would have to pull off to the side of the road until I could quit crying. Utterly frazzled, I couldn't cope with the kids fighting or crying. The one blessing was that my kids were tired and slept some of the way.

As I crossed the Arizona border into Mexico, I felt freedom—like a caged bird flying away from its cruel captor.

I looked back at the life I lived and the life I nearly ended and vowed to be free from the hell I lived in.

I was going to get well.

After we arrived in Mexico, my children and I stayed with my mother, but I knew our stay could only be temporary. We needed a place of our own. There were seven of us and we were adding stress to my mother's life and that put more stress on me. One afternoon my Mom and I went for a drive.

I wasn't sure I was going to stay in Mexico, but when we passed a vacant house, I told her to stop and we got out. We both walked through weeds up to our waist and peeked in through the windows. The house had been vacant for quite some time and it was rather small for a family of seven, but I was excited.

"Mom, this is it," I said. "This is where I need to live until my divorce is final."

With my mother's help, we talked to the owners and an agreement was reached. This little red brick house, facing Main Street built over 100 years ago, was soon to be my first real home—far enough away from any threat of violence.

The weather was humid and hot, but I had help cleaning the inside of the house. I painted kitchen cupboards to give them a bright, new look, and I knew that underneath old and worn vinyl was a hardwood floor so we stripped the vinyl away and then began scrubbing and polishing the wood. Every window was opened to let the warm summer breeze be the only air-conditioning we had.

I saw new life all around me. Even though our small, two-bedroom house appeared shabby in the beginning, it was more than a palace to me. Outside in the flowerbeds, tiny flower buds, so filled with promise, seemed to whisper sweet promises of new beginnings. For the first time, I felt that I had a life and I could do anything I wanted with it. I wasn't weeping at the drop of a hat; instead I was finally starting to live.

I had very little contact with Bobby. I returned to Mesa long enough to file a divorce petition with court, but I didn't have to see Bobby.

Summer was soon over, and the children began a new school year. They seemed to be thriving in a new environment without living under tremendous stress. They were playing as normal children and bringing friends into our home where they knew they would be respected and treated with dignity.

Once Bobby was served with divorce papers, I believe he knew our marriage was over and that I wasn't returning, but he wasn't ready to give up. He fought the divorce and filed a petition with the court alleging I had left the country taking the children without his permission.

I fought against his petition, but in a court hearing I was unable to introduce allegations of child abuse because none had been reported. Instead, he was allowed to introduce hospital records and suicidal letters from me to my children, and the judge decided I didn't appear to be a stable mother.

Temporarily, I lost my battle to keep my children in Mexico. I was ordered to return to Arizona even though we had no place to live, I was unable to work, and Bobby refused to pay child support. The Judge didn't want to hear this, and I left the courtroom vowing I would never allow that to happen.

Soon after I returned home to Mexico, my husband called late one night. He said if I would come back to Arizona just to talk to him about our divorce, he would reconsider and sign a document allowing the children to stay in Mexico. As part of the agreement, he also wanted me to pay him the money I received for the furniture that was sold prior to my leaving Arizona.

My mother gave me the money I needed, and so with a check in hand, I flew to Phoenix and he picked me up at the airport. The moment I saw him standing in the airport holding a bouquet of red roses, a feeling came over me warning me to stay away from him. But I didn't listen. Our plan was to exchange the check for the agreement at a local restaurant, and then he would drop me off at a friend's house.

Instead, I let him drive me to the home we once shared. He said he only needed to pick up something, and we wouldn't stay very long.

Like an idiot, I believed him. Before he opened his pick-up door, he told me to go inside the house with him and get photo albums and other keepsakes that belonged to the children and me. I went inside even though I knew I shouldn't.

The house was cold, and dark, and I was immediately reminded of why I had fled from there in the first place, but it was too late. He grabbed my purse away from me, dumping the contents on the floor. He quickly seized the check and forced me into the bedroom, throwing me down on the bed. His eyes were cold and menacing, and he was unmerciful as he tore at my clothing.

I begged him to stop, but he said I was still his eternal wife, that I belonged to him and he could do what he wanted. With all my strength, I fought to keep his hands from hurting me, but it was to no avail. He was stronger than I and he forced himself between my legs. Feeling him thrusting himself inside me over and over sickened me. As he breathed heavily into my face, I tried fending him off with my fists. I screamed, and kicked, and I thought for sure I would suffocate as tears streamed down my face.

After what seemed like an eternity, he finally stopped. He walked into the bathroom and closed the door. I scrambled for my clothes, and grabbed my purse, stuffing my things inside, while dressing as I ran from the room.

I finished dressing on the front porch, and then I sobbed as I looked around me. Familiar surroundings of what used to be my home felt strange and uninviting.

What had I been doing living here in what once seemed like a home to me? Had I ever lived in a real home with Bobby or had I just existed in hostile environment? Had Bobby really changed that much over the years or was the man that just raped me the same man I married 15 years ago? This was the ultimate betrayal and reminder of my horrifying past. Should I call the police and report a rape? Would he say I was his wife and went to his house willingly?

I had been fooled by my need to believe in the humanness and decency of Bobby. My married life was based not only on my fear of him, but also my belief that there was a spark of decency left in *him*. For many years I told myself I just needed to find it.

The cruelty of his acts that fateful afternoon woke me from another deep sleep. Bobby was an angry man who had a need to hurt and destroy anyone who rejected or abandoned him. The innocence of his childhood had been silenced forever and pain and anger became the only force in his heart.

Humiliated, I ran to his pick-up, grabbed my suitcase and walked several blocks to a pay phone and called my friend. Sobbing, I begged Patti to pick me up. I stayed over night with her and returned home to Mexico the following day.

Boarding an America West jet, I found my seat next to a window. Tears soaked my face, smearing my make-up and causing my head to ache. But I cried tears of relief; grateful I was going home to the only place that offered refuge for my children and me. I vowed that no one would ever take that away from us again, and if I had to be a fugitive and live south of the border for the rest of my life, that would be a small price to pay. My children would never be forced to leave the only safe home they had ever known until they were ready.

Twelve

Healing begins

Learn to get in touch with the silence within yourself.
And know that everything in this life has a purpose.
-Elisabeth Kubler-Ross

L ife is not a fairy tale, and frogs don't turn into princes when you kiss them. Instead, I was the one that turned into the frog. My own self-reflection frightened me, and I was angry at the conditions in my life.

Too embarrassed to tell anyone that Bobby had raped and deceived me, I said nothing, except that Bobby refused to sign the agreement allowing the children to remain with me in Mexico.

Bobby called me begging for reconciliation. He even asked the judge to force me into reconciliatory intervention before my divorce was granted, but it was too late, I was never going back into his violent world.

For months, I traveled back and forth from Mexico to Mesa so I could continue my therapy with Jori as well as appear in court when necessary. At the beginning of my sessions with Jori, I blamed Bobby. I was angry with him. More truthfully, I despised him. I wanted him to pay for what he had done. If he was suffering from the loss of his family it was at his own doing.

If I thought I was in bad shape when I left Bobby that was nothing. For years, I was willing to hurt—be the sacrificial lamb. I didn't want Bobby to hurt, although I despised him, I didn't want him to suffer, but now I wanted to kill him—I wanted to wring his neck just like you would a chicken, skin him, and put him in boiling water. I wanted to see him suffer the way I was suffering—all those years of pained silence felt like a bomb explosion and it was too late to stuff it all back in as though it didn't matter.

That one tormenting feeling of rage felt like a vengeful volcano, one that had remained sleeping for a thousand years. In its mighty fury it began spewing hate, revenge and bitterness at the bottom of my feet, then rising up to consume me with its rage.

When I awoke early in the morning, I was angry, and when I laid my head down to sleep my tears would soak the pillow. I remember feeling exhausted and discouraged with more burdens than I could deal with. How was I to cope with my own anger, six hurting children, financial stress and complications with the legal system?

During those awful days, I felt like yesterday's trash, and for the most part, really didn't care. I don't know how others coped, but I faced each day with a tear-stained face too tired to take care of myself, emotionally drained and obsessed with revenge.

Have you ever been at the breaking point and one little thing takes you over the edge? Once I went over the edge there seemed to be no end. I had fallen into a bottomless pit.

It wasn't until after several weeks of therapy that I knew I was in serious trouble. I wanted to wear a bandage around my head that read, "Beware. Don't mess with me, I'm volatile." It was difficult to be around my children because they were as angry and hurt as I was and it seemed as if everything they did pushed my buttons and made it even harder for me to function.

Then I was angry that I had to start over. I was angry because I didn't have a way to support myself. I was angry because I didn't have a life worth living. Soon there was nothing but my anger. I'm still amazed when I remember how angry I was driving down the street screaming obscenities at people because they blocked traffic. Often drivers would retaliate by flipping me off and screaming back at me.

I hated Bobby for so many things. He went on with his life. Nothing changed for him except that he didn't have a wife to abuse or children to hurt, but he still had his mind. He could think and function and blame me for everything.

"Hate" isn't a strong enough word; I loathed Bobby not only for his abuse, but also because he deprived me of many precious moments. I would never be a young woman again experiencing her first time as a wife and a mother.

By doing everything in his power to destroy me, he hurt his children. They needed me and for many years I hadn't been there for them. And because I left him, he was willing to hurt them even more just to get back at me.

It didn't take long for me to realize that I had stopped the process of healing—I was trapped. I was too angry. Nothing in my life felt right and I resented it. I wasn't just angry, I was miserable and blaming everyone around me and I didn't know how to go beyond it.

Being true to my natural stubborn tendencies, I wallowed inside trapped feelings. I just couldn't let go of anything and my need to have control where I didn't, until I couldn't stand being so miserable.

In reality, I think I just needed to feel angry long enough to remind me whom I was angry with and to *never* let this happen again.

In the beginning, I wanted Bobby to acknowledge what he had done as if that would make everything all better. But since Bobby wasn't going to show up at Jori's willing to beg my forgiveness, and tell me how sorry he felt for all the pain he had inflicted on me, finally, I was willing to do the next best thing.

I used imagery! I visualized scenes in which I was being beaten. This time, I couldn't allow myself to shut down. I had already done that; it's a natural human instinct to protect the mechanism that keeps us functioning, which is our mind First, I told him why we were in therapy and how angry I was at him for hurting me.

It was difficult to relive moments of sheer terror. I felt helpless and terribly afraid, but I knew that I was safe in Jori's office and that provided the security my mind needed to play this game with me.

When I lived with Bobby, I was always conscious of whether or not I felt safe in a room. I would stay close to any door that offered a quick escape, and I was always frightened of going into the bathroom or closet where he could corner me. So in my mind, I pictured an open door, an easy escape if he lost his temper, and then I mustered up my most vivid imagination, which isn't all that bad, and I recreated actual memories of violence.

The terror I felt remembering the rage in his eyes and his strength was enough for me to say, "I'm not going there." But I had to relive it—somehow it had to become real enough for me to feel the terror and pain and associate with it in order for me to deal with it.

My most vivid recollection is the time he used the golf club. I can't even begin to describe the terror or the pain. It was excruciating, but what frightened me more than anything was the thought of my unborn baby.

There was no way I wanted to go through that again—my wounds were still raw and bleeding and I still felt extremely fragile—anything could send me over the edge, but I trusted Jori and somehow I knew I would be okay.

As I described the scene to Jori, I closed my eyes. I remembered watching him as he ran to the golf bag standing in the corner and in haste grab a golf club. Everything happened in split seconds, there wasn't enough time to run, but I knew exactly what he was going to do with that awful thing.

Then I watched, as if in slow motion, as he swung the club into the air and brought it crashing down on me. That's when the pain hit me also. I actually felt it rip into my skin. I wanted to stop, but I didn't.

I let my mind carry me all the way through it, each painful swing after another. I remembered crawling on my hands and knees, trying to escape the next blow. Anyone that has been pregnant knows how difficult it is to gracefully climb out of bed in the morning or bend over to tie shoelaces. It's just not that easy to maneuver an oversized body. But much more than that, if I moved the wrong way, Bobby easily could have slammed that iron rod across my tummy.

He could have crushed the baby's skull; he could have caused internal bleeding and the baby would have died.

I was scared; not only for my life, but also for my baby's life, and I relived each terrorizing moment until the beating stopped.

When necessary, I would reenact another situation in which I felt helpless, I had fifteen years worth of accumulated memories so it wasn't that difficult. I brought it to life the best way I could and instead of cowering, I stood up to him.

There were times I beat the pillow until the stuffing was scattered all over the floor. It felt good to get in touch with my anger and to react in a way that restored my power. It felt good to strip him of his dignity and make him huddle defenselessly in a corner pleading for mercy like I had.

In my make-believe game, I was the one that could do anything I wanted. I needed to play it over and over just long enough to say, ***"No one will ever do this to me again."***

Then I took all the humiliation I felt over the years and handed it back to him. "This is yours," I said. "I no longer need to feel it. It's your turn to feel what you did to me."

In time, I found I didn't really need to hurt him; I just needed to stop him from hurting me. I didn't feel better by causing him to huddle defensively in a corner—I didn't want to be that horrible giant hurting someone else. But it felt good to stand up to him and take away the power he had over me, and it was a necessary step in my recovery.

As often as I needed, I played this scene over again and never once did I give in when I remembered how often he blamed me or attempted to gain my sympathy. Never once did I allow him to turn me into a victim again.

Each time I replayed this scene, truth would hit me in the face. Bobby was an abuser when I married him—he always had been and never changed. I was the one trying to change him. I wanted so badly for him to see the dysfunction in his behavior that I forgot to look at mine. What seemed astonishing to me was that he never once saw any need to change his behavior; he was too busy trying to change me.

Associating anger with its cause is imperative. It's the only way we can end it. But old negative thought patterns don't just disappear. Often I would question my feelings until Jori helped me understand that battered women disassociate with their feelings and they identify with the abuser more easily than with their own feelings, therefore; recognizing where the anger is coming from is essential for healing.

No one has the right to hurt anyone, but when they do we have the right to protect our self. Living with an angry man doesn't allow that right. To be angry and express it would only bring about more violence and because of that fear, I had to hold back not only anger, but also my pride and my dignity and all the pain that accompanies self-betrayal.

I had been tortured at the hands of my husband and the reality of the abuse awoke me from a deep slumber—where had common sense and dignity been during all those horrid years?

Once I felt safe enough to be angry, I also gave myself permission to *feel* my pain! I mattered. How I felt mattered. I was able to say, "I'm angry as hell. You had no right to do this to me and I don't have to take it."

Knowing that I didn't have to take it was the most liberating feeling of all. In triumph, I felt renewed with a power I hadn't experienced before.

Coming out of a relationship where I had been riding on an emotional rollercoaster powered by Bobby's skillful ability to lift me up or bring me down with ridicule had completely distorted my self image. I didn't believe in myself. From this, I learned to be patient and good to myself.

Most of all, I had to accept that I enabled—I was co-dependent. With that awareness, I took responsibility for my recovery. But I also made many mistakes during different stages of recovery—patience and understanding made a difference for me.

I also needed to understand why I turned to others for answers. While this is common for battered women, women of my faith are taught to be dependent upon their leaders, and not to go outside that authority.

In view of all that had gone before, I couldn't possibly understand why my Bishops hadn't understood what was happening inside my family enough to do something about it when I asked for help.

They knew of the abuse, so why didn't I receive their support to leave my husband?

What difference did it make if Bobby attended his meetings? It didn't change him.

What difference did it make if I attended the temple with my husband?

Attending the temple didn't heal either one of us because it isn't possible to find healing inside an abusive relationship. I had to get far away from it before Spirit was able to work with me.

It is important to listen to my instincts. If that channel isn't clear, then something is wrong that needs my attention. I am my own authority. From my Higher Self, answers to all my questions are available as well as divine guidance.

Discovering inner-peace didn't happen for me for quite some time. In facing my past, I faced a lot of ugliness. My behavior had been humiliating, but my behavior also has a name, it's called "codependency." Instead of hating myself, I needed to put my arms around myself comforting the little girl in me.

So I did. I sang lullabies to her pain and spoke to her of love. I needed to know that my pain and all the abuse I had lived with mattered. Sometimes I felt as though the little girl in me would surely die from her broken heart if someone didn't say, "You, my little one, are more precious to me than all the shining stars in God's vast heavens."

Unfortunately, my Fairy Godmother didn't appear waving a magic wand erasing all my bad feelings or rewarding me for my wonderful new and wise choices. And my wounds weren't magically healed. Healing really didn't come until years later, but I do know my time with Jori is where my healing began.

Thirteen

Family in Crisis

Each day it was my prayer to find my saving grace—what did I need to make it through each day? Sometimes I just needed help with my children.

While the judge was deciding Bobby's petition for custody, I was ordered to bring the kids across the border on weekends so that Bobby could pick them up. I didn't want to. I made up excuses, and I made sure the kids knew they didn't have to go, but if I didn't comply, the judge said he would rule in Bobby's favor.

During this time, I felt completely helpless. There wasn't anything I could do to hold Bobby responsible for the irrational things he would do. Bobby would always do or say something to hurt the kids just to get back at me. One time they were to stay with their Dad for two weeks during Easter vacation.

A few days after they arrived, Bobby became angry over something that happened and told the kids to get out of his apartment. Robby called me collect from a pay phone telling me that he and the other kids had been told to leave and they were forced to sit outside in the parking lot. It took me seven hours to get there and during that time they waited in the sweltering hot Arizona sun.

I can't begin to imagine the rejection they must have felt. Remembering those awful years is difficult—my children endured so much. So, in between nursing my wounds, I tried dealing with their problems.

Robby and I continued to struggle in our relationship. Terribly defiant, he didn't want to get up in the morning. He refused to attend church and he was disrespectful. He got angry when I tried forcing him and accused me of being a liar.

I wanted Robby to tell me exactly what lies I had told. Immediately, Robby was defensive and he said that his Dad had worked hard during our marriage and I destroyed him financially. He told me that his Dad had never accepted money from my mother; of course, the list went on and on. Then Robby told me that he could never respect me as his mother. Frightened by the hostility in his voice, I asked him why.

Anger and tremendous pain spewed from his mouth. "How could you have an abortion, Mom? God will never forgive you because of the things you did."

I was stunned. I asked Rob who told him, he answered, "Dad told me, and he said you would only deny it if I asked you." Apparently Bobby wanted his son to know exactly what kind of mother he had.

Shocked beyond words that Bobby would do this to his own son, I tried to explain to Robby what had happened, but he didn't want to listen. In anguish, I wanted to wither and die. I was humiliated in front of my son trying to defend my actions and explain why I had opted to have an abortion, but he was only thirteen years old.

"I can't believe anything you say, Mom; you lied to Dad and destroyed our family."

What I saw in Robby's eyes went deeper than his Dad could ever have imagined. If he'd wanted to hurt me, he had, but in doing so, he destroyed his own son's self-respect and damaged his love for his mother.

Many times, I don't know how I made it from one day to the next. I remember one evening in particular when Rob tried to light a gas stove.

Built-up gas exploded and blew him across the room, burning hair and skin on the upper part of his body. I was hysterical and couldn't think rationally. The kitchen walls were closing in on me, and I felt panic rise into a suffocating swell.

The madwoman in me returned with a vengeance. I felt overwhelmed with the stress in my life. Unfortunately, stress doesn't separate or categorize itself into neat little packages that say, "Today you only have to deal with me." And this happened to be a day I had more than I could cope with.

Rob's 12-year-old brother drove him to the doctor's office, (we lived in a small rural town and the doctor only lived down the street). When they returned, I was overwhelmed with guilt, but grateful that his burns weren't serious.

I was writing my own obituary by the way I was living. I was afraid that "If I should die before I wake," my children would write on my headstone, "Here lies the remains of an emotionally unavailable, exhausted and irritable mother, may she finally rest in peace."

The severity of my emotional problems deeply affected my children, in fact, early on my children learned to be on their own. They didn't know how to just be children because they had to take care of me as well as themselves.

Long before dawn, my children had fixed each other breakfast for quite some time. When I finally tried to take over, they didn't trust that I would be there for them. They were angry with me, and they let me know it.

Often, Nate would say, "You've never been here for us, Mom, and we don't need you anymore."

Gradually, I was learning how to be a mother and allow my children to be children.

It sounds like a simple thing; children should instinctively know how to be children, and adults should know how to parent. This isn't so with abused women and children. Their sense of normalcy is extremely distorted. The family doesn't know how to function; they just learn how to survive. Once the family becomes unbalanced because someone pulls away from their dysfunctional role, the whole family is thrown into chaos.

You learn to take the bad and cherish the good. I feel it was the laughing and the sharing that started our family healing. We started spending time talking and doing things together.

Even though some incidents are rather insignificant, I remember one afternoon when Darinn and Westin were playing a game they called "Cowboy." Darinn would throw a looped rope around Westin's head and pretend he was roping a calf.

One afternoon, Darinn got the rope out and said, "Come on Wes, let's play."

Westin put his little hands on his hips and said, "Okay, but I'm tired of playing that way. This time I'll be the boy and you can be the cow."

We laughed until we cried, and for the first time, I realized that we could say or do anything without being afraid.

This one little incident taught my children what so many kids know instinctively—when it is safe to play and when it is safe to laugh and when it is safe to simply act like children.

I also struggled in my relationship with my mother. She was overbearing and protective, but my problems adversely affected her. She wanted to control my life in little ways that didn't seem like control at all, but rather assistance. She didn't have safe boundaries and this created tremendous stress in her life, as well as mine.

Afraid that I wouldn't get out of bed, she checked up on me. Afraid that I would overspend, she tried controlling my money (which was really her money anyway). We were both trying to survive and while she thought she was helping her help was hurting me. I felt controlled. This is part of the dilemma, I did overspend and my behavior was unhealthy, but I needed to feel some control in my life.

My problems also spilled over into my children's lives and their problems impacted my problems. When I couldn't deal with my problems, I took more pills.

The only antidepressant that seemed to help was Prozac, but that wasn't enough. I already had prescriptions for Ambien and Xanax from my doctor in Arizona, and our family doctor in Mexico prescribed Ativan for me—even then I was abusing the medication. I was depending on prescriptive drugs to get me through each day.

Before long, I was also plagued with chronic fatigue. I don't know what brought it on so suddenly, but most of the time it was incapacitating. I found it difficult to hold my hairbrush or walk the short distance to my bathroom.

The judge finally ordered a family evaluation, so I had to prepare my children. This made them even more confused. What were they supposed to say against their father? Were they supposed to hate Bobby? In fact, they didn't want to talk about the abuse with anyone, they just wanted their lives to be normal, and they wanted their father to treat them with kindness.

Rob has told me many times how much it hurt him to hear me put down his father, most of the time I didn't know he was listening. My mother and I talked often about the custody battle. It wasn't right. We both knew what Bobby's ulterior motive was for petitioning the court in the first place. He wanted me back.

We thought about taking the kids to him and giving him custodial rights just to prove our point—he wouldn't keep them. But I couldn't do it. That would have sent a message to my kids that I didn't want them.

Even though my children hated their father's abuse, they still loved him, and they needed to know he loved them. When we, as parents, are angry and feel the need to get even, we should remember how devastating it is for our children to hear insulting remarks about either of their parents, however true they may be, because both parents will always be a part of their identity.

My children knew the truth about their Dad, because they experienced his cruelty, but hearing about it didn't make them feel any better. I did my fair share of spouting off about their father. It was difficult at best to keep my mouth shut when he said and did unloving, cruel and vicious things.

Much later my son, Robby, allowed me to read part of his diary. He wrote: *"My mother is having a hard time, I feel bad for her. I wish we could stay here but my*

Dad is trying to make us go back. I like my new home if only my mother wasn't so sad." I wonder how this story would be written from my children's perspective.

Nine months later my divorce was final, but the child custody issue had not been settled. The day I received the news from my attorney, I celebrated. Yet to be truthful, there wasn't much to celebrate—I witnessed too much damage that had been done, and I had to wonder if we would ever heal.

We had been living in Mexico nearly 16 months when I returned to Arizona with my children for psychological testing and found the process to be very complicated.

After a few days of evaluation, I cancelled the visits and refused to have my children continue with the process. Bobby also refused to attend, and the court appointed psychiatrist was blackmailing me into paying for the children's evaluation. The afternoon of our second day, the psychiatrist took me in his office, closing the door behind him.

"As you can see, your ex-husband has cancelled every appointment we had made with him, but someone has to pay for your six children and obviously, he isn't here to do it."

Shocked by our conversation, I answered him, "Take that up with him, I'm doing exactly what was instructed of me. I've paid you for my evaluation [just as the judge had ordered], now Bobby is responsible for theirs."

I got up to leave but he insisted I hear him out. What he wanted me to understand was the fact that it was up to him to decide our fate.

"If you don't come up with the money by tomorrow morning, I'll write an unsatisfactory report against you."

Infuriated, I stood up and told him, "Do what you have to do, but you won't receive one dime from me." I hardly had the money to pay for mine, and since I refused to pay him for my children, he did write an unsatisfactory report against me.

Life can be anything but fair, but the judge didn't control every aspect of my life, and thank Heaven angels were still busy at work. Even though I struggled with my children, I wasn't discouraged.

During the next few months, intuitively, I felt excitement in the air. Something wonderful was about to happen that would change my life forever and that of my children.

Fourteen

No sweeter love than this

The union of Twin Flames is the most sacred of ceremonies ever performed; it is a reunion of spirits created as one, embodied in mortality as two. This love is incomparable, and it is the essence of this pure love that heals and inspires others.

Renewed by a sense of immeasurable hope, I felt discouragement slowly fading in spite of the chaotic state my life was in. I was drawn within myself and spent time meditating and asking for spirit's guidance.

Mysteriously, I lived in two worlds. While the outside of my world was spinning out of control, at times I felt deep inner peace.

Gracious and loving people came into my life bearing spiritual gifts— knowledge and answers I needed. They were always there when I needed them and when I was ready to hear what they had to say.

Patty, a spiritual healer, who channels from the other side, gave me invaluable assistance. I owe much to her.

She opened the door to a whole new side of me and this was the beginning of my spiritual journey. I believe it is true that when the student is ready the master will appear. The universe has a magical way of responding to our needs.

Precognitive dreams, which are vivid dreams that feel so real they are strongly with you once you wake, became part of my life. Some dreams came in the form of a warning of what would happen should I not change my behavior. Often, I would dream of things that were to happen, and later they did. In the beginning, I resented these dreams. They frightened me. Later I saw them as a gift and another way spirit communicates with us.

In the meantime, I felt magic in the air. The countryside was aglow in vivid autumn colors. Early morning walks gave me time alone to experience the wonder of this special feeling. My children were busy in school and looking forward to the upcoming Christmas holidays.

They hadn't seen their father for several months and the court date for the custody hearing had been changed until sometime in January. Bobby and I hadn't called a truce, but the kids needed to find a place of neutrality. Since it was court-ordered, the kids stayed with him during holidays or weekends when I could take them, and even though Bobby wasn't physically abusive during this time, emotionally he played havoc with their minds.

Bobby had been dating someone he met from his apartment complex and it wasn't long before they were married. Bobby hadn't been paying child support, and when I learned he was given a temple recommend, I called his current Bishop.

His response was ice cold. I was accused of causing severe suffering in the life of my ex-husband. It was his opinion that Bobby had done nothing to deserve the abandonment of his family or my harassment for child support since Bobby could barely maintain his own needs. This was another rude awakening for me.

It was late November when my mother told me about her plans to be with my sisters in Salt Lake City, Utah. She tried to encourage me to go with her, but I felt certain I would have other plans. Call it woman's intuition, but I had no doubt that I wouldn't be alone on Christmas Eve.

During this time, I was blessed with many spiritual experiences, but the most sacred and memorable one happened when I first began to dream of *him*.

At night, I entered into a glorious state of dreaming about a man without a face, and yet the love we felt for one another electrified my being.

While in his presence, peaceful serenity filled my being. I wanted to run to him, and have him hold me in his arms, but not once did we touch. In awe, I would awake. In disbelief, I made my way throughout the day longing to dream the same dream again. Yet, I couldn't help but wonder, "What is happening to me?"

The love I felt for him was as much a part of me as my own heart.

For weeks to come I felt him close. Then a few weeks later, I had the same dream again and just before dawn, I felt the presence of angels in my bedroom. I don't know that I was sleeping or dreaming it felt so real.

A being filled with love softly whispered, "You have known him for all time." An infusion of knowledge poured into my being. Dormant knowledge dimmed from many years of separation was awakening reminding me of another time and of the sacred love we shared.

In naïveté, I didn't fully understand, but it wasn't long before I did. A few weeks later, I was in Mesa visiting Belle. She had made an appointment for me to see Patty, and it was Patty that had the answers I needed.

During our session, Patty told me that I would soon meet someone special. "Are you referring to my soul mate?" I asked.

A smile came over her face when she answered me, "Oh no my dear, this is much deeper than that, he is your Twin Flame."

This was a word unfamiliar to me, but I didn't question a word she said, my dreams had already prepared me and my heart simply understood that time would reveal all I needed to know.

Patty also cautioned me to let things happen.

"They will happen, you know," she said several times and, of course, I assured her that I would not interfere with nature (or the angels that were watching over us).

Driving home the following day, my heart rejoiced. I felt close to the angels who had stayed with me, and I gave thanks for the joy I felt.

A few weeks later, I was visiting with Aunt Marene. She wasn't my aunt at the time, but I had always thought of her as someone special. Often, I rode horses with her two sons, Lee and Jay, as they helped fill many empty hours since I didn't have any other friends. That afternoon, as Aunt Marene and I were mindlessly chatting, she mentioned her nephew.

"I would love to introduce you to him," she said, "but since you still have six children at home, I don't know that he would be interested."

Then she went on to explain how Richard had been married before…the moment she said the name Richard, my heart stopped.

"That's him!" I exclaimed. I don't know *how* I knew, but I knew that Richard was the one Patty had spoken of.

He was the one I dreamed of. Richard was my Twin Flame.

She looked at me rather strangely and said, "Who?"

I answered, "Richard, he is the one."

In my heart, I had no doubt. Oblivious to my new discovery, Aunt Marene went on to tell me that Richard had plans to meet a girlfriend of his sisters.

"They are all flying to Cancun together," she said.

"Oh no, he can't," I said rather forcefully, and before I could stop myself I added, "He belongs to me."

I left that afternoon feeling desperate to stop this ill-fated introduction from happening. I remembered the words Patty spoke when she said, "Janice, don't do anything to make things happen, let them happen on their own."

At that moment, I didn't trust anyone. I felt I had to make things happen or they wouldn't happen by themselves.

Late that evening I called Jay. Together we schemed. Jay would play Cupid and call Richard and get us together.

"Leave it up to me," he said. I put the phone down with such relief. The wheels were in motion.

Jay called Richard. He waited until the following day, and in their conversation Jay told Richard about me. In fact, according to Jay, he made me sound exciting enough that having six children at home seemed (almost) insignificant.

Richard was to call me the following Sunday. Anxiously, I waited for that day. I counted the hours. I was excited and extremely curious and finally it was Sunday. I made sure my kids were busy watching television.

All of them cooperated, but Justin was suspicious. He wanted to know why I didn't want him in the same room with the telephone and me.

Finally, I told him that I was waiting for a guy to call me. That was a big mistake.

The minute the phone rang, I knew it was Richard, but Justin grabbed the phone before I could. Reluctantly, he passed the phone to me, but then started to argue.

I didn't want Richard to hear the commotion, so I begged Justin to wait until I was through talking. I had tried explaining to Justin that this was just a friendly conversation and that he shouldn't feel threatened.

Finally, I asked Richard to hold on. I ran for Rob. Rob was strong enough to drag Justin out of the room and keep him away from me and Rob was only too happy to oblige.

I ran with the phone, closing myself off in the bathroom while Rob and Justin fought with one another. Rob grabbed Justin by the legs and pulled him outside then sat on him. Unfortunately, I could still hear Justin screaming.

We stayed on the phone for nearly an hour. There I was huddled in the bathroom, sitting on the toilet seat with the water running and the door closed so he couldn't hear Justin. His voice was soothing, loving, kind and gentle with a wonderful sense of humor.

I melted into a puddle of emotions sitting on that toilet lid. I had no idea what he looked like, but that didn't have any bearing on my feelings. How I felt was beyond my control—the love was simply there—a deep love that transcended any other feeling I had ever felt before.

We also made plans that afternoon. I was to take my children to Mesa on December 21st to drop them off at their Dad's home, then I was to spend the night at a friend's and return to Tucson by noon the following day. That day soon arrived.

I left the kids with their Dad and stayed with Kristi. Early the next morning, I woke to Heaven's melody, my soul's love song, feeling happier than I had ever felt before.

Just off the freeway, as you first enter Tucson's city limits, is a McDonald's. Richard said to stop there and call him. He lived just minutes away, and once I called he would meet me there.

Nervously, I pulled into the parking lot. The telephone was inside the restaurant near the restrooms. Timidly, I walked in knowing I had to call him, but I was so nervous. I went into the bathroom, stared at the face in the mirror and couldn't help but wonder, am I still pretty enough?

I left the bathroom and stood by the pay phone. Hours could have passed or just minutes, but I know I stood there for a long time, still I didn't dare dial his number. That's when a stranger walked up to me and looking right at me he started to speak.

For a moment, my heart stopped. *If this is him*, I thought to myself, *I'm running*. I wasn't the least bit interested in the looks of this man.

With a blank look on my face, I didn't let him say a word before I asked him if he was waiting to meet someone and he said, "No, but I would like to use the phone, so if you're not going to call anyone, would you please move out of the way?"

Relief washed over me as I nervously laughed and said, *"Thank God you're not Richard."* That's when I found the courage to call him; he couldn't look any worse than that stranger.

His voice, and I still love to hear his voice, was quick to answer. I told him what I was wearing, and that I would be waiting outside the front door of McDonald's. I thought I would die a thousand deaths before he got there, and then all of a sudden he was there. He recognized me instantly. He knew my mother and said I looked just like her.

I was still so nervous, I hardly said a word, but I remember following behind him in my car. Over a dusty, unpaved road, I sped to keep up with him.

I thought about many things in a short period of time. Life had given me many hard lessons and I was still trying to grasp the strangeness of this whole situation. His face wasn't familiar at all, yet my feelings were overwhelming. For a split second, I wanted to turn my car around and drive across the desert and disappear into the fading sunset.

Then I thought, *"No I'll stop and sit in the hot, scorching sun until reason returns,"* that shouldn't take long, even in December the desert is hot in mid afternoon. I was willing to ask anyone who would listen, even if my only audience were prairie dogs, if they thought I was a fool allowing my heart to feel again, to love and to trust again?

I didn't turn around instead I followed him to his front door and once inside, I felt at home. It was as though I had been there before. We talked for hours, not as strangers, but as one in heart and spirit. When I looked into his eyes, the windows to his soul, I knew I had no secrets from him, *he knew me, he really knew me.*

Years of pain dimmed, a heart scorched and withered felt renewed, alive and so filled with joy. I felt myself wanting to reach out, and hold on to him, love him or curse him for making me go through life without him. *"Where have you been?"* My heart screamed. Part of me was angry with him, but I loved him. I had no doubt.

Richard wanted to know everything about me, including my past. I was open and honest with him from the very beginning, and he knew that my family had been shattered by domestic violence. I was recovering, but I still had a long way to go. For years, I had battled against debilitating depression and it wasn't that long ago a breakdown had left me unable to cope with tying my shoes, taking a bath, or combing my hair. But worst of all, depression had been a thief robbing me of time with my children.

I couldn't tell him enough. It was the sharing I longed for, just conversing with him was healing and somehow he was part of my past. He felt my pain, and I was in awe of his compassion. Our journeys in life had been similar.

Once I had been a battered wife; his ex-wife had many faces and sometimes she had been violent. There was a parallel of different experiences that bonded us together, yet he was not wounded. His soul remained untouched. What he experienced gave him understanding and compassion, but he remained strong and resilient. I knew he would have to be if he were to live with me.

That afternoon passed so quickly. It was sundown and we hadn't stopped talking. Even in the shadows, I felt his light. My eyes drank in each line on his face, mesmerized by his smile and captivated by the way his eyes warmed my soul. I didn't want to move from where we were sitting, as if that would awaken me from my dream. In his presence, I felt at home. Curled up on his couch, I was where I belonged. I had finally come home, and sharing my heart with him reminded me of a fire burning warming the soul from the chilling winter's wind.

Later we dressed for dinner, and then drove to Red Lobster where I hardly touched my food. After dinner we returned to his place and it was early morning when we finally decided to say goodnight. I stayed in his guest room upstairs, yet felt close to him. The next morning it felt wonderful to wake knowing I was there with him. As I look back over those first few days being with Richard, *they remain the most precious and sacred memories of my life with him.* It is difficult to recreate those memories in writing.

But it's here in my heart, and tears easily flow as I remember how dearly and deeply he has always loved me. I knew it long before he said the words.

That morning, Richard shared his innermost feelings with me. The night before, after we said goodnight, he closed his bedroom door behind him. Since the minute we met, he felt a rush of emotions swelling in a river of love. Wanting to feel me close again he finally drifted into a restless sleep only to awaken.

"I'm in love with her," he said, "but I can't take on six children, seven with my own." And yet, he said the love he felt went beyond physical desire and any love he had experienced before. Richard was torn between his love and reality. But later that night in his dreams a messenger appeared to him. Vivid and so real he felt more alive and in tune with each word that was said to him. "Your love is not a love of this world, and this love will carry you through difficult times, you need only trust in your feelings."

As he spoke, gently I touched his hand. He turned to me and unexpectedly held me close as though he would never let me go. A rare love flowed from his heart to mine from a place in time that has no beginning and it has no end.

Inside the hearts of Twin Flames there is an understanding, and we knew that from the spiritual realm of existence, we descended into form sharing the same blueprint that is not duplicated anywhere else in the universe knowing that some day our souls would find one another. And after walking across the fiery bridge of adversity, we were prepared to fulfill a sacred vow we both made before God.

This is our divine mission and deep within all doubt was erased.

Then softly he whispered, "I love you."

My heart stood still. I found refuge in his warm embrace. As wings of a bird open and take flight, my soul soared and drifted into another realm, and I felt the heavens open and rejoice at the reunion of Twin Flames. I felt his heart beating, his breath upon my hair, and his hands gently wiping away my tears, and my soul wept.

The power of Twin Flames is the essence of one flowing into the essence of the other creating wholeness and in his sacred heart, Richard confirmed his commitment—he would help me heal and bring me safely home.

Richard wanted to marry me. He didn't want to wait since I would have to return to Mexico in a few days and we would be separated. Right now, I can't say that reason was with me. I can't say that I made a sound and wise decision when I agreed to get married as soon as possible. But I did.

I can only imagine what this must sound like as my words are read, and if my daughter were saying this to me, I would grab hold of her and freeze her until she was thirty. I don't know that relationships like this happen very often, but without a doubt, Richard is my Twin Flame —the love we share is pure soul love.

That morning we knew we could not wait. We both weighed our options and knowing that if I remained in Mexico, more than likely the court would rule in Bobby's favor. Bobby was persistent and clever. He knew how to manipulate the system for his benefit, and because I had taken the kids into a foreign country, it didn't matter whether it was in their best interest to remain there. Bobby claimed he had no assurance I would ever allow him to see them or bring them back into the United States. Our hearing was scheduled in January and I really felt certain I would lose.

Even though the custody issue was of great concern, I must also be honest and admit that I had never lived a life of stability and I didn't sort through all of the ramifications of a hasty marriage or the disruption of my children's lives in Mexico.

Perhaps I was acting out of selfishness, if so, it was not intentional. I had no doubt that my marriage to Richard was nothing less than a marriage of deep, eternal love, but I didn't have the right to uproot my children without involving them first or giving them time to get to know Richard. Perhaps I was also afraid that if I did, Richard would change his mind or my children would not accept him.

Yet, I was happier than I had ever been and on Christmas Eve, holiday music played throughout his house as Richard prepared dinner for his Mom, Dad and siblings. If they were shocked by our engagement, they didn't say a word, instead they were happy for us.

Richard's mother and father had also been born in the Mormon Colonies, and Richard spent most of his youth there. He knew my family and even though I was much younger than Richard and, therefore, did not know him, I knew his family.

Monday morning Richard took me to the mall. He wanted to buy me a ring. We went inside Helzberg Diamonds and there was one that I fell in love with.

Once he purchased the ring he asked for my hand, right there in front of the sales clerk and I whispered in his ear, *"Now this isn't exactly what I would call romantic, can't you find somewhere else to slide that ring on my finger?"*

Without hesitating, he swept me out of the store, dancing through flocks of Christmas shoppers, he guided me to a more romantic place...in-between racks of clothing in Dillard's Department Store.

Bedazzled by his overture of rapture and romance, I looked around. *"How* appropriate," I said, *"Now that we're alone, hidden behind women's intimate apparel, how could any other place be more romantic?"* Giggling with girlish laughter while Richard took my hand in his, he placed the ring on my finger and gently kissed my lips.

We must have been in a world of our own that day because it didn't enter our minds that someone else might think we were a little too hasty in our decision to marry, but the Bishop did.

As soon as we arrived home, Richard called his Bishop to ask him if he wouldn't marry us that evening. Without knowing all the details, the Bishop gave us the hour to be at his home. The only suitable dress I had with me was one of black lace. Knowing that black isn't exactly what one should wear to her wedding; I hastily gave the dress a blessing.

We arrived on the Bishop's doorstep at 8:00 p.m. The moment he heard when we met he said, "What do you mean you've only known each other for three days?"

No one gets married after knowing each other for three days, unless they are insane. I know that's exactly what he was thinking, but you must remember, this happened eight years ago and today we're still happily married and very much in love.

Before the ceremony he sat us both down to give us a Bishop's Counsel. He sat behind his desk and we sat across from him. Carefully, he opened his book, as if to stall this marriage for a few more precious moments, but no matter what he said, each time he would roll his eyes around in complete circles. Exasperated, he simply closed his book exclaiming, "Are you sure about this?" Then waving his arms he said, "Of course you must know what you're doing. "

Richard was 54 and I was 39, *that's old enough isn't it?* But I'm sure he was thinking, *"Age doesn't have anything to do with it."*

Knowing that we weren't about to change our minds, we followed him into his living room. Standing before him we exchanged our vows.

The Bishop and his wife gave us both hugs and said they were happy for us, but I would have loved to remain behind as a fly on the wall to hear their conversation once we closed their front door. Without any fanfare we simply drove away.

The following day, I called my mother. She was still visiting with my sisters in Salt Lake City, and when I first told her that I was married she said, *"You're kidding me aren't you?"*

When I said no, she handed the phone over to my sister. I could hear her say, "Janice is playing a game with me, tell her it isn't funny."

My sister, Marsha, immediately grabbed the phone and said, "Janice, you're not really serious are you?"

When I said, "Yes," she laughed and said, "I don't believe you."

Several times, I tried to convince her I really was married. She just couldn't stop screaming, *"No you're not! You couldn't be."*

Finally, I realized how crazy I sounded and so I said, "Don't panic, Marsha, of course I'm just kidding."

We said goodbye and I hung up. Richard walked into the room and asked, "How did it go?" I told him they wouldn't believe me, so finally I agreed with them and said we really weren't married.

A few hours later, I called my sister back and told her not to say a word, but just listen. I explained to her how I felt and what had happened between Richard and I, and that yes, we were married. There was a long silence at the other end of the phone. This time Marsha believed me.

Stunned, she didn't say a word until I said, "It's okay, I know how you must feel, but just tell Mom for me."

A few days later Richard and I flew to Salt Lake and talked with my mother and sisters in person. It took my Mom a while before she could talk without crying. My mother had witnessed many years of my unhappiness and I know she thought I was making another mistake—until she spent some time with us. Later my Mom said to me that had she not *felt* right about my marriage, nothing I said could have convinced her that the marriage would work.

Our deep love resounded within their hearts and they also felt the conviction of that love. The day we left Salt Lake City, we had my family's blessings.

Fifteen

Newly Wed with Children

The complexity of my spinning world only grew more bewildering. Two hearts joined together as one found little peace together, we were married with troubled children.

My happiest memories begin with Richard, but they are bittersweet in that we both had troubled children. From the day we met my husband swept me off my feet, but our marriage didn't place me in a mystical garden of paradise. Instead, our life together with our children was stormy, demanding and unrelenting.

It started with Justin. The day before Richard and I drove to Mesa to pick up my kids, I told them about my marriage. Even though they were shocked, they seemed to be okay with it, but Bobby wasn't. Once he found out I had remarried, he demanded that I pick the kids up immediately. The following day Richard and I drove to Mesa, and on the way home Justin was obstinate, sullen, and ill tempered.

When we drove into our driveway, he refused to get out of the car.

"I hate you, Mom!" he screamed over and again.

I had had enough of his bad temper the whole way home.

I was ready to skin him alive. Instead of making a good impression, like I had hoped they would, Justin argued over everything, causing everyone to be in a bad mood. All six kids bickered back and forth.

"That's enough," I hollered at Justin. "What's the matter with you, anyway?"

Justin didn't waste any time in telling me how angry his Dad had been the

160

day before, "and he took it out on us," he said.

Apparently, Bobby did a real number on the kids while they were at his house. The moment he learned I was married he went into a rage, and Justin was more than eager to unload it on me.

"You never cared about us," he screamed, "and you're the one that's trying to destroy my Dad. He's really sorry, but you won't give him a second chance."

"A second chance, Justin? I gave your Dad 15 years' worth of chances."

"But you didn't try hard enough," he said.

"This is insane, Justin." Your Dad and I have been divorced for nearly two years and you didn't have a problem with that before, so why now?"

I wanted an answer from him, but he wouldn't give me a reasonable one. Justin's attitude threw me. He lived with his Dad long enough to know exactly why I left him. He had spent time with him during the summer. He was there when his Dad married his deceased uncle's wife just months after our divorce was final. He saw how quickly that marriage dissolved and his Dad had already re-married soon after his last divorce—and Justin was blaming me?

We were both yelling, but I was furious when Justin said, "You sleep with men just to get what you want, Dad says you're nothing more than a slut."

That was it. I wasn't feeling guilty for the mess Justin's life was in and I didn't feel bad for his pain. I was mad. Justin knew better and yet he sounded just like his Dad.

"Live with your Dad then," I yelled. "If he is the poor victim, then take care of him, ruin your life, but I won't let you ruin mine."

For a moment, Justin almost seemed repentant until angrily he said, "Why did you marry him? Richard doesn't want us. He'll get rid of us as soon as he can."

Pleading just one more time, I said, "You don't even know Richard, why won't you give him a chance?"

"Because you're the one that has ruined everything and I hate you."

Slowly opening the car door I said, "If you really believe that, Justin, then I won't try and keep you from living with your Dad, but I know you know exactly what kind of father he is."

Why did his Dad so easily influence Justin? It wasn't as though his Dad had never raised a hand to him. It wasn't as though Justin hadn't witnessed his father beating me time after time. But I was the one who destroyed everyone's lives?

From words that stung, I was hurt and I was angry. Bobby was a vile creature without any conscious. He would have destroyed everyone of us rather than see me move on in life, especially if that meant I was happy.

I left Justin alone in the car with his bags still packed while I went inside the house to talk with Richard. He asked if I thought it would help if he talked to Justin. "Go for it," I said. "We have nothing to lose."

Richard talked to him for quite some time, but he came back and said, "He's angry Janice, and he won't listen."

We left Justin there for several more hours. I went back and forth asking if he wanted to give this some time before he made a decision. Each time he said, "Take me back to my Dad's. I'll never stay here with you."

I called Bobby to explain the situation and the first thing he said was, "Can you blame him?" Then he went on to remind me how sick I was and that Richard was a fool to marry me. I felt sick all right: heartsick. This battle between us, the one he instigated, was destroying the kids. I don't think Bobby's wife was happy about it, but Justin went to live with his Dad anyway. This was only the beginning of the unraveling of my family.

Later that afternoon, when Richard called his daughter, April, she laughed. She couldn't believe it. When we picked her up she just stared at me.

Once we were all together, Richard genuinely wanted my kids to feel welcome, and I wanted a good relationship with April. Bedrooms were arranged to accommodate each one and then Richard suggested we do things as a family. He included my boys in buying furniture for their bedrooms. He took an interest in how they were feeling and in what they wanted to do. It wasn't long before Darinn respected Richard and didn't hesitate to let me know that our marriage was okay with him.

In January, Richard and I attended the custody hearing, and even though Bobby tried to convince the court that I was an unfit mother, the fact that I was living inside the country satisfied the judge. The judge also informed me that had the children not been living in Arizona prior to the hearing, he would have ruled in favor of my ex-husband.

Bobby and I were awarded joint custody, but I was the custodial parent. Then as soon as the judge ordered Bobby to make his $400 a month child support payment (for all six children) Bobby stormed out of the court room vowing that I owed him and he would never pay me.

In the months that followed, I noticed how quickly my kids were changing. They were growing up. They weren't children anymore and each searched for his or her identity. I don't know that they ever felt safe in their individuality and while stepping into a new horizon; their teen-age years drastically changed our family dynamics, one that was barely holding on.

I also had other problems to worry about. Richard's job required a great deal of traveling and he hated to go alone. He wanted me with him all the time.

I've always had a problem saying "No!" when necessary. Therefore, I tried to say "Yes" to everyone. That behavior was emotionally draining, and each time I traveled with Richard, guilt overwhelmed me because I wasn't home. If I stayed home, I was afraid that my husband would complain about my children.

When I stayed home, there was constant conflict with my children. Having friends of their own, they were also making lives of their own. Little by little they pulled away from me, and I didn't agree with what they were doing.

By this time it wasn't going well for Justin. Even though he denied it, he didn't sound happy when we talked on the phone. I knew he was having problems, but he wouldn't talk to me about them. I know living with his Dad brought back the same anxiety he suffered from in the past. In time he was failing in school.

I spent time with Justin whenever I could. When he had a basketball game, I went to watch his games, and we would spend time together on weekends. I knew he wanted to live at home with me—he seemed so vulnerable—but he had his pride, and it was hard for him to admit he had made a mistake.

To avoid going home after school, Justin told me that he spent time with friends who smoked cigarettes and marijuana. I was worried about Justin's welfare, but when I approached Bobby about my concerns, he said it wasn't any of my business.

He said, "If Justin has any problems, you are to blame."

After this he made it more difficult for Justin to free himself from the emotional hold he had on him. All he had to do was make Justin feel sorry for him—the 'poor me' syndrome! Over and over, he would tell Justin how hard his life had been and how much he needed his family.

Then there was April. She was Richard's troubled 12-year-old daughter and had been living with him at the time of our marriage. She wasn't ready to share him with six other children or me, and she had become increasingly difficult for her father to control.

Richard had already encountered severe problems with April long before he married me. He was unable to date anyone without April interfering and causing problems for him. She seemed incorrigible after I was around her for a while.

But then April bounced back and forth from her parents. She wanted to live with her mother, but for several reasons her mother didn't want her there. Since childhood, April felt unwanted, and when I entered the picture it wasn't long before I became the wicked stepmother and it wasn't any easier for me.

I spent time alone with April trying to bridge the rift between us. I have fond memories of afternoons shopping at the mall trying on similar clothes, and modeling in front of the mirror giggling like two teenage girls.

In spite of her negative behavior, I saw another side to April and she was a compassionate young girl. She had a sense of humor that could lighten anyone's mood, but she also had layers of hurt and resentments. She was angry with both her mother and her father. She had been for years and she certainly wasn't ready to surrender and allow my children or me into her life that easy either.

One moment she was sweet and innocent, laughing and kind, but the instant her mood changed—watch out. When she didn't get her way the walls in the house vibrated and doors were broken as she slammed them back and forth. She could throw a larger tantrum than anyone I had ever seen and I was shocked at how far she would go to get her way.

Richard and I forced April into a home for girls. She would stay there for a week and then return home if the counselor thought she was ready. She was always ready to come home until she walked through our front door.

As for my own children, Darinn's my wild child. Once he had played the role of the family peacekeeper, but that all changed. Like a sponge overly saturated with water, Darinn had had enough and all he wanted was to escape from his pain.

As a family, we were fractured. I knew my children were angry, but I couldn't reach them and they rebelled in every way possible. From taking the car without permission to staying out all night drinking and running with a wild crowd, I nearly lost my mind.

Then Darinn wanted to live with his Dad. First, he said he just wanted to be with Justin so he wouldn't be alone, but I also knew he didn't feel like he belonged in our home either. April caused a lot of problems for Darinn. They were close in age and April got too involved with his friends—she had a way of causing problems by making up stories and Darinn was always the bad guy. After many blow-ups between April and Darinn, I consented and asked Bobby if he would keep Darinn.

What was I thinking? No one should have been living with Bobby.

I'm appalled at my behavior. I shouldn't have consented or allowed either one of them to live with their father but it wasn't easy to fix problems or find solutions. I had six children that were acting out and they all had needs. Frankly, I don't believe an easy solution existed.

Bobby told Darinn he was welcome to live with him if that's what he wanted. I don't know why it was okay with Bobby when it wasn't okay with his wife, because as soon as Darinn unpacked his things, she wanted to throw him out. The situation didn't improve over time in fact it only worsened.

Then Darinn started telling me exactly what was going on inside Bobby's home. Bobby and his wife had serious problems—only this time it wasn't as much Bobby beating his wife, as it was his wife beating him. They had been sealed in a temple marriage and Bobby often flaunted his worthiness in my face and yet the police were often called to their apartment. I begged Justin and Darinn to just walk away from that whole situation.

Even though my boys faced many problems with their Dad, neither one wanted to live with me, either. I know there are those who would say, "These are just kids—you make them do what is in their best interest." I wish it had been that simple—just make them—if I had been able to, so much pain could have been avoided.

Darinn and Justin lasted about nine months at their father's. Even though Bobby refused to send Justin home, Darinn was free to leave anytime. But once Darinn returned, I wasn't about to leave Justin behind.

I waited until Justin was in school one morning before I went to see him. I took him out of class and demanded that he tell me *why* he wouldn't leave his Dad.

"You're miserable, Justin, why do you stay?" Justin looked down at his feet but he wouldn't answer me.

"I'm okay, Mom," he finally answered.

"No, you're not." I said. "I want you out of there, I want you home where you belong."

Still, Justin wouldn't budge. When I confronted him with his smoking and possible drug use, he denied it. I looked at his clothing. My heart ached to see this young boy dressing in extremely baggy jeans that two of him could fit inside; they weren't even around his waist. Chains were hanging from pocket to pocket while his pants dragged below his waist and made a puddle around his feet.

With tears in my eyes, I demanded to know, "Why do you want to dress like this?"

He answered, "I'm a skater, Mom, this is how we dress."

His hair was shaggy and he looked forlorn and lost more than any child I had seen before.

Adamantly I told him, "You're coming home with me, whether you want to or not."

Then he said with tears in his eyes, "I can't, Mom, you'll get in a lot of trouble if you try. Dad has custody of me and he will have you thrown in jail if you take me."

"That's not true," I said.

"Yes it is, Mom, I signed a piece of paper telling the judge that I wanted to live with my Dad."

"Why would you do that?"

"Because I felt bad," he said. "No one likes Dad. You don't and Rob and Nathan won't hardly talk to him."

"That's not your problem, Justin," I answered.

With resignation he said, "But Dad cries all the time, you just don't know how sad he is."

Pain twisted my heart. Overtaken with guilt, I felt responsible for all that had happened. For many months Justin was more afraid of the trouble he would cause me than the hostile situation he was living in.

I told Justin he had been lied to, but just the same, I felt panic. I left Justin at school and told him to wait for me; he was not to go home. Quickly I drove to the county courthouse and searched through every record concerning Bobby and me.

I found more than I anticipated. I ran across divorce decrees in Bobby's name. In disbelief I stared at the records.

This was the first time I knew that Bobby had been married six times before me!

Startled by the information staring me in the face, I didn't have time to think about them. I had to make sure I was still Justin's custodial parent. I found the document Justin was referring to, but amazingly, it had been forgotten. A date for a hearing had never been set and the line for the judge's signature was blank. I hurried back to school. I took him out of class and told him we had nothing to worry about.

Justin didn't pack his clothes that day. We immediately left for Tucson and later on returned to gather his belongings.

Perhaps all I needed to do was stand my ground from the beginning and *refuse* to budge an inch. Perhaps I should have ruled my children with as much force and discipline as possible but I hadn't. I didn't know how to and yet even if I did, I might not have been anymore successful.

Still, I did as I had been taught to hold my troubled family together. Every Sunday, we attended church and I tried to get them to attend Church activities during the week.

At first we didn't have problems with church attendance, but in time my kids felt threatened. They didn't fit in. The more I complained about how they dressed, the more they tuned me out.

"This just isn't acceptable," I screamed day after day.

"What do you expect parents to think, Darinn, when you show up to church with an earring in your ear?" Even though they tried hiding it, I could smell cigarette smoke on them when they came home. "Now you'll never be included with your Mormon friends," I cried.

When Darinn first came home with a pierced ear, I thought I would die. How was I going to explain that to my family? Later, not only did he have a pierced ear, his leg boldly displayed a magnificent dragon tattoo that covered most his leg.

In reality, the boys felt ostracized from the mainstream. And what they were taught in their young adult classes didn't cause them to feel any better about themselves; in fact, they felt worse. Everything that had ever happened to them was either in the form of physical/mental or sexual abuse.

They saw themselves as damaged goods. They were rejects in the Lord's Eyes and nothing I said changed the negative reinforcement they received from their religion. Later on it didn't help when no one inside the church wanted to befriend them either. So they befriended those that accepted them.

My kids weren't products of a "picture perfect family," but I still felt the pressure to raise them that way. They were children raised in violence and now they had a voice and the ability to exert their will and I was at a loss in knowing what I could do.

In need of a social life, and friends with whom they felt accepted, the friends they brought home dressed exactly like they did. I was so indignant. They were going against everything I had been taught and the teachings I had tried to instill in them. I was beyond consoling. According to the way I had been taught, my children were fast approaching the gates of hell. I don't know that I was more frightened by their behavior or embarrassed by their appearance.

So when did I lose control? Did I ever have *any* control? I think the answer to those questions is quite obvious—I never had any control. Obsessed with controlling life from the outside I don't think I realized how unmanageable my life had become.

I allowed others to control me and felt victimized as a result. Not only did people do things wrong, from my perspective, but they did it to me. Always feeling betrayed, and hurt, I was furious that no one listened to me.

Helplessly intoxicated with obsession, I wanted change from everyone else but me that behaved inexcusably.

Although painful, I believed my behavior was honorable. I thought I was doing everything right. But later I learned how impossible it is to be an effective parent when you are bound up in such pain and anger.

At the time, I didn't realize how detrimental I was to their healing. I always turned to my church leaders for answers. I had never been taught to seek help outside my religion—those on the outside didn't understand our beliefs, therefore, I faced our family crisis with limited skills and understanding.

I disregarded reality and wanted them to be picture perfect both in dress and behavior. I wanted them to be just like every other adolescent in the ward— clean cut and obedient. I wanted them to go on missions when they came of age; I wanted them to live worthy lives so they could attend the temple. The simple truth is, I wanted them to live their lives *my* way, because I thought it was the only way they would find happiness.

When they were trying to find their *real* identities, I tried forcing one on them that had never worked for me either. My children didn't fit the mold, they were different and nothing I did changed that—they needed loving acceptance without fear of rejection or blame and they certainly didn't' need to feel anymore guilt. What I needed was help in understanding their behavior and how I could deal with it more appropriately.

It has been difficult for me to admit this for many years, but I was confused with what I had been taught and terribly angry. How many years had I been told how to mend my marital problems? How many years had I tried? Was I the one who failed or did a system in which I believed fail me?

During those agonizing years I didn't live my life—I allowed someone else to live it for me. They had all my answers and the secret formula for happy, eternal families. In the end I found myself facing cold facts—much of the teachings and counsel I received prevented me from controlling my own life.

I believe that too many of us inside the Mormon culture live according to how we are told to live. While this may work for some, it doesn't work for everyone. We're given a model to emulate and when it doesn't work, we feel like such failures. Unintentionally, I had gone outside the paradigm. I wasn't the "perfect Mormon mother" and my children weren't models of the secret formula for eternal families. I was angry with myself, and I was angry with my children. The phrase once said by a Mormon Prophet, "No success compensates for failure in the home," only made me feel worse.

Each day seemed to be worse than the day before and I felt drained. My home was a battlefield, and I was determined to force my kids into compliance. Relentlessly, I pounded each one of my teen-age sons like they were tiny square pegs into a round hole in which they didn't fit.

Sixteen

Frightening days ahead

Sometimes you have to hold on until the storm is calm and the sun warms the Earth again, and during troubled times the only solace you will find is prayer. Praying for strength knowing God sends angels to watch over you.

was still attending therapy sessions with Jori. Once a week I drove to her office in Mesa. Sometimes I was spaced out enough from all the medications I was taking, I had my son drive me. I also located support groups in Tucson for my kids. The only problem I had was in getting them to attend.

Early mornings we battled because Darinn didn't want to attend school. Robby didn't want much except the keys to the car. If he wasn't involved in a fender-bender, he was speeding like a demon. Darinn seemed to be the hubbub of his social circle. Friends were over all the time, friends that were rebelling against any authority.

I'll never forget an experience I had during this time inside a Tucson shopping mall. A woman had a small booth and was giving people spiritual readings as she held their hands in hers. I stopped and insisted Richard wait so that she could read mine. This woman was gifted. She spoke of many truths and one that stands out was about Darinn. Among other things, she said, "This son will do things that will make your hair stand on edge."

At one time they may have hid their bad habits from me, but not anymore. Completely unafraid of any consequences, my three older boys would sit outside smoking their cigarettes. This wasn't any small matter to me. I detested seeing their young little fingers holding that terrible vice to their lips as the smoke curled up around their heads.

Just the sight of them smoking sent me into a rage. Their behavior was an insult to me and I loathed their cigarette smoking. I had been taught well. Breaking the Word of Wisdom was the ultimate appearance of evil.

Robby and his friends had desert parties where they would stay out all night drinking. Many times he came in at 4 a.m. so intoxicated he couldn't make it up the stairs to his bedroom.

Sometimes, Darinn didn't come home at all. When he did, he slept during the day. He had NO direction in life and he didn't care. He was looking out for himself and doing whatever he felt like doing.

One afternoon, during a heated argument to get him off the hook for his drinking, Robby shifted my attention to his brothers. He swore that he knew Darinn and Justin were also using drugs. As soon as Justin walked in the front door I started in on him.

"I want the truth," I said. "Are you smoking pot?"

The look on Justin's face was a dead giveaway. Justin wasn't as adept at lying as Darinn.

As if drinking or getting high on illicit drugs wasn't enough, together with their group of friends they also found it exciting to break and enter someone's home while they were gone. They would take stereos or other items just for fun.

Darinn became streetwise and never got caught. He lived on the streets with a rough crowd hell-bent on self-destructing, but Rob couldn't quite figure it out. He was the one that always got caught. If it wasn't Robby then it was Justin. I seemed to be spending more time in juvenile court than I did at home. In no time at all I was on a first name basis with the judge.

"I remember you," the judge would often say, "weren't you just here yesterday?" Perhaps I should have taken up overnight parking to save myself another trip.

I was exhausted and humiliated and sick of appearing in juvenile court. None of the kids were ever punished enough to make any difference for them— just fined and I had to pay the fine.

It wasn't just my older kids that were facing a crisis in their lives, the atmosphere, the rebellion, and lack of control had a rippling affect on my younger children. Nathan was only eight years old and had already tried smoking with one of *his* friends.

The straw that broke the camel's back happened one afternoon when Darinn returned home after a four-day hiatus. The moment he walked in my front door holding on to his *beyond baggy* pants so he wouldn't trip on them, dirty and blurry eyed I hit the ceiling. First, he tried to walk past me. I wasn't about to let him walk out of the room without getting the answer I wanted from him.

Getting into his face, I pointed my finger at him screaming, "How could you do this, Darinn?"

He mumbled a few incoherent words. Knowing that he was high, I didn't stop. Then waving his arms in the air, he raged, "Get the hell away from me." Still I wouldn't budge an inch. He tried to go around me and I grabbed on to him. He dragged me as far as the garage. I was still screaming at him to stop when he exploded. First he shoved me away from him and I fell to the floor, then I watched in horror as he went wild. Our garage looked bombed out, as he pounded his fists through the dry wall from one end to the other. He was completely out of control and the rage I saw in him scared the life out of me. His fists were bleeding but that didn't stop him. Only seconds had passed before I ran into the house to call 911 but before I had a chance to pick up the phone, Darinn ran out into the streets. He jumped over a retaining wall fleeing into the desert.

Scared for him, for me and my other children, who stood by in horror watching their older brother, I put my head in my hands and wept. Crumbling into a heap on the cold garage floor, I didn't want anyone to touch me, and so when Nate tried to put his arms around me, I turned him away from him. For an instant I wanted to push them all away—pain consumed me and I was terrified for my son. But this is how I always reacted—I went to pieces, which is something my kids hate about me.

That night I paced the floor. Every few seconds I peeked out the window in hopes that he would return. With tears of agony flowing, I wept. The night was still when finally I fell to my knees and I prayed for his safety.

I wasn't alone in my living room that night. God's Angels were with me. Shimmering outlines of bright light surrounded me and I felt the warmth of their luminosity. As I continued to pray, mentally I could see a host of angels protecting my son. They weren't like the angels that stayed with me. These spiritual beings were large in stature exuding power and protection.

I was comforted, but my fear was greater than my ability to trust in the powers of Angels. I knew I needed to let go and let God, but the night was too dark. Shadows frightened me, and the thought of Darinn overdosing or being in other danger was a real threat for me.

A few days later, friends of Darinn told me that he was now hanging out with some pretty tough kids from the south side of Tucson. He wasn't playing around with small stuff, this time he was using crack cocaine, heroin and stealing cars.

The one that frightened me the most was Darinn. He was the one who had been at the brunt of his father's vicious verbal abuse. In his father's eyes, he never did anything right. Since he was a small child he had been ridiculed, and according to his father, he was certain never to amount to anything. His wounds went deep and I knew how terribly hurt he was. But how was I to stop him from hurting himself?

Finally, Richard convinced me there was nothing I could do. Eyes swollen and my head throbbing, exhausted I went to bed, but the following morning that horrible knot was still in my stomach. Days went by and still no word from Darinn.

I filed a runaway report on Darinn and then several weeks later he finally came home on his own, but he didn't stay. By then I had no doubt that Darinn went beyond marijuana; hard drugs had become his way of life. Off and on he would show up at a friend's home that knew Justin. That's when Justin started staying away from home also. By then I wasn't just afraid for Darinn, I was angry as hell with him. He seemed magnetic—what he did the others followed and Justin was one of his favorite little cronies.

One afternoon, out of the clear blue sky, as if nothing was wrong, Justin and Darinn came home together and both of them were high. Richard told them it had to stop. They couldn't keep this up. Instead of making things better, I believed Richard made them worse when he told them they weren't welcome in his home.

That was it. Both my boys were gone and I was so angry with Richard and he was angry with them. All the begging, threatening and reporting them as runaways did nothing to help our family crisis—still I tried to handle things MY way and I resisted any help or suggestions from Richard. Finally Richard reached the end of his rope.

Searching through the Yellow Pages, I made phone calls to different drug treatment centers. We didn't have health insurance; therefore, none of the treatment centers would agree to take them, unless I paid cash. Unable to afford the cost, I really felt helpless.

April wasn't involved with substance abuse, but her temper and lack of discipline continually wore me down. She fought with Lynsey. She resented Nathan and Westin. Quite often April was heartless in the way she treated my younger children. But in fairness, she was fighting her own battle for survival. She was afraid of losing her father.

Amidst the chaos, April was the only sister Lynsey had and she was good to her. But abandonment was a real threat to April. Unfortunately, I didn't know how to reach her anymore than I could reach my own children.

"What else can possibly go wrong?" I asked Richard one night after a heated argument with April. He sadly shook his head. He didn't have any answers either. We had yet to find a solution that actually worked because grounding her, taking away privileges or possessions had no affect on her.

The only thing I can say for certain is that Richard really did love me. Physically and emotionally I wasn't well, and he was more concerned about me than anyone else. I battled with depression, along with other autoimmune disorders that only worsened with the stressful problems I continuously faced.

At night Richard would hold me tight. I was terrified of slipping into that deep, dark and terrifying black pit. He was frightened for me. Unless I stabilized, my children wouldn't either. During the day he would take me with him and often we found quiet places to sit and talk. Being with him was healing. The energy around him was calm and he always reminded me of his love.

"Can't you just wave a wand and fix everything?" I'd ask. The manner in which he remained centered in a crisis and the way he loved me reminded me of my father.

"I need you to make things better for me, Richard, and if you love me, you'll do it."

He'd always look at me and say, "I can't, Janice, you've got to become strong and do it for yourself."

I hated it when he said that. I wasn't getting stronger—I needed the chaos to stop so that I could.

I felt the inside of me was a cesspool filled with toxins that were destroying me. I was seeing two different doctors searching for a cure. Depression wasn't my only illness; I also suffered from chronic fatigue. Between the two of them they prescribed Xanax to calm my nerves, Prozac for depression, Amytriptlyn to treat pain caused from Fibromyalgia, and Ambien so that I could sleep at night.

There were days that I was in and out of coherency. Several times I left home unable to find my way back without help. When a friend of Richard's found me at a neighborhood convenient store disoriented, he called Richard.

With each passing day, Richard became increasingly concerned. He took the keys to my car and begged me to see another doctor. He saw many changes in my behavior and attributed my problems, in part, to the medications I was taking. But as my depression worsened my doctor only increased my dosage of Prozac. By then I was taking 80 milligrams of Prozac a day.

One particularly bad day, Richard took me into our bedroom, sitting me down on our bed he said, "Janice, let me take over with the discipline."

My heart froze.

"No way," I said.

Holding his hand up he said, "Hear me out…"

"No, I'm not going to step aside, you can't do it Richard. You don't know how to do it any better than I do."

"They are walking all over you Janice, You've got to stop protecting them and you need to follow through with some pretty tough consequences."

"Right," I said, "as if you know how to do that..."

I just wasn't about to let him take charge—I knew exactly what that meant and I really didn't know if a relationship had been established enough between Richard and my kids. I was afraid they would resent him if he became their disciplinarian.

I reassured Richard that I could handle the situation. With runaway reports filed on both Darinn and Justin, I finally found a drug treatment center that would take them. That solved ONE problem, but I had many more to face. First I had to locate Darinn and Justin, and then I had to face the fact that I was unable to adequately care for Nathan, age 8, Lynsey, age 7 and Westin, age 6. I asked my mother for help and she offered to keep them for a while.

The day Richard drove away with them I knew I would never see sunlight, feel laughter or joy again. Today the haunting memory of their little pleading faces still reminds me of their pain. They didn't understand why they had to leave, and Nate could only ask, "Mommy, what did I do wrong to make you send me away?"

I tried to get him to understand that I was doing it because I loved him but how could he possibly understand?

One afternoon in late May the police contacted me. They had found both Justin and Darinn inside a trailer house within miles of our home. I asked them to take both boys to Cottonwood, a drug treatment center. I met them at the facility and both were admitted that afternoon.

Even though Robby refused treatment as an in-patient, he did attend the family sessions. During these sessions he couldn't help but feel his pain. Being able to talk about it gives way to feeling what you try so hard to forget. Robby wasn't ready for healing any more than his brothers, but just the same they were affected by what went on during this time.

As soon as the school year ended, April went to stay with her mother and for the first time part of my family was in counseling together. I was amazed at what I was learning about my children, but the family sessions with my boys were almost too painful as they finally allowed me to see everything through their troubled eyes.

One of the counselors explained that it might be difficult for me to hear my boys express their pain. "It won't be easy," she said. "They are angry with you as well as with their father." But nothing quite prepared me for the agony I felt. Listening to them tell the story of their childhood abuse was one of the most excruciating experiences of my life.

Unable to escape reality, the faces of my growing boys ripped my heart a part. Is this what I had done to them? Between bouts of agonizing remorse, and unforgiving anger, I would leave the center and go home wounded and hurting and then crawl into bed and cry myself to sleep.

The next day, I returned to help them face their anger. Because of what they were learning about addiction, Darinn and Justin accused me of having a chemical dependency. How absurd, I thought, I didn't have a chemical dependency since mine was "prescribed" medication. I denied it; in fact I resented both of them for saying it.

I honestly believed that I wasn't to blame for the medications I was taking. Bobby was responsible and my boys were. Could they not see what their choices were doing to all of us? Truthfully, I hated the fact that I didn't have a life. I felt like I was walking around in shock amidst the ruins of what once I believed was my family.

I just wanted the pain to go away. I wanted to feel better. I hated waking in the morning with a knot in my stomach. I hated existing in a world of darkness and I hated myself as a woman and mother more at that moment than at any other time.

I didn't have any control in my life and the only skills I had to change my life were the old ones that hadn't worked in the past.

It was important that we receive counseling, and I hoped Bobby would accept responsibility for the damage he had caused.

Both Darinn and Justin asked him to attend the family session, but he chose not to, and this was a tragic mistake. They needed this healing time with their father before it was too late. I was angry with Bobby. He had failed me in every way, but I couldn't help but be angry with myself also for the expectations I still had of him.

Even without their father's presence, the family sessions were an important aspect of the treatment program. I will also have to say that placing Darinn and Justin in a safe facility was more important for me than it may have been for them. They didn't ask for help. Every chance they had they tried running. Once they were successful, but within days both were located and returned to the facility.

Perhaps one of the most vivid memories I have of the family sessions began one morning when the room was filled with victims and their families. Some of the in-patients were teen-agers and others were close to my age, but the one thing they all had in common was their inner pain.

One young man, who was close to six feet tall, even stood on a chair because he needed to feel larger than his father had once seemed to him when he beat him as a child. The scene was almost unbearable for me. Everyone inside that room felt this young man's anguish and need to take back his power.

Witnessing the intense emotions from this 26-year-old man brought to life my children's pain. Through him I saw my children. Vivid memories of little boys standing in their bedroom while their father beat them with his weight belt left me in agony.

Allowing painful childhood memories to surface is essential to recovery. It's important, at any age, that victims own their power, and that means taking it away from the one who took it from them.

It's the journey between childhood and adulthood that is often dismal and dark. What they find on their journey adds to their pain and often is just as controlling. This is certainly what happens with substance abuse. What starts out as rebellion results in habit-forming behavior just as self-destructive.

Life has a way of forcing us to see what we don't want to see and facing what we don't want to face. This happened to me the morning I awoke in place of Chicken Little to find the sky falling in and I felt like my world was coming to an end. Chicken Little may have been able to run for cover, but I couldn't. Besides, Chicken Little is a fictitious character that only thought the sky was falling in. Mine had.

Having been victimized in my previous marriage had many consequences. The worst came to light when my children reached adolescence—their teen years were filled with rebellion and anger. Their behavior turned my world upside down and I wasn't ready for it, but frankly, I don't think we ever are.

Time passes so quickly. One moment, I was a young mother raising her children. I didn't understand the repercussions I would face later on—I was too busy.

I had to survive, and I had responsibilities, my most important one being that of trying to change my husband. Caught up in illusions prevented me from stepping outside this paradigm long enough to see the sickness inside it—one that has the power to wipe out a whole family.

Regardless of the pain it caused and the upheaval, I will always be grateful for the short whisper of healing time with Darinn and Justin. I learned that it wasn't just I who had been severely wounded.

For the first time I was feeling my deepest feelings with my children. Together we cried. We expressed our innermost feelings of anger and deep emotional pain.

Heartbroken from the severity of my older boy's problems forced me to face reality.

What part had I played? What had that role done to my children?

In my darkest hours, I reached out to hold onto a sense of security, but, once again, severe depression had a hold on me, and my children's pain was a current stronger than I could withstand. I wasn't ready to face my children's demons and dragons before I conquered mine.

Seventeen

When does it end?

Never-ending is the soul's seasons to grow in wisdom and understanding and the seasons to grow from life's most difficult lessons.

The time for Justin and Darinn's release from Cottonwood came all too soon. Richard and I had already decided that we would move from our neighborhood. We found a perfect place to build a home. We hoped that being in a different environment would help them choose different friends.

Unfortunately, after we moved, nothing really changed. Darinn ran away from home again and Justin just found new friends with the same habits. Even though he was attending school, he was failing in most his classes.

Several months after moving into our new home, Nathan, Lynsey and Westin came home. They had been with my mother for the past school year and anxiously wanted to be in their own home. At the same time, April's Mom insisted we take her also. I wanted time alone with my children, but that wasn't to be and the moment April walked through our front door, I knew our problems were only starting over.

April was worse than she had been in the past. As soon as she was forced to move in with us she was angry and resentful. I don't blame her. She felt rejected by her mother and rather than adjust, April bitterly fought with Lynsey and Westin. I wasn't able to leave home without April threatening to hurt or hurting either one of them.

To make matters worse, April's mother and grandmother criticized me and interfered with any discipline measures I tried to implement. They sided with April, which only reinforced her negative behavior in my home. When I was criticized for the problems in my home, I repeatedly asked that her mother take her back. But that wasn't going to happen.

To add to our problems, Richard and I were worried Nathan would follow in his older brother's footsteps. He was failing almost every subject in school and he wanted to drop out. Nathan is an angry child. He was so young when I left his father, but not once in his short life had he felt safe. The reasons for our divorce didn't seem to matter as much as what the abuse and my emotional illness did to him. He was undergoing counseling, but he resented anyone who wanted to help him. Finally, he was placed in a special program for students at risk but in time we realized that even this did not help him.

Darinn was still a runaway. I had no idea where he was and I worried about him night and day. Little bits of information made its way through his old circle of friends and the news about Darinn wasn't any I wanted to hear. Several of his friends were now serving time in prison and I felt it was only a matter of time before my wild child joined them.

Rob turned 17 that summer. He was drinking with his friends almost every night and he wouldn't get out of bed long enough to look for a job. Sick of pleading with him and allowing his problems to get me down, I warned him that if he didn't change, he would have to leave.

The morning I finally said, "I've had enough," I awakened him. I told him it was time for him to leave our home. I'll never forget the look on his face when he said, "Where will I go Mom? You can't do this to me."

Just the fact that I desperately needed to have some control in my home forced me to do this. But it ripped my heart out. And, frankly, my heart had had enough.

Later that week, I drove Robby to Mesa and dropped him off at his Dad's. Bobby agreed to keep him while Rob looked for a job or until he found a place to live. But Bobby's new wife refused to allow Rob into their home. Soon after I returned to Tucson, Robby was forced to leave his father's home. He slept in his Dad's car and during the day he looked for a job. Bobby helped Robby find an apartment once he found a job.

I could hardly stand to see him. On weekends when I drove to Mesa to visit him, the sight of him, depressed, forlorn and so angry seared another dark hole through my heart.

Darinn contacted me for the first time in over a year and wanted to come home, but I knew that nothing had changed with him. Because of the problems with my other children, I couldn't let him move in with us.

My sister agreed to let Darinn live with her. He came by the house for a short period of time before he left for Salt Lake City and I hardly knew him. I felt my heart break when I saw him. Drugs had completely changed my son I didn't know him.

I don't remember when it happened, but I stopped getting out of bed in the mornings. Richard prepared meals and took care of other responsibilities while I seemed to fall deeper into depression. Unlike the depression I experienced in the past—I experienced extreme highs and lows. No one knew what to expect when they walked through the front door.

If I wasn't in bed, I was racing in and out of stores wildly buying needless items to decorate my home.

I could take a room apart, repaint and rearrange in several hours. I had boundless energy and then suddenly my mood would change. Unable to focus any task was overwhelming. The ups were euphoric only to hit the lowest point of existence with despair.

Living in chaos it wasn't enough to run wild or disappear in despair, sometimes; another demon controlled me. On certain occasions, I didn't bother to pay for what I needed—I shoplifted. That is so hard for me to say, but it's true, I took things.

What frightened me and angered me more about myself is that I was right back where I was when I left Bobby and I couldn't stand to be in my skin. I hated myself. Richard gave me more than enough money to take care of my needs. But I didn't want to buy things, I wanted to feel powerful and alive—I guess in shoplifting there is a certain shock to the system. During a short period of time, fear accelerates the heart into frenzy, the body feels euphoric and the mind's insatiable need for control is satisfied, quite a different experience than the avoidance of pain or the numbing of sleeping pills.

After living with my sister for nearly a year, Darinn needed to be on his own. His drug habit was just as bad in Salt Lake as it had been in Arizona.

Robby was living in an apartment by that time and so Darinn moved in with him. This only made the situation worse for Robby. Hardly making it on his own, Darinn didn't work instead he stayed at home stoned out of his mind. It didn't take him long to make friends with other addicts and this made Robby's life a living hell.

Richard's advice to Rob was to throw Darinn out, but that was easier for Richard to say than for Rob to actually do it—between me and my children not one of us had the ability to keep ourselves safe from the destructive behavior of others.

Then I started thinking about dying. I didn't want to live. I resented Darinn for the turmoil he brought with him no matter where he went and as long as I was angry, I didn't hurt for my son. Or did I? I don't know that I felt anything except intense grief, anguish and unbearable guilt.

I don't know when I actually became addicted, since I had been abusing prescription drugs for nearly three years, but when the medication no longer seemed to work, in desperation I combined alcohol with my sleeping pills. Since any use of alcohol was against my religious beliefs, I became a closet drinker. Late at night (or any other time of the day), I huddled underneath my clothes in my closet where no one would catch me and drink. But it only seemed to have a reverse effect on me; instead of sleep, it wired me with extreme anxiety, so, I drank more.

I just wanted a life of my own. I wanted to leave my home and return without having the police at my door or my kids screaming at one another or something broken or destroyed because someone lost their temper. I was sick of putting out one fire after another and feeling terribly responsible. Frankly, I wanted to run away and never look back.

Not only was I angry with my children, they were angry with me, and it was Nathan that felt betrayed more by his mother than any of the others. Each day that he came home and I was still in bed added one more strike against me. When he awoke each morning and fixed his own lunch for school that day added another strike, but then one afternoon when he caught me in the bathroom holding a bloodied razor against my wrist was the last strike he needed.

Anyone looking from the outside may have thought, "What is wrong with that woman?" as if I could wave a magic wand and dissipate my illness or just snap out of it.

But I couldn't.

Depression isn't a choice—it is an illness. It happens when the mind is overloaded with stress. It happens when a woman's life is not her own. It happens when her soul has no other way to grab her attention, but I couldn't let go long enough to let someone else make decisions that would help me.

Then I met Sheri. She moved into our neighborhood the same time we did. We became friends, but she was also a miracle in disguise. Since Sheri is a nurse she immediately knew I was over-medicated.

Sheri also found me in my bathroom with a razor blade—trying to get the courage to slit my wrists. She emptied my home of almost every sharp object she could find. She talked to Richard and then called a friend of hers, a psychiatrist, and made an appointment for me.

I started therapy with Dr. Johnson several times a week. He wanted me off all my medication. He then started me on a lithium treatment for manic depression but still prescribed Ativan for me. Richard joined me in therapy.

For obvious reasons, I couldn't do anything about the interference and problems created by April's mother and grandmother, but Dr. Johnson strongly recommended Richard be more aggressive. But I don't know that Richard felt there was anything more constructive that he could do.

After spending a weekend with her mother, April returned hostile and accusatory. She ridiculed me for my emotional state. She said she didn't have to do anything I asked her to. She slammed doors in my face. When I tried to put her in her room, she fled into Richard's office and tried calling her mother, I grabbed the phone from her and she shoved me, I pushed her back and then she slapped me.

My problems with April, her mother and grandmother climaxed one afternoon just before spring semester was over for April. April saw Lynsey as a nuisance and treated her as such and Lynsey retaliated. One afternoon, while Richard and I were not at home, Lynsey wanted to talk to April while her friends were over. April shouted at her to get lost. It didn't take much for a war to begin and both were at fault.

When Richard and I returned home, April had already left with her grandmother for the weekend. It was Nathan that told us what happened. April had physically hurt Lynsey and Lynsey had then put holes in her bedroom door with a sharp object. Richard and I both talked to Lynsey and decided how we would handle the situation. April's grandmother had different plans.

April's grandmother was hell-bent on telling me just how I was to discipline my own daughter; it was not my right to discipline April. She forced her way into my home screaming at me.

"You're way out of line," I told her and when she continued mouthing off at me, I asked her to leave. Even though she left, the problem had only started.

April's Mom drove to our house from Phoenix that weekend. She barged through my front door demanding to talk to Richard. They both went inside his office and when I tried to follow, she slammed the door in my face.

"This is none of your business, Janice!" she yelled, "Get out."

That was the straw that broke the proverbial camel's back—I was furious. I felt the problem was indeed my business so we yelled back and forth at each other. Finally, I forced my way into the office and demanded that she leave.

Bottom line, I couldn't take any more. Richard didn't stand by me this time. He tried to remain neutral and that wasn't a wise thing to do. He wouldn't stand up to his ex-wife and I had had enough!

It was an ugly situation that day. But I was so angry—angry enough to pack April's belongings and put them inside the garage. I told her mother and her grandmother I didn't care which one picked her up, but she was *out* of my home.

April did leave that afternoon and she moved in with her grandmother.

That wasn't how I'd wanted things to happen. I cared about April, but it was hopeless, as long as April got away with whatever she wanted with the support of those who wouldn't take responsibility for her.

As if things couldn't get any worse, several months later I received a phone call. Darinn and Rob had lost their apartment and they needed a place to stay temporarily. Since I was still trying to save them, I allowed them to move in with me.

We were all part of the problem regardless of what role we played.

The night Darinn brazenly traipsed back into my home; he didn't care what he brought with him. He really didn't have an ounce of remorse or responsibility in his bones. Although I warned Darinn and Rob about the consequences if they didn't find work and move out soon, Darinn didn't hear a word I said and apparently neither did Robby.

Darinn brought drugs into our home. Rob had his drinking problem and since he had a roof over his head, he wasn't motivated to find work.

Nathan ditched school. During parent/teacher conferences, I was made aware of the possible dangers Nathan faced, but Nathan wasn't listening to anyone. He was running with friends who had a negative affect on him and his attitude completely changed. He wanted to dress just like his older brothers. He wanted to run with a crowd just like his brothers.

They smoked, so why couldn't he? They had dropped out of school, so why shouldn't he?

Heartsick and filled with anguish, I had failed.

One by one, I lost each one of my children as they reached adolescence. The first three were close in age but Nathan was four years younger. I had hopes for him. I felt that it would be different for him. He was only five when I left his father.

With each child who slipped away, I wallowed in guilt. I couldn't move beyond it. I felt so responsible for what Bobby and I had done to our children that I felt it was my obligation to save them. I would have given anything to turn their lives around. Even though I knew my behavior was irrational, I couldn't relinquish the control I foolishly convinced myself I had.

Many times I told myself, "If I just help them this time, they'll get on their feet." I always felt there was something more I could do that would make a difference. Richard didn't agree with me but he didn't force me to see things his way either.

Many times he said to me, "Janice, you have to let them go."

"But you don't understand," was the answer he received. I lived completely inside this emotional circus ring. I couldn't see the forest for the trees, I couldn't think clearly.

My thoughts were completely irrational, but each time Richard said, "Something drastic needs to happen to wake you up."

I resented him. How could he possibly understand a mother's sorrow or guilt?

Even though I had to ask myself, "Have I completely gone over the edge?"

I honestly believe that at the time I was willing to go down with the sinking ship. I was determined to save my children regardless of what it took.

But I wasn't parenting my children; I was allowing their behavior to control me. I wasn't saving them by becoming part of the problem, but I couldn't see how dysfunctional, irrational and destructive my behavior really was. Instead, I became a mother bear ferociously guarding her cubs. No one was to ever hurt them again—it just never occurred to me that I might be hurting them with my help.

The problems inside my home were at an all-time high. Although, Robby appeared to be looking for work he spent more time with his girlfriend. Late in the evening he would return home as though he had been out looking all day. He would come into my bedroom in the evening to see how I was doing.

"Mom, will you be okay?" he'd ask. With tears in my eyes, I couldn't answer him. I wasn't okay.

I was living the only way I knew how and it was as unhealthy with my children as it was with Bobby. I lacked the skills necessary to enforce consequences and to step outside the drama of each angry child. I can only imagine how different our lives would have been had I been healthy enough to be their parent.

I don't believe a magic formula exists in mending families of violence. There is help available, but it is also true that no one can be forced to receive help if they don't want it and often everything falls apart before families can begin healthy living.

Not one of us was any less hurt than the other and desperately we fought our separate battles to survive. My children were hurting. I was hurting and not one of us had been able to find a foothold.

In retrospect, I never once "controlled" my children. The truth is, my life was just as unmanageable. And I had no idea how to stay emotionally safe as long as I believed I was responsible for their pain.

Recovery is a family matter. It wasn't enough that I received professional counseling, my children also needed a safe place to vent their anger and express emotions, a place that offered information, love, and support but my children weren't willing to receive help. They made their choices, and with every choice there is a direct result or consequence. It's also difficult, as a parent, knowing what consequences need to be enforced when teens are abusing drugs and alcohol—I certainly didn't have the answers.

Tough Love is an organization that offers help to parents with troubled teens. While I didn't have the ability to implement family rules and follow through with tough love consequences, another parent can. There is support between families and most of all, education.

If you are a parent, don't wait until it is too late. I lived my life doing the best I could but what about my children? What choices did they have? While they may not have had choices while in their youth, when they grew up the story changed and so did their behavior. Not that they weren't responsible, but lacking in healthy life-skills and a strong self of sense they imitated what they learned.

Nothing works as well as prevention but that also means your eyes must be open to the dangers you face as a parent with children at risk.

Eighteen

My Saving Grace

We all have angels guiding us... they look after us. They heal us, touch us,
comfort us with invisible warm hands.... What will bring their help?
Asking. Giving thanks.
-Sophy Burnham

One weekend, my husband thought a trip away from home would be just what I needed. Helplessly he stood by until he wasn't able to take it any longer. I know secretly he worked through his options. If he even tried talking to me about what he felt needed to happen. I tuned him out.

Together he and I spent several days at my mother's in Mexico. While riding horseback I was thrown from my horse, breaking bones in my shoulder that required surgery. It was too far to travel back to Arizona, and so I had my surgery done in a local hospital.

After nearly four weeks, I returned to Arizona. In my absence, chaos had erupted. Richard had been planning to sell our home and had already put it on the market.

For quite some time Richard felt compelled to take drastic measures in our life. Several times he said, "Janice I need to take you away from here."

I knew what he really meant was, "I have to get you away from your older boys." I wasn't ready to abandon them, and, in my mind, forcing them to leave my home meant abandoning them.

My drug abuse increased considerably during this time. Along with pain medication, my doctor in Mexico also prescribed Ativan for me. By then I had quite a supply of the drug, but even that wasn't enough. Obsessive worry controlled me day and night. I imagined the worse that could possibly happen—I wasn't at home, and I had no idea what my kids were doing. From past experience I knew whatever it was, it wasn't good news. To escape reality, I started out with several pills in the morning and by noon I needed a few more. As the day went on, I slept more than I was awake.

Finally, it was time to go home, but just before I left Mexico, I had my doctor prescribe extra medication for me. I picked it up from the pharmacy and stashed it away. When Richard arrived at my mother's, he was concerned. My mother told him I was taking a lot of pills and slept more than I should. Since Richard was aware of the problem I had with pills before the accident, he went through my make-up bag and counted how many pills I had with me.

We left Mexico the following day and a week later, he overheard me asking the receptionist in my doctor's office for a refill of Ativan.

"What are you doing?" he asked in the middle of my conversation.

"I'm out of medication and I just need a refill," I answered.

He shot back, "Tell her you don't need it."

"What?" I exclaimed, putting my hand over the receiver so the receptionist wouldn't hear him, "Of course I do."

Richard promptly took the phone away from me and told the receptionist, "Don't give her a refill, she still has enough pills that she brought with her from Mexico to last her several months."

"Mind your own business," I screamed, but he wouldn't listen.

"You're NOT getting any more, Janice, you've got to stop, you're taking way too many," he said.

"Oh my gosh, Richard, you don't know what you've just done. I have to have them."

Then I admitted, "I'm out, I don't have any more," I cried.

"Well then, you'll just have to go without."

By then I was frantic. I called the doctor's office back immediately after Richard left the room, but the receptionist said she wouldn't be able to refill my prescription.

The first night without medication, I lay awake all night. Restless and nervous, I was exhausted by morning. After two nights of not having the drug in my body, I was coming unglued.

To make the situation worse, early on a Monday morning a police officer appeared at my door. Bobby's family didn't have my telephone number and they needed to get hold of me.

The officer simply said, "Here is a phone number—it's urgent that you call." I hurried and dialed the number.

Darrell, Bobby's brother answered the phone.

"What's wrong?" I asked.

He answered, "Bobby died Saturday night. He wasn't found until late yesterday afternoon in his apartment."

Nathan hadn't left for school yet. He was standing by me when I made the call. I put down the phone and turned to Nate, "Your Dad passed away."

His face drained of color and then he cried, "No, Mom, it can't be true, he isn't dead."

I tried to comfort him, and briefly, he let me hold him as he sobbed, but he wouldn't hold still. He ran into his room slamming the door behind him. After I told Richard the news about Bobby's death, he left to pick the other kids up from school. That afternoon, I watched as my children tried to absorb the news of their father. My heart ached for them. So much pain in such a short span of time and they were still children.

Several days later, my children and I attended their father's funeral. Together we sat on the front pew in the chapel. The casket was closed and it all seemed surreal. Inside the casket was the body of a man I hated and yet had spent 15 years of my life with—we had children together and they loved him.

Regardless of what Bobby had done, his children never stopped loving him, and I couldn't stop crying. I'm sure family members thought I was grief stricken. I don't know what I was feeling, but I ached for my children, and I know I was an emotional wreck.

After the service, Bobby was taken to his final resting place, and his children looked on in bewilderment. How were they to heal without him? As the casket was lowered into the grave, emotions that I can't even explain tore at my soul.

I wanted to stand up and scream, "This isn't fair, how can he die without making things right?" If possible, I would have dragged his body from the casket and made him face misery with me.

I was still so angry. Dying seemed like the cowardly way out, and yet I knew Bobby hadn't opted to die. We stayed as long as we could with his immediate family, who still treated me as part of their family. My children felt comforted, and somehow we made it through that day, but that ended all too soon.

We returned home in the early afternoon and later that night, I slipped into a world different from any other. It was filled with inner darkness, covering my body with a heavy blanket of terrorizing fear. My mind was entering a place that could only be known as hell.

By morning, I thought I was losing my mind, as I continued to experience paranoia and extreme agitation. I made many phone calls to my doctor telling him about my situation, but my doctor thought I was having another mental breakdown. Since I didn't have health insurance, my husband was trying to find a hospital that would take me.

That's when an Earth-angel came to my rescue. Belle, my friend who had been with me for years, felt she needed to be with me. She was not in the habit of coming very often, as we lived hours away from each other, but that day she showed up at my doorstep and I don't know what I would have done without her. As soon as she saw me, she knew my behavior was a reaction from chemicals, and that I was not losing my mind.

Richard had doubled his responsibilities with work, the house and the kids. Then a situation on one of his job sites made it necessary for him to leave town for a few days. Even though Belle stayed by my side, it was an extremely frightening experience. I thought I was going to end up in the insane asylum and someone would throw away the key.

Knowing that a hospital was not going to admit me, Belle tried to calm me by telling me the worst was almost over.

"If you just hang on, Janice, the drug will soon be out of your system enough for you to feel better—you're almost there."

I didn't believe her. I knew my mind was gone forever. Finally late into the third night, a calm feeling filled my being.

"Belle," I said, "someone is here with me. I can feel them sitting next to me."

Of course, Belle didn't see anyone, but she listened. Fear and paranoia completely left me. I wasn't hallucinating or imagining—the feeling was powerful and yet loving. I felt the presence of an angelic being as a voice gently, but forcefully, spoke to me in a clear and calming manner.

The voice adamantly said, "You have had time to get well. Many opportunities have been placed in your hands, but you have remained ill. It is important for your future that you fully recover. There will be changes in your life but they are necessary."

I knew the message meant, "Janice, you are going to move again."

I had spent most of my life packing my belongings and moving. In 17 years, I had moved over 20 times and I distinctly remember answering, "Oh no, I won't. Wild horses cannot make me move one more time."

The voice simply said, "Wild horses won't be necessary."

The next day, Richard signed a contract. Our house had been sold. Belle had also successfully communicated my problem to my doctor, and he authorized one last prescription of Ativan. I was to slowly taper off my medication over the next six weeks. I couldn't wait for Richard to pick up my prescription. The moment the drug was released in my system, it didn't take long before I felt its effects and I soundly slept for the first time in four days.

Once again, my hands were pried from a situation in which I was wasting away. Another door slammed shut, snapping me back to reality, and once again, I was not to return to pick up old shattered pieces. Instead I had to let go of my children.

They weren't babies anymore and I couldn't save them or fix them. They needed to learn how to save themselves, even if that meant they would learn the hard way.

I knew we wouldn't find another home in Tucson. Richard had talked about moving often enough—this was his chance. I argued with him every chance I had, but then he calmly expressed how he felt.

"You can't continue the way you have, Janice, you've got to make major changes in your life. We'll find a home in Mexico where the kids will be much better off. Nathan will have a chance if he is in a better environment, and you won't be in a position to enable your boys to live the way they are."

I disagreed. I was frantic.

Where would my older boys go? How would they survive? In my head I came up with several wild and crazy plans, but Richard continued talking without giving me a chance to argue.

"In the meantime," he said, "I'm taking you to your mother's, and the three younger kids will stay with their cousins until you are feeling better."

I knew I needed serious help, and I was relieved that my kids would be taken care of, but I was scared. When I'm frightened, I get angry. For the first time, I threatened Richard with divorce, which wasn't a smart thing to do after I thought about it—he might welcome the idea. But he wasn't the least bit worried that I would leave him—I didn't have anywhere to go. My arm was healing and I still had to have the pin removed. This time not only was I an emotional wreck, I was crippled.

I was so certain Richard was making a terrible mistake. He had worked hard to build his business.

What would he do if we didn't stay in Tucson? I don't know if he understood at the time how important financial stability was for me. After living for many years on welfare, the life Richard offered was one of dignity. I didn't see any good in what he was doing.

I wasn't willing or able to pack, so Richard put me in the car with my overnight bag and shipped me off to my mother's. I rode in silence with tears streaming down my face.

I wasn't happy about moving to say the least. I left behind three troubled teen-agers and I was leaving a home I loved. What I didn't realize was that my home had become my prison, one from which I hardly left. Unable to stop it, my behavior was wildly unmanageable and I wasn't about to let go of problems I couldn't solve.

Nathan, Lynsey and Westin weren't any happier with the move. They said goodbye to their friends and reluctantly packed their own things. This was a sad day, another unhappy ending—I believe they were as frightened as I was about the future.

Isn't it amazing how our mind can play tricks on us? I really believed the world would end if I weren't the one holding it together. It didn't matter if I was invading upon the right of my children to grow through their own experiences. Even though I took them away from a violently abusive situation, My children were angry with me and it didn't seem to matter that I struggled just as they did to piece my life together—life seemed terribly unfair to them and emotionally they needed much more than what I offered.

Still, I will always remember that in the midst of chaos and at the bleakest and most troubled times, I strongly felt the presence of angels. I knew that I was being protected in every possible way, and so were my children. When I felt frightened, light surrounded me and nourished me with love.

And today, my writing is for my children and for all those who have been robbed of a safe and happy childhood. Some day I hope to be forgiven of the life I offered my children. In the meantime, I pray that my children will know my love runs deep for each one of them.

Robby has always been my fragile one—in him I see myself as a child. The love in his heart, which has been shattered and almost irreparably broken, hides behind his anger and dies beneath his pain, but still it shows in his countenance and breathes upon his face.

Darinn, my son who left home before he was fourteen, was the family scapegoat and he took it for as long as he felt he could. Driven by his anger and blinded by his pain, he took to the streets in search of little boy lost. I see what he wants me to see, resilience and determination, and yet my heart sees behind his face and I feel his inner pain.

Justin, bright and caring, has learned to follow and has yet to test his own strength. When I couldn't save his older brothers, I threw my heart into saving him.

Nathan, my stalwart warrior, analyzes his family and is frightened by the breakdown that he sees. He is angry that he lost his father he never got to know—he is angry with his mother because he still doesn't understand the choices she had to make.

Lynsey, strong-willed and outspoken always has to be in control, perhaps because she felt it was her job to take care of her mother. I worry more about her than my other children. What has she learned that she will take into her role as a woman, wife and mother?

Sweet and caring, Westin is my child of peace. He just wants to live carefree with a loving mother. He seems untouched by the turmoil in his life—he has faith and believes in many things.

Nineteen

Rainbows and Treasures

At the end of every storm is a rainbow, and at the end of each day is a new beginning—believe in miracles and never lose faith that tomorrow holds treasures untold.

My three youngest children stayed with their cousins, and I settled in at my mother's. I had time alone, and it was exactly what I needed. My body felt like it had been through an old-fashioned washing-machine wringer. I still remember the one my mother had when I was growing up, and I felt like someone had pulled me through it, but the storm was lifting, and I felt a rainbow rising within.

With no other place to hide, it was time to realistically face the conditions in my life. While medication may have been necessary at one time, more harm was being done than good, and I don't know that I had any other choice but to take responsibility for my healing.

Slowly, I tapered off. Each day I lowered my dosage of Ativan. Within four weeks I stopped completely. I wasn't able to sleep, but I also didn't experience a painful withdrawal.

Even though I was walking every morning, chronic fatigue made it almost impossible to walk very far. Between severe body ache and mental fatigue, I wasn't sure feeling better was an option. But I read everything I could concerning chronic fatigue syndrome, and I knew that not only did I need to eliminate stress from my life, but also sugar and yeast products. Just by being in touch with my inner-self, instinctively, I was aware of my needs. This is an important part of self-nurturing. Listening to what our body is trying to tell us. We receive signals, messages and warnings all the time.

Fortunately, I was able to sleep often enough during the day. I listened to music and felt safe just being alone. I didn't want to be around anyone, and I certainly didn't want to feel responsible for anyone's needs. Reading romance novels swept me away into someone else's life—I didn't want to think about my own.

Self-care hadn't been part of my daily ritual for many years. In my head, Janice wasn't important enough to take care of. She was too absorbed with everyone's problems and how she was going to solve them. I didn't know whether I lost myself during some inexplicable time in my life or if I ever existed! But something was so wrong about the way I felt about myself. Although, after my divorce, I learned about co-dependency and what needed to change inside me, time didn't stand still long enough for me to catch my breath and begin working on me.

For a while, Richard stayed in Tucson making sure we had closure to our life there. That was okay with me. I needed to be away from him and everyone else. Frankly, I was in a blaming mood.

It seemed almost ironic. After four years I was back at the beginning, where I once moved my family to find safety. Somehow I felt defeated.

Our new home was quite different from the one I left behind. So I got busy painting. I love to decorate, but with this house, nothing I did could take away from its worn appearance so I decided to enhance it. I painted my walls sunflower yellow, and my kitchen cupboards barn red. I was making this house a home, but I was also making a home within myself.

I cleared away an area for a garden. Some days, I worked until I could hardly stand. This was my therapy and it kept me busy enough to where I couldn't dwell on my problems. While I was still concerned about our future, I knew Richard and I were starting over and for the first time it felt right. I was where I needed to be.

But I also worried about Justin. He was only 16, and I wanted him to finish high school more than anything. Several times Richard and I drove to Tucson to see him. It was quite obvious that he was still using drugs. Everything about him bothered me.

He was living with a friend and so I asked his mother to evict him.

"Don't give him a place to live," I begged, "If you don't, he won't have any choice but to come home with me."

Richard felt if it weren't Justin's choice, then he wouldn't be willing to make necessary changes. Justin wasn't willing to change but he did ask for money.

I might have given him some if Richard hadn't been with me but instead Richard said, "If you want to live on your own then you'll have to take care of yourself."

I was heartsick the following day when we drove home leaving Justin behind.

"This isn't the way it is supposed to be," I said to Richard. "Justin is only 16, he needs to be with us."

"Janice, give him some time. I think he'll come around."

I wanted to believe him.

Even though it took Justin four months before he decided he wanted to come home, he finally did. He called me one afternoon and said, "Mom, come and get me."

I drove out alone to get my son. What I picked up later that afternoon was a son high on marijuana. His eyes were dilated, blurry and red. He was also irritable and agitated.

I searched through Justin's belongings to make sure he didn't have any drugs with him. I also made him empty out his pockets and take off his shoes. He didn't have anything he shouldn't with him, but drugs were still in his system. The drive home wasn't an easy one. Three hours after we left Tucson, he changed his mind and didn't want to go with me.

Justin began swearing and yelling at me to turn around. We got this far and I wasn't about to turn around. Then Justin started fighting with me.

"I said, turn this damn car around," he screamed as he grabbed the steering wheel.

I managed to pull off to the side of the road as Justin fought for the keys.

More afraid of him taking my keys and forcing me out of the car, I jumped out with my keys.

I waited for nearly an hour in the hot sun, upset and angry that he had control over me.

Finally, we made a truce.

"Give yourself time," I said, "If in several months you still hate it in Mexico, then you can go back."

Finally, he agreed.

It took time before the drugs were out of Justin's body, but Justin was true to his word. He gave up smoking cigarettes and he quit using drugs. That fall he enrolled in high school and studied hard. I was amazed and so proud of his progress.

Robby and Darinn struggled. This was a rough time for them, but they were also slowly learning. Neither one of them had a place to stay, so they bummed a couch off different friends and often slept in the desert. My fear has always been that they would never find stability, which meant a job and a decent place to live.

Darinn is an addict and I had to face that fact. Nothing Richard and I did helped him. Robby made unwise choices—sometimes he didn't think at all he just acted irresponsibly.

Many times, I wanted to rescue them, but sometimes I couldn't. When Robby had unpaid traffic fines, he spent thirty days in jail. I suffered every day thinking of the worst that could happen to him.

I didn't bail him out, even though I wanted to. While he had time to reflect upon the choices he had made, I had time to reflect on how I could help him. Finally I was able to say, "He is where he needs to be, and it is for a lesson he hasn't learned."

I then turned to prayer and asked that he be protected.

It felt like an eternity before he was released, but we both got through this difficult time. Later, he let me know he felt comforted and protected (he needed protecting from an inmate who thought he was a birdie in the window).

How difficult is it to stand one's ground to save their sanity? From writing perhaps you can see it is very difficult.

The worst part of co-dependency is that we try to control everything outside our self. There is madness to this disease that defies all logic. Strange as it is, all the energy that I exerted never accomplished any worthwhile result.

How long does it take to learn important life lessons, and what do we need so that we can begin learning? The love I received from Richard gave me the freedom and the security to go through all that I needed to learn. I had the desire, but he had the love that kept me safe. He understood, and he gave me space to work through my anger and my pain and yet not once did he enable me.

Throughout the years we have been together never once has he been demanding, jealous, impatient or angry with my children or me. But this confused me. He didn't seem normal. I don't know what I expected, but being around someone who didn't react or expect anything from me gave me more time than I needed for soul-searching. I couldn't fixate on him or his problems—there was nothing to fix.

Why is that we can be our own worst enemy? Why do we make choices that ultimately hurt us? It's because we don't have healthy life management skills. Even though it was more painful living the way the way I did, I didn't know how to change.

It isn't that difficult to let our lives turn into a run-a-way train, and feel helpless and unable to slam on the brakes. Many of us live that way. In my situation, I was afraid of the outcome if I did.

But when life hurts *enough*, maybe then we'll fall on our knees. Maybe this is the only way we release those around us to their highest good while we trust in a Higher Power. For those of us that have a high tolerance for misery, life can really get messy before we find our Selves in that position, and, without a doubt I had reached that infamous plateau of intolerable suffering. When we don't learn from our negative experiences we repeat them until we do. Since this is true, I guess you could say I repeated the same grade over until I had outgrown the size of my chair. Learning *how* to detach from the behavior of those we love and establish safe boundaries isn't easy.

If there is any lesson I want to share with battered women with children it's this—you aren't alone in your suffering. Heaven only knows what your children will do when they become of an age to stand up for themselves. They are angry children, and angry children don't conform.

From experience, families are shattered from abuse. Before healing can begin family members have to find their own way. It is a painful personal experience and painful for others to watch from the outside. No one has a magic wand that saves children from hurting themselves, and no one has a magic wand to comfort a mother's heart.

Nothing compares to a mother's sorrow believing that she failed in one way or another. I still remember many nights without end. Grief filled my waking hours. At times, I was angry that I was even a mother.

While I may have been in recovery, my children's behavior sent me reeling. I was right back in raging waters trying to save them and myself at the same time. It doesn't work that way any more than the blind can lead the blind.

Richard is my saving grace. From the time we married he has remained steadfast. We both made mistakes in our limited understanding of the severity of my family's problems. I believe we thought everything would just fall into place, but they didn't.

Over the years I've learned more about the love between Twin Flames and it has helped me understand the staying power Richard has had with our relationship and I would like to share this with you.

In order for the Twin Flame relationship to flourish and accomplish its unified spiritual mission, both individuals must be at a certain spiritual level in life. They have reached a state of inner wholeness. The personality does not exist inside this relationship. Their love is selfless. While many people idealize and romanticize the concept of the Twin Flame, the Union of the Twin Flame is carefully orchestrated by the Divine Mind for the bringing together of their souls to accomplish a humanitarian mission. The Twin Flame would not be brought together unless they had the absolute ability to complete their Mission of transcending their male and female attributes. Together they can accomplish more than they could as two separate beings—together they multiply their powers.

When God created the individual Spirit, he formed a sphere of light, which then split into two separate flames. From these spheres, two souls descended into form. The frequency of their vibrations is powerful on the physical plane in that it carries and holds Divine Love, thus becoming a stabilizing force and the most powerful healing energy that we are all in need of.

My spiritual path had been unfolding long before I met Richard. We both had gone through similar experiences in life preparing us for one another. Because Richard's love is pure and unselfish, he provided a safe haven for my recovery. It is his firm belief that he was aware of my soul's journey, and that I would need him when the time came. His love has been unfailing. He is my Knight in Shining Armor and it is because of him, I am where I am today.

But I didn't recover overnight, and a major contributing factor to my illness is that I didn't know how to take care of myself around other people.

But now that I was gaining a foothold, I needed to fasten my feet to the ground. I felt like a tiny seedling just sprouting her roots. The world I was trying to create now included me. I was important enough and how I felt mattered.

Sometimes, blessings can be wrapped inside meager offerings—Richard offered me a chance to have a life by taking what life I had away from me, and yet I was afraid. Mistrusting in everything, I waged a mighty battle against surrendering to the inevitable.

But this time, it wasn't just a lull in the storm that brought me inner peace; this time it was the beginning to the end of the storm I had created. And just as it is after rain has fallen, a rainbow appears in the lives of those who find safety beneath wings of an angel. It is here they find healing from that sacred place within, and the love they find is the key to a treasure chest. The one they have always wanted—it's a dream come true—restoring love to the heart of the one who is hurting.

Nurturing the seedling

The greatest gift we can give
is the love that allows souls to learn
And wings to fly

A mother's gift to her children consists of her happy heart and idealistically; they also create a warm, safe and nurturing environment in which to raise their children. But life isn't always fair, and typically life isn't really all that idealistic either. It's sad but true; families are being destroyed everyday from abuse and neglect. And it's not just happening out there somewhere. We are living examples of that destruction, so how do we repair what has been broken?

Healing begins with us. We have to make a difference in our own lives before our strength is realized in the lives of our children. Our children learn only what we teach them and one of the most valuable gifts we can give is to follow our dreams. If we allow ourselves to dream, love, and fly again, they will do the same.

For the first time, I realized I had to put myself first and then I had to be strong enough to make it last. It's easy to do something right for one day! The difficult part is in carrying it out long enough so that new behavior becomes a healthy habit.

I was so proud of myself after establishing new rules and creating a house of order. For the most part, my stress had been eliminated—I left it behind in Tucson. Darinn wasn't close enough to be a constant threat to my new house of order. Robby didn't have a telephone or enough money to call me, except collect and I had the option to either reject his call or except it. I was feeling a little more in control.

And this time, I really meant it. I was going to take care of me and my kids were beginning to cooperate. After all, it was clear to everyone that "Mom was really sick." But I will have to say; cooperation, or even feeling sorry for mom didn't last.

Cooperation for my kids wasn't a problem until it didn't feel right to them! After all, you know how unfair parents can be when they say no.

To keep myself safe, I drew an imaginary line. I decided that when I didn't feel good about doing something, I wouldn't do it. The problem with that is generally saying no meant depriving my children of something they needed to be happier. So, as soon as my children wised up, which didn't take very long, they knew what to do. Every day they challenged my imaginary line, and then they challenged my ability to keep them on the other side. They knew all they had to do was wear me down. Have you ever felt like you just walked through a minefield to get to the other end of the house? That's how I felt at the end of the day.

Some days my children seemed like the enemy, and I was the invisible invader no one took seriously. When I tried to enforce rules, Nathan would immediately remind me I hadn't been the one raising him so why should he listen to me now? The accusations he threw at me would rattle anyone's resolve.

I returned to my old ways of dealing with conflict. I hated conflict. I was afraid of it and my children knew it.

The mantra, "Just wear her down and she'll give in," must have kept them at it for long periods of time. I was exhausted every time I had to say no, and often I said yes just so that I would have a break.

Being controlled by other people is demeaning. When I gave in I hated myself for doing it. I was angry with the one who controlled me, and I was angry with myself because I allowed it.

My behavior was making everyone crazy, but how do you stop it? How do you gain control when you're afraid of what your son or daughter might do? You start by saying no when you have to and asking for support if you can't enforce well-defined consequences. But it also takes patience.

I struggled with balance. If I wasn't acting like a doormat, I was dancing around like a War Chief. Some days I had my head on straight and other days I didn't like myself at all. I never imagined it would be so traumatic for everyone. I couldn't believe how my children panicked and rushed to protect their freedom. I pushed everyone's hot buttons just by saying, "I'm taking control." Once again I was a threat to them.

Sometimes I just wanted to throw away the rulebook and say, "Who needs rules anyway?" It was more exhausting trying to come up with a few rules that they could all agree with. I was still trying to win their approval. Approval must have meant a lot to me, because it was difficult for me to give up.

For a time, I fought back, like I had in the past. Sometimes I surrendered to weeping and wailing and begging until I finally learned to remain steadfast.

My children, all six of them, have always been a challenge. They didn't grow up with love and nurture or rules and boundaries that were fair or consistent. Trying to change that in later years hasn't been easy. To this day, they can still wear me down, and cause considerable guilt and worry.

Not only was I learning new ways to parent, but I also found myself struggling in my relationship with Richard. Richard doesn't have a violent bone in his body—he is kind, patient and even-tempered—it takes a lot to upset him yet it was hard for me to trust him. Many issues in our relationship were insignificant to him, but not to me. I continually saw small things as huge threats that would destroy my marriage.

From past experience anything that involved money was something I hated. I tried to hide any new purchases I made, along with receipts and price tags. It was incredible how frightened I was of making Richard angry with me. Just getting me to act normal was a challenge for him. Even when I left home, I would start calling him the moment I arrived at the store and seconds before I left to let him know where I was.

Perplexed and completely unaware of my feelings, many times he would say, "Why can't you just trust that I won't be angry with you, no matter what you do?" I would always tell him, "I do trust you," but I would still hide the receipts anyway, just in case.

Expressing dislike was also a real threat to me. I was always afraid of what would happen if I rocked the boat, and so when my husband would say, "Janice, what do you want?" I would invariably say, "Whatever you want," as if I couldn't think on my own and feel safe expressing that I wanted something different than he did.

Richard certainly isn't a mind reader. He only knows how I feel when I tell him, and it's okay with him no matter what I say.

Then why is it so hard to simply express how I honestly feel? And yet it isn't difficult to say things in anger.

I was afraid to stand up for myself, which is common for those who have been emotionally abused. They fear anyone that appears intimidating or threatening. I cared about how others felt about me and I didn't want to disappoint them. It seemed as though a little mechanism inside me malfunctioned every time I needed to stand up for myself. I just couldn't do it.

I'm certainly not trying to paint a picture of a quiet and shy person, because I'm not. In fact, I've never had a problem with talking, other people might have a problem with it, but I don't. Once I asked my husband why he was always so quiet and he looked at me as if to say, "You've got to be kidding?" "My dear," he said, "when you stop talking long enough, maybe I'll have something to say.

With patience, Richard tenderly nurtured another side to me, a loving and caring aspect that finally felt validated. He never lost sight of what was important and with his love I didn't have to be anyone else but me. Love has its own allegiance—in feeling loved, I wanted to be my best. He taught me that loving isn't controlling or changing another person and love isn't found in care taking or enabling.

For such a long time, I didn't know myself. I suffered from self-loathing because I repressed all that was sacred to me, and I accepted intolerable behavior just to have the illusion of being loved and of being obedient. I gave into people who used their emotions to control me. I had been conditioned to play the victim's role and anyone in authority was intimidating to me.

Was I to receive a medal for playing a martyr's role? Absolutely not! So many times I kept silent because I thought I was keeping the peace and that was the honorable thing to do. But peace came at a lofty price.

In time, I understood that there isn't any authority greater than my own— I needed to be the steward of my own life, and reclaim personal power. We, as women and individual souls have the right to question anyone that teaches differently. But perhaps the most startling revelation I received was that God is part of me—His Spirit is my spirit, how could we be separate? Even in wrong choices, which by the way, is when we need inner guidance and love more than any other time, God's Spirit did not vanish. We separate from that feeling inside the mind, but not in actuality and our suffering is a reminder of that separation.

It also took time before I realized that my opinion was important, but no one had to be wrong so I could be right. I didn't have to agree with anyone to be loved and nothing disastrous happened when I simply said, "I don't agree."

Amazingly, my spiritual life followed an intriguing plan. I hadn't taken the wrong path even though I lingered longer than necessary in learning, but once I learned and made necessary changes, my feet moved forward traveling the same unforgotten path.

Richards's support is my guiding light. Always as a lighthouse guiding me, not once did he give up. With hindsight, I was able to see how synchronized my life has always been, it was my stubbornness and fear of change that hampered the natural learning process.

In all honesty, I can't say that it was always easy for Richard. I'm sure he (temporarily) felt discouraged when I wouldn't give in. It's certainly no secret that I am a stubborn old soul.

One morning after a difficult time, he awoke completely mesmerized by his dream. He couldn't wait to share the following with me: In his dream, he was carrying me across a river. Small stepping-stones made the crossing possible, but with each step, crossing became increasingly difficult. For a moment he would panic, but just when he thought he would lose me into the raging waters below, another stone would amazingly appear up from the water. As he continued crossing the flooding waters, he felt encouragement and support.

Each day brought wonderful surprises and blessings into my life. It's amazing how spirit works giving us promptings, warnings, and directions and how the Universe provides the help that we need.

Opening my heart to Spirit's Love captivated my inner child and brought her out and into healing and simply by asking the answers came in wondrous ways. I am convinced that each experience in life serves only one purpose and that is to learn. Not to be judged or prove our loyalty to God, it is for our experience alone. And that is the power and the gift of unconditional love.

All the help that we need is inside. When in charge of our destiny, our outlook changes. No one is controlling anything about us and they can't change what is in us. But every relationship offers an in-depth look at our Selves and without fail each situation offers us another opportunity to grow. Without opposition, we don't learn. Without suffering we can't experience compassion—this is the path to spiritual enlightenment—the freedom of the soul to experience itself without limitations.

Detachment along with enforcing boundaries just means being uninvolved on the emotional level. It doesn't mean that we are indifferent. Indifferent people do not care. On the other hand, a person that can detach from the over involvement and suffering can be very active and caring.

As we evolve, the soul's natural gifts and abilities offer guidance and insight. Dreams are part of that guidance.

As I felt drawn into my spiritual path, dreams happened quite often. One night, in my dream, I saw myself behind a desk, writing. There was a book, but I wasn't able to read its title. When I awoke an overwhelming emotional current ran through me with the words "Beneath Wings of an Angel."

Without knowing it, the stage had been set. A place was provided in which I could nurture the seedling of self-care that blossomed into a woman with a deeper sense of her identity. And when in desperate need, God sent His Angels to guide me. My past held the secret to my future and in Richard's love; he created a safe place that allowed me to heal my wounded inner child giving wings to my dreams.

Twenty

Gifts of the Soul:
Love is First

Our happiness is measured by our capacity to love, and with the gifts of the soul every thought, every desire and every breath becomes a melody of devotion, until the heart is filled with a glorious song of compassion, mercy and understanding.

With each passing day, my desire to write filled my waking hours. It echoed with my every thought and each morning when my feet first hit the floor, I wanted nothing more than to put pen to paper. There was a knowing that this was vitally important to me. Richard knew how I felt, and with his encouraging support, I embarked upon an incredible new journey. But I wasn't ready to delve into my past so I wrote about God's Love—the irresistible force of the Universe.

Each morning, before I began my work, I knew that I wasn't alone. Angels and spirit guides spent many long hours with me. In awe of such love, I felt the sun rise and warmly kiss my face—I was finding peace.

A new computer, a gift from Richard, replaced my old, worn, word processor, and I turned a studio apartment adjacent to my home into my office. Fragrant flowers blooming outside my window spoke of rebirth and angels, wise in their knowing, were quietly preparing me with a safe foundation for my past to surface.

Meditating often, I visualized showers of light flowing through me. This light was lifting pain—I could feel the negative energy surfacing and slowly dissipating. Working with this light and healing from within, it wasn't long before I opened to channel, which is the ability to receive divine guidance (from a Highly Evolved Spirit Guide) for others and myself.

There are four channels—seeing, hearing, feeling and knowing—from which everyone has the capacity to receive divine guidance, those new to channel may use one or two even though it is possible to use all four. Even though my channel involves hearing, the ones used most often, and more readily accessible for me are feeling and knowing.

In time, everything was changing about me, including my physical appearance, my moods, how I felt and my priorities. Step by step, the healing process was bringing mind, body and spirit in harmony and I felt divinely guided—intuitively an inner knowing let me know what my emotional and physical needs were. This Love was bringing my life into balance both spiritually and physically.

Often, I received messages that came as a warning about my children and I was able to help them. In time, they learned to trust me. Rob once told a friend of his, "Be careful with my mom, she can see right through you."

Having their respect, and gaining a deeper understanding as to their trials, it was easier for me to let go and let them learn.

Intermittently, between writing about love, forgiveness and gratitude, I would write different chapters of my personal story. It was difficult at first. I didn't want to dig deep. I cherished the new stability I had in my life and was afraid of emotionally upsetting that balance by dragging up the past but I also learned that I couldn't prevent healing from happening either.

My writing evolved, as cautiously I touched the tip of my inner pain. I thought I was over much of the hurt from what went before, but my unhealed wounds were still very much a part of me. My past held memories of a young girl who had failed and her life was a story of her painful choices. Nothing I said or did could change the past, and to be honest, I still loathed the reflection of shame I saw in the mirror each day.

Quickly, my world began to turn from peaceful interludes into dark, and stormy periods of time. As much as I didn't like what I was experiencing, I felt safe enough to walk through my past in my writing. But as this unhealed fear or negative energy surfaced, my body felt sick all over again. At first, I felt certain I was having a relapse. Terrified that I would slip into depressions dark pit of hell, my first reaction was get myself back on medication fast.

Then I met a woman who is an experienced iridologist.

I won't go into too much detail, but the tiny circles around the iris reflect what's going on with the body and by looking into the surface of the eye, she is able to tell you important things about your body.

She assured me that emotionally and mentally I was strong. She also suggested that I allow the healing process to happen and not to suppress buried, negative feelings (energy) from surfacing by using medication.

As if it wasn't enough to deal with fluctuating emotions that took me from highs to lows, my children became angry because I was writing about their deceased father. To make matters worse, Richard still wasn't able to find work. Even though he spent most his time and what money we had traveling back and forth to El Paso, work wasn't available. Deeply discouraged, I doubted everything around me. The peace I once felt disappeared into thin air.

The pressure to finish my book was tremendous—I felt the weight was on my shoulders to provide for my family and that sent me into waves of hysteria crying, "I can't possibly do that—I may never be published."

Nerves frazzled, a few weeks later I had had enough. I stopped writing. Not only was I emotionally spent from the negative energy that had infiltrated our home, I had also become that pitiful woman again, and I didn't believe in anything except doom and failure. The stereo that had played was silent in my office while years of work collected dust.

My heart ached when I walked into my office knowing that I was throwing away my soul's most fervent dream, but I was finished with my writing. Heartsick, I reacted angrily toward everyone. Then as if I needed to prove to myself, I took a printed copy of the manuscript and burned it outside my office door.

My kids ran outside! Nathan was hysterical and Lynsey just stared and shook her head at me, Westin tried to put out the fire.

Then Nate grabbed me by the shoulders and said, "Mom, you're coming with me." Being the "theatrical" person that I am, while crying my head off, I said, "Nate, forget it. It's too late. I'm through with this book, everyone is angry with me and I can't take it anymore.

"That's your problem, Mom. You give up and then you run to your bedroom and hide." I didn't say a word; I just listened as he continued. "If you give up then we'll all give up, but I will never forgive you for throwing away all those years of work—you weren't here for us, you were always outside in your office saying you were too busy and now you're saying it was all for nothing."

I tried to stop him from talking but he wouldn't listen. He was too busy trying to make me listen.

Finally, he said, "Mom, it's okay that you're writing about Dad."

Tears welled in his eyes as he continued, "I know what he did to you and I'm proud of what you've accomplished."

Nathan thought I had burned the one and only copy to my entire life's work and he was furious with me. He wouldn't stop lecturing me long enough for me to tell him my work was still safe—in haste and a little show of theatrics I may have burned *a* copy but I'm not crazy enough to burn the *only* copy!

This was healing time between my children and me. I needed to know they believed in my work as much as I did. It wasn't an easy choice to write this book in the beginning and I was worried not knowing how it would affect them.

Lessons always come when we need them, but I don't always embrace them. Stubborn as I am, no one knows better than I how to run my life and yet I really don't know much of anything, that wisdom belongs to my soul!

Without a doubt, many lessons remained, waiting patiently for me to learn. My burdens weighed heavily upon my shoulders. The truth is, I had yet to learn when and how to let go of trying to control the outcome of every situation.

It wasn't long before I received another message. Asleep and dreaming, I heard a voice say, "*Janice, before you can finish your book, you must first go through the process of deep inner healing—this is what you are doing. You can't teach what you have yet to learn.*"

Instantly, I awoke but the dream didn't stop—I could hear the voice telling me, "*Fear has always been your greatest obstacle. Everything that you are facing is to help you overcome it—this will be your greatest trial.*"

With this message came a glorious power of inner peace. I wasn't alone in my healing and within my being the spark of light and love enfolded me in my hour of need.

I sobbed! I wept, and I cried tears of joy and sweet gratitude.

I wasn't alone as I once thought, and Richard had not made a mistake. I was exactly where I needed to be and so were my children.

Cleaning out dusty cobwebs in my office, I returned to my desk and my soul rejoiced. Over the following months, my writing continued, but it was still shallow because I held back just enough of my dark secrets to keep them safe from anyone ever knowing. Yet, I knew I wasn't being honest, and I was deceiving others.

Through a twist of fate, Kitty came into my life. A kind and loving kindred spirit offered to help me with my writing and she tirelessly worked with me. We had never met in person, but we were closely bonded and I relied on her. Without her, I never would have been able to put my life story on paper. She was the force pulling me forward when I gave up, and she was my faith when self-doubt over powered me. No one could possibly ever convince me this life is not filled with miracles, and when it came time to walk through one of the most painful times in my life, Kitty was there to hold my hand if only in spirit.

After years of dancing around the real reason I was writing, I was ready to open my heart and write from the depths of my inner pain.

But for months, I wrote with a heavy heart. Self-doubt was deeply embedded and too many painful memories surfaced when the same quiet and soft angelic voice softly whispered, *"Oh, little one, if you could only see what we see in you."*

The love that filled my heart overwhelmed me. I *felt* my inner beauty and I rejoiced knowing I really was a courageous woman. This was the silver lining inside the fear that had always prevented me from reaching beyond the imprisonment of the glass bubble.

At that moment, I knew the Savior cared about me. Kneeling before a love greater than us all, unable to hide my past, I felt loved. Nothing had really changed about me except I allowed Love to open my heart center and in God's love I felt spiritual healing begin. His Love was doing what I had not been able to do alone.

This was the beginning of a miraculous journey and a long healing process. My writing brought every dark aspect that existed inside me into the light. In fact, it is this very light I used for comfort and guidance—this light is the source of all existence. It is the purified energy that sustains all living things—it is God's Love.

Once the heart center opens, Love radiates from this inexplicable source inside the body and darkness surfaces, which mean all unhealed wounds, rise into the conscious mind. It's a process that can't be stopped. Whatever is in need of healing will surface when its time. As if an automatic response takes over, the all-shining light searches inside the body. It may only take insignificant situations to trigger the memory but it will happen.

One night, as I entered my living room, my eyes fell upon a picture of my two innocent little boys taken when they were about four and five years old. Grief filled my heart as I remembered the sexual abuse they had suffered through. That painful incident along with the physical and emotional abuse they endured at home had scarred and changed the lives of my precious little ones forever. This one photograph triggered a profound feeling in me and suddenly, in agony, I feel to my knees.

Not wanting to bear such pain, I begged for the torment to stop.

"I've already lived through this once," I cried.

Then a loving voice began to whisper: *"Yes, you did, but you still carry the pain and now you must let it go."*

I knew that my Savior had taken upon himself not only the sins of the world, but his love for the heartache and sorrow of the Earth, and so with tears streaming down my face, I placed my pain in the hands of love.

I ached to gather my little boys to me and tell them how sorry I was for not being there to protect them. Instead, I felt the Savior hold me in His arms and as the healing began a soft voice whispered once again, *"You are not to blame, and you must forgive yourself and let me carry your pain."*

Day after day, I continued to write, as tears blurred my vision. Writing about my children caused a flood of anguish sending me into a world of torment.

I lived inside my children's world as abused children. I felt the terror, denigration and shame of my children. Abuse became real in a way I cannot explain. Writing brought it to life, and I had not the power to turn back the hands of time.

In writing about my life with Bobby, wounds opened that hadn't even begun to heal. I grieved for the woman who hid in shame. Memories of broken bones, bruised and emotionally wounded didn't stir the anger in me; I had long since put anger to rest. I had yet to grieve. Memories ran through me washing dreams away; wrenching heartache left me unable to see beyond a swollen river of pain.

As my fingers typed, childhood memories surfaced, and I remembered myself as a young girl. I could still feel my sadness, and how afraid I was of criticism, but in searching through my memories not once could I find a time when I felt proud of who I was.

When the memories of childhood sexual abuse surfaced, I could not see the face of the one who was humiliating me, but I could feel the shame as he touched my body in a way that hurt and felt demoralizing. I had carried this dark secret for many years and it had altered the direction in my life and the lives of my children. Finally, my tears began to release what I had held inside for so many years.

I wept for the little girl, who was afraid to tell her mother, and I wept for the little girl, who felt defiled as though something was wrong with her, and I wept for the little girl, who carried her secret as if she really didn't matter.

It was a time to be alone, and oh, how I cried. I needed to know I had done nothing for which to feel ashamed. The hurt I felt went deep and no one could share my inner pain, but me. No one could change what had happened, but it was time to heal something that happened over 40 years ago.

The reflection in my childhood mirror was of a pretty girl, but I couldn't feel her self-worth and my physical appearance had never been enough to take away my shame, but the light of God's Love healed the barrier between my heart and my soul.

When I was ready, I gently opened the lid to my beautiful satin box inside my heart, the one that held pieces of my shattered past. Truth was revealed in the face of my dark and pitiful little shadow. When I looked into her eyes, I saw her pain and her self-doubt. For many years I had been disappointed in her, but I wasn't in need of self-pity; I was in need of self-love.

For the first time, I wept with the arms of love comforting me. I had lived my life doing the best I could, and I needed to feel compassion for the small child and the hurt she experienced at such a tender age. My tears flowed for all the things I failed to do and for the love I withheld from myself.

Then I wept for the woman who was beaten by her husband. Is there anything more shaming than that? Stripped of all dignity, pride and courage and in all my soul's nakedness, I saw myself as a whimpering child.

When I had had enough, the door closed. Memories didn't surface. There was a lull in the storm and I basked in the sunlight rejoicing that it was over. But it wasn't long before another haunting memory begged my attention.

First, it began as a rough draft but through my writing, the memory came alive in a way that had never happened before.

"I can't do this," I cried. "I'm not ready."

For a while I even convinced myself that this memory wasn't important. Besides, there's no need, I told myself. No one will ever know, this is my secret and I was sure Bobby took that same secret beyond the grave with him.

Keeping secrets contradicts everything I believe in, they imprison the soul, and so for weeks I agonized with a decision I would have to make. Back and forth, my mind argued against the many reasons why I should and why I shouldn't. Then, without a doubt, I knew I would have to and so I went back into my first chapter and made revisions.

For the first time in 24 years, I faced the unforgivable sin in me. The tiny unborn life I ended. Even though I knew how deeply wounded I had been, I had no idea how deep those scars really went.

During the following months, I mourned unremittingly. I grieved for loss of this child, and for the pain and guilt had caused me for so many years. A mother feels the bond with her unborn child—the love is there, the need to protect and nurture is there—it's not something she thinks about or waits until the child is born to decide whether she will love the baby.

At night, Richard held me. He dried my bitter tears. His words were comforting and I knew he was right, but I couldn't accept what I had done. And although Richard was with me, I have never felt more alone. Many times I asked, "Why had all this happened?" As far back as my memories took me, crippling emotional pain pierced and seared a black hole through the middle of my heart.

Astonished that I had buried such intense sorrow and guilt, I was even more astonished that it still so powerfully remained with me. This taught me many things. Each trial that we go through has eternal purpose and it serves no purpose to hide it or to allow guilt to corrode the soul's light. This is the purpose of God's Perfect Love—It is Love without hesitation, without restrictions or conditions—It's simply a Love that heals and instantly forgives.

Without a doubt, I realized that no one could judge another. It isn't really possible; we haven't the eyes to see beyond the surface or the understanding to each soul's life purpose. When we do we are simply seeing an unhealed aspect of our self.

Life is a puzzle. Gradually, over time, and from many of our experiences we are given one piece at a time. Clearly I saw how mine were teaching me eternal principles and they all begin with love—loving myself enough to embrace acceptance, and loving myself enough to honor my soul.

I thought about Christ's Ministry and for a moment I saw a glimpse of myself as a small child kneeling before him—my life was an open book and my sins had been etched in bold ink. Carefully, with love in his face, He turned each page. Lovingly, He took me in His arms. I wasn't a disobedient child or one that He sent to her room.

I really understood how deeply scarred I had been for a choice I regretted, and how that guilt destroyed my self-image. Remembering the Church Court and how it was to have been a Court of Love saddened me.

I truly believe the process I went through further damaged me—I had suffered incredibly. I paid the price, and when it was all said and done, I never once felt any better about myself. And for years to come, deep down I believed I deserved physical beatings and humiliation. How far had I strayed from the teachings of Christ? How far had I strayed from His love? The answer to that can only be measured to the same degree as my suffering.

If only someone had said to me, "You were raped. You don't need to be forgiven," I would have welcomed those compassionate words, but to send me to my room or prohibit me from participating in God's Church seemed contradictory to the way Christ loved. To this day, it's still incomprehensible to me.

The tears that flowed were nourishment to my soul and as the tide began to ebb; I felt deep inner pain wash out into the middle of the ocean. In place of sorrow, love softly played a melody in witness of my Savior's love.

Over the following days, my feet graced the floor and humility filled my heart—a love more precious than sunlight, more glorious than blooming flowers and more beautiful than singing birds healed and cleansed my soul. It was the very power of Heaven placed lovingly in my hands, with a promise that if I were to live this love, speak this love, until its melody sang forth in devotion from every breath and silent prayer, my life would become a glorious symphony played on into eternity.

It wasn't long before a sweet and tender voice gently reminded me to stop running from my shadow long enough to turn around and love her, that's all she really needed was to be loved. In loving her, I was no longer frightened of my own weakness; instead, I was willing to let go of fear and allow it to become my greatest force propelling me further than I had ever dared venture and believe in myself in ways I never dreamed before.

From this I learned that we each have characteristics we detest and aspects of ourselves we don't want anyone else to know, but unless we can accept that negative facet of ourselves, that part we detest will never let us be who we really are.

Today, I understand that this light, God's Love, has the power to reach into the very darkened corners of the heart such, as I have never felt before. Without a doubt, no human being is so lowly, miserable and destitute that he cannot be perfected by this one gift. I believe this divine love has the power to find its way through the hallways of the past and heal the injustices that have left wounded hearts.

Gently, I closed the lid to my satin box and quietly put it away—it no longer had any value. I was ready to accept the things I could not change, and embrace my pain, my past, and each one of my painful choices.

Today, my heart still aches to comfort my older sons, but they are grown and I can only hope they will heal themselves in their own time and way. Nathan, Lynsey and Westin still share their lives at home with me, and I am grateful they have caused me to reach inside and test my strength to love with all my heart and soul.

Twenty-one

Gifts of the Soul
Next comes Forgiveness

How can I forgive when my heart is still grieving? Where is the fairness, if forgiving is required of me? Can I not be justified in my need to hate my enemy? The answer seemed almost too impossible to believe, forgive others so you can forgive yourself; in this there is healing peace.

There was a time when forgiveness meant self-betrayal—if I forgave, no one would be responsible for their horrific acts of brutality, and I wasn't about to let certain people off the hook that easily. What they had done was reprehensible, especially in light of the damage that had been caused to my children and me.

As much as I tried to heal my bitterness, the pain I carried begged to be remembered after so many years of abuse. Finally, I quit trying to forgive. I believed God would have to understand my reasons if I never forgave the man who betrayed me, and even if I forgave him, what about the man who raped my children? I felt I had a right to be angry, and I didn't want anyone telling me that it was one of God's commandments to forgive and go on.

When I started writing this chapter, it wasn't my idea! I felt inspired to begin but I wasn't ready to forgive and besides, I really believed God understood my reasons and He was with me on this one, but I didn't understand the laws of the universe—I really didn't understand God at all.

In spite of my hesitation, I was willing to try. First, I learned that when Christ taught us to "turn the other cheek," He wasn't talking about staying in an abusive relationship.

In fact, had I known the devastation of domestic violence long ago, I would have fled in the beginning with the blessings and help from Heaven. When the Bible tells us to forgive so that we can be forgiven, it isn't God who determines who is forgiven, in fact, God isn't the One who needs to forgive anyone. His Love is unconditional and it is something very few really understand!

Then I made a mental list of all those I thought were in need of being forgiven. If you've ever done the "stone tossing" exercise then you know what you have to do.

First you gather a basket full of small stones, then you make a list of all those who have offended you (or unhealed feelings) and then you toss a stone as far as you can for each person or situation in which you were emotionally wounded.

My list was quite lengthy and God was right at the top.

For years I went to the temple. Inside, before people enter specific sessions, there is a waiting room where soft music is played. I would sit in that room and silently pray. With my husband at my side, I would hold his hand and beg God to bless us as a family. When my prayers went unanswered, I bargained with Him. I made sacred promises to do my part and be obedient in all things. I wasn't asking much, I just wanted God to soften my husband's heart and help him find work. But each time that I left the temple, and Bobby's wrath ripped welts into my children's skin or bruised my body with a broken rib, I held God responsible—He wasn't fulfilling his part of the bargain.

Next on my list, and this one was a big one: What about my church leaders? I was really angry with the one who convinced me I should give Bobby another chance in the first place! I allowed him to stir feelings of guilt because I wasn't any better than Bobby. At least Bobby was a worthy member of the church (and this is important when you're adding or subtracting points) while I wasn't. I had been disfellowshipped for a very serious sin and never once had Bobby been stripped of anything.

How could I possibly overlook the Bishops and a Relief Society President with whom I entrusted my soul to know what was best for me? Aware of the beatings from my husband, this woman in my ward saw the bruising on my face, and yet I was a burden to her. She just wanted me to go away and stop calling her.

I had no doubt that they failed my children and me and I was angry. I had always been taught to "stay" within the church for counsel and guidance because no one outside our religion knew our values; therefore, they may guide us in the wrong direction. But what good did it do me to "stay" within the walls of my church?

They knew Bobby was abusive and yet they did nothing except ignore the problem as if that would make it go away. Perhaps they didn't know what to do, perhaps they advised me to the best of their knowledge, but that didn't change the fact that we were a family in crisis—an endangered family during those dark and frightening years.

"Be obedient, Janice, and you will be blessed"—How many times had I been told that? Enough times to cause me to feel completely victimized by life itself, and enough times to really fear and resent God.

I was surprised that Bobby was third on my list, but that didn't lessen his responsibility for what he had done. Memories of the times Bobby would say he loved me, after beating me so badly it hurt to be touched were bigger than life, was I to forgive him? When I felt raped by my husband and then shriveled with shame when he touched me, was I still required to forgive him?

This little exercise of tossing stones only increased the hatred I felt for my ex- husband. I could still hear my children screaming, begging and pleading for him to stop hurting their mother.

Completely taken back, I then added myself to the list.

With each wretched memory, I couldn't help but remember that I hadn't saved my children when they hid from their father or when he found them and yanked them from their place of hiding to beat them for some silly thing they had done. Sometimes I even forced them to stand still just so he wouldn't hurt them more because they ran from him.

Memories of my children searching through empty cupboards for food that wasn't there, and wearing dirty clothes, because I wasn't able to wash clothes or I didn't have enough money to buy them food tormented me.

Finally, forgiveness didn't make any sense at all. I knew that I had ultimately failed my children. I had neglected them, left them to fend for themselves and even worse than that, I had failed to protect them. I felt disgraced as a mother. Not only had I failed my children, I had failed myself.

I wasn't angry anymore. I was so filled with sorrow for the conditions in my life that forgiving my ex-husband or anyone else for that matter seemed to be a little thing, minor and almost insignificant when I recoiled and hid from my memories of being a woman and a mother.

My anger and resentment were only beginning to surface. But was it just my ex-husband I needed to forgive? Was it my religious beliefs that had betrayed me? Although, I believe the answer to that is yes, in my heart a voice resounded a million times, *"Janice, you are the one who can never be forgiven."*

Once upon a time, I needed to cling to and love my feelings of resentment more than I needed to forgive Bobby. He deserved every harsh word I said about him. Foolish Bishops who believed him and cared little for his victims angered me. But I realized how easy it had become to condemn the faults I saw in others rather than admit how I felt about myself.

In paraphrasing the words of Christ, I wanted to say, "Take this bitter cup from me." Forgiving was all entangled with incomprehensible crimes of the heart and I wasn't any less guilty than the One at the top of my list.

One afternoon, I sought solace in a grove of trees along a riverbed. On horseback, I rode as far as I could along the shady riverbank, and then I stopped. My heart was heavy, and I didn't understand what God wanted from me.

"What am I to be learning?" I cried. "No more riddles. Just help me understand what it is that I must learn so that I can end my pain."

Sitting at the edge of the river the past silenced the present. Confused, I couldn't help but feel that if I forgave all those who had betrayed me that would mean I didn't matter.

If I were to forgive, would forgiveness overshadow the importance of my sorrow? What about my children? My heart ached for the lives they lived. And this is where I couldn't forgive. Not me, not Bobby, not anyone who had a hand in shaping their destiny.

Where would I be without God's Emissaries? When I needed them they appeared. I felt their presence that sultry afternoon along the riverbed.

"Let it go," the words reverberated over and again. "Trust and just let it go."

"How do I do it?" I cried. In all things there is a reason, and as you forgive, my little one, you will be forgiven."

That quiet afternoon, I held a ceremony. A weeping ceremony!

Tears freely poured from a heart that had known more heartache than joy.

Lost in the silent breeze, I whispered, "I am sorry for the pain I have caused my children." More than anything, I just wanted to be forgiven. I carried a burden that only nourished my pain. Never once did anger or guilt resolve pain for anyone.

I dearly love my children, they are part of me and their sorrows are my sorrows and their joy is my joy (a phrase my father once said to me). And as their mother, I have never harmed them intentionally.

A certain, undeniable knowing, told me that my family was not circumstances. The abuse we suffered together had eternal purpose—as I worked through my sorrow, they would also work through theirs. It wasn't important to know why my little family chose to be together this lifetime, but I knew that I wasn't to feel guilty because of it.

"You have nothing for which to be forgiven—just love your children as we love you." Those words flowed through me like a gentle stream—erasing years of guilt and taking it far away from my heart.

From dark clouds overhead the heavens opened, and I felt the Earth respond to my pain. Gentle summer rain fell and danced upon the waters. Embraced with caring love, I knew the angels wept with me understanding a woman's pain. A soft breeze flowed through my hair and for a moment I felt peaceful. Mesmerized, I didn't dare move. Raindrops kissed my face, and my mind, in quietude felt communion between her spirit and her Creator.

On that late, sultry summer afternoon, something mysterious happened. I was feeling whole again. Tranquility filled the air rendering its sweet melody while leaves gently swayed reminding me of God's unseen power. My spirit rejoiced that afternoon, because I was finally learning the value of the gifts of the soul. I understood that there is a perfect ness to life's existence regardless of our circumstances and forgiveness allows us to continue forward and ever onward as the soul evolves.

Each shattered piece in my life is to always be a reminder of what happens when the heart forgets—love lives on and can never be destroyed, but the heart needs to be free to remember.

Today, I have compassion for my ex-husband. Bobby was an angry soul who experienced misery and sorrow all the days of his life—I pray his soul rests in peace. I pray he knows that in spite of his atrocities against his children, they love him and they always will.

Perhaps he knows that I am healing and he is grateful for that. I am the mother of his children and just maybe he is proud that I took all the pain and suffering he had given me and weaved it into a tapestry of which I am proud.

I believe we joined together in a union meant for our souls sacred missions. Even though our marriage had been written in the stars, I was not to stay with him. He was a reminder of what needed to be done before I could walk across the fiery bridge of adversity and join my Twin Flame—there was much to be gained from my marriage to Bobby, from him I learned the most about myself, and I am only beginning to understand the vastness of the soul's infinite journey and the role we each play giving many opportunities to heal from the past.

In awe, my eyes opened to a new understanding of life's most sacred purpose. From the beginning, my life has offered me the exact experiences I needed to be where I am today. Before I was born, I understood my life purpose, and I was willing to go through each and every trial knowing what joy I would experience at the end of my trials. But I haven't been alone to find my way. When I first meet Bobby, I knew him at soul level, and I didn't love him. I didn't even like him. I felt drawn into his world as though I didn't have a choice, and yet, as I look back, I was given a choice and many opportunities to back out. I didn't do it and I rejoice in the knowledge my soul had.

Remembering much suffering through many years of heartache, I can also see doors that opened with an opportunity to walk away and not look back. I didn't do it, but still I gained more awareness and deeper compassion as a result.

Today, my life is rich with spiritual blessings and not one is greater than the other. I am living the life of which I always dreamed with a man who gave me freedom to begin a new life with dignity. He has nurtured my soul into wholeness.

If at one time I lived in a fantasy world, then all I can say is "Welcome home, Janice." I have arrived with my feet firmly planted in the sacred commitment of my soul's journey.

The most difficult paths are often filled with heartaches and sorrow, and yet it is through this journey the soul opens to greater joy and enlightened consciousness. How great is the Holy Spirit's joy when we bring one soul unto Him—especially if that soul is our own.

Our responsibility in life is to become the light of love and from our light within others will follow.

Nothing you do erases the past, but to have a forgiving and compassionate heart is the greatest gift we can share. Forgiveness is permission to be the divine and loving soul that you are and to share your light with others so that they may follow.

Twenty-two

Song of the Soul
Gratitude

How blessed are the hearts that sing, for life shall bless them with inner peace.

One quiet afternoon, Richard gently offered me his opinion as to why he hadn't found work.

"Honey," he said, "maybe there's something you need to be learning and once you do we'll be okay."

I hit the ceiling!

"What do you mean it's because of me?"

Whatever he said that afternoon didn't go over quite as he expected. "I'd always been blamed for everything that went wrong (at least in the past) so I was astonished that he would say that to me.

Months went by and nothing changed, every job he bid on went to another contractor. The longer he went without work, the more miserable I became. Once again my writing stopped. I took to my bed. I pulled the shades down when the hot sun was blaring through my curtains begging me to get out of bed.

Yet, as a family, we weren't suffering. Our needs were being taken care of, but I couldn't see the goodness that was in my life, instead I complained.

Finally, one day I had had enough.

"Okay," I said to Spirit. "I'm listening, now let up on me!"

Frankly, I was tired of learning the hard way, especially because I wasn't doing it intentionally. Change can be difficult when you're learning new ways to think and to believe and to feel, but maybe Richard was right. Maybe, just maybe, there was a lesson to be learned in our situation, it wouldn't be the first time—our life together brought about tremendous spiritual growth especially for me.

Willingly, I emptied my head of all MY reasons and I waited for Spirit to give me better reasons for Richard's unemployment. Nothing came to me. Weeks went by and I didn't feel any different—stubbornly, I still believed I was right, Richard shouldn't have left Tucson, but misery also accompanied that belief and deep down I knew I wasn't right.

I couldn't help but remember the feelings I first had when I left Bobby. In such dire circumstances, I found thanksgiving for little things to be a sweet melody that lifted my soul. But it was when I listened to a sweet and touching story told by a close friend, Erin, a first grade teacher in the elementary school in our community, of a little native boy named Rafa that gratitude took on even a deeper meaning.

One morning, Rafa stood before his second grade class. With folded arms he bowed his head; eyes could not help but see his tattered clothes, buttons missing and shoes that were well worn, but still too big for his small feet.

Slowly he began to pray, "Dear Father, thank you for our many blessings. You have been good to us and so we ask, please bless those who have less than we do..."

No one, not even I, had less than little Rafa. If he could find something for which to be grateful in a life of poverty, then surely my heart should overflow from blessings I received every day.

This is the answer, I thought. Stop complaining and just be grateful. Count your blessings and stop worrying about the future. Knowing that the Hands of Providence had been taking care of me, I really tried living gratefully each moment, and knowing that giving thanks would also help my children, I asked them to count the blessings they had been given. It took time and effort, but from that day on, gratitude took on a powerful form of joy that spread like wildflowers dancing in a summer breeze. Attitudes within my family, ever so subtle, began to change.

Then one morning, working in my garden, I felt the warmth of the sun. As I basked in its comfort, my mind was aware and conscious of what was going on around me. Golden sunrays felt nurturing, and I felt part of the Earth's spirit. This glorious ball of fire gently faces the Earth each morning promising to be there again tomorrow. While there are many things in life we cannot rely on, the sun isn't one of them.

Feeling joined with the miraculous beauty of the Earth wasn't my first encounter with gratitude and it wasn't Earth-shaking, nor was I forever changed in the twinkling of an eye, but as the days went by I took notice. I made an effort to open my eyes and appreciate what was happening around me.

I wasn't preoccupied with my future, nor did I live in the past. Instead I made an effort to do my part, finish my writing and ask for spirit's guidance. Each time worry crept in; I simply remained focused on what was happening.

This was a new dawn with a new beginning for me. Just as each season gives birth to something wonderful, being grateful ushers in the Angels to join in harmony with sweet songs of praise.

On that day, I changed. A feeling of joy stayed with me and as the sun set below the Earth that evening, stars across the sky became a shimmering light as love gently fell upon my world.

Another burden lifted. My soul felt light. My world was bright, and I felt positively encouraged about everything I was doing.

In my most desperate hours of doubt and fear my soul was learning. I've lived with a lot of fear and it is something that I have needed to overcome. Slowly, I was learning to weed out all doubt thus allowing the positive energy to flow, but my dream still seemed far-fetched and so far away.

One morning, while sitting on the sandy beach in Mexico, I asked Spirit to teach me what I was still lacking in understanding. The answer came to me by way of passionate feeling. All around me, I felt a tremendous living force guiding the Universe. I could feel it in the waves as they crashed upon the shore. I felt it in the clouds as they gracefully swept across the sky.

Every living thing was working together in perfect harmony.

Suddenly, I felt a change inside me, a change that created intense doubt and then everything stopped moving. I felt the waves rolling backwards, the sun spinning out of control and then I realized this same powerful energy is in my thoughts. As long as I fervently believe in something, the energy from my deepest thoughts flows in perfect harmony joining with the Universe bringing to me situations in which my dream would manifest into reality.

I felt the power of that energy and it made perfect sense, but as soon as a thought about my future as a writer entered my head, doubt returned tenfold.

"How can I possibly find success when the odds are against me?"

I hear it from everyone around me. It's a given that writers experience rejection time and again before they find success if fate turns their way. Yet in my heart my only answer is, "If you believe that way then that is what you will experience."

But I also understood the magnitude of my sacred promise to be a light worker and help heal the suffering. First, I would experience, and then I would learn so that I could teach. At that moment, sweet melodies of gratitude moved through me with an intensity I hadn't felt before. "Believe in yourself," I heard over and again. "We do."

From this experience, I learned to give up my need to control the outcome, and I placed my faith in God's Hands and in His almighty Universe. I surrendered and in giving thanks to the spiritual realm; in return I felt their love as they gave me a message of my own. "Richard has been true to his mission. He has stepped aside to give you time to grow. He has done well and the time is near. He will move on in his life and work will come to him. You need not fear."

It wasn't long before he was introduced to a man who hired him as a subcontractor on a large project. We both saw this job as a blessing brought to us by providence, and we felt a loving force guiding our lives gently along the path we have chosen as spirits. We are fulfilling our destiny, he and I together, united as Twin Flames.

Today, as I write, I will count my blessings and name them one by one: I am grateful that my past has offered many mountains for me to turn into a stairway taking me further than I have ever dreamed.

I am grateful for the woman I am, because it released my need to be someone I wasn't.

I am grateful for the love that is in my life, my sweet, loving, kind and wise husband. His love is without end.

I am grateful for my children. In times of great difficulty, we have learned to pull together and we are learning to trust one another, to love and go on.

I am grateful for the tears I've shed, for they are nourishment to my soul's garden bringing forth new life after the rains have fallen.

And in my heart I've saved a special place for kindred spirits who have graced my life with their love and open hearts.

Rowena Gardner, I see her smiling face and in my memories we're walking arm in arm, autumn leaves rustling beneath our feet in the cool Arizona sun.

My hand still feels her soft touch as she stayed by my side in the hospital emergency room.

My most cherished and dearest friend left his Earth before I could say goodbye—softly whispered words of gratitude are sent her way, as tears glisten and fill my eyes, I long to hear her voice.

Comforted, I know her soul feels the love in my heart. She will always be remembered, and revered in my choicest memories of Earth-angels that cared for me and helped me find my way from inner-darkness.

There is another place in my heart that sings with a continuous song of gratitude for the angels on high who write with me each day.

Each word of gratitude resonates with the stars above as the melody of love plays on throughout eternity. If I desire happiness, I must give another person a reason to smile; if I desire love in my heart, I must heal another with sweet and tender compassion.

Over the course of several years, the angels encouraged me to be willing to open my heart to love. From their teachings, I learned that in loving and forgiving, we find the pathway to perfection. We learn to love our self and to forgive our imperfects by embracing our dark side. Only then can we go out into the world and touch the lives of others with the Pure Love Of Christ.

Each gift of the soul has its own virtues. Intricately they go hand in hand and in writing about thanksgiving this is the message the angels shared with me: *As each day unfolds you have the power to gather it into your heart and bless it and give thanks that it is yours to live. Then when evening shadows fall, you can send the day into eternity a glorified light with joyous strains of gratitude because your heart embraced it, your life touched and you lived it.*

Twenty-three

The Awakening

When we least expect it our Spirit awakens and softly whispers… "You are accepted in God's Sacred Heart just as you are," giving meaning to a past, comfort to heartache, and wings to our dreams

Over the years, the colors of my life seemed to fade away as each season passed before me. Who am I? I asked the wind one day. A wind song, rustling leaves beneath my feet and bending flower heads, did not answer me.

Sun-dappled memories of a child are still calling out to me. Longing to grasp her tiny hand and bring her safely home takes my breath away. Distantly, her eyes fade in morning light, and my eyes begin to see. Her golden hair of honey melts against my face, mysteriously reminding me, she isn't gone she's still here with me.

Years have passed and vanished into thin air, and although I'm certainly no longer a child, I hold to her dreams imbued with the same fears of yesterday. I'm a grown woman who has felt her share of pain. Yet, is it possible to integrate this little girl with all her innocence and wonder into the woman I am becoming?

Victimized by low self-esteem, for many years I felt less than other people. In later years, locked inside a loveless marriage brutally bludgeoned my true nature. My pain, a silent scream of despair begged for release—disquiet between heart and soul grew in strength and intensity until it became a roaring rage. With blatant expression of grief, the silencing of my heart returned with misery, and the only thing standing between my broken heart and wholeness was *truth*.

As real as it gets, I journeyed through disappointments, heartache and anguish until my heart felt nothing but rage and betrayal. After years of pent up anger and resentments, an emotional breakdown crumbled the walls that imprisoned me. Only then was I faced to let go of a life that wasn't mine and start over.

Peering behind immense intimidation, every aspect of myself was open to anyone who listened to the latest gossip. But it was the small child in me that felt vulnerable to outside voices and opinions knowing how scathing that can be.

In spite of the passing years and all the wisdom they have instilled in me, I still want to paint my world with living color, restore shattered dreams, feel good about myself, and feel joy in simple pleasures. I want to walk along a deserted beach in windblown skirts and sun-kissed shoulders; I want to feel young again.

I want to be strong enough to stop taking the blame, and feeling a rush of panic when things fall apart, and I can't repair the damage. I want to live my life in peace. I want to hear singing birds, and feel rapture in each breath I take; I want to know I matter.

I certainly don't want to leave this Earth a troubled woman filled with remorse and regret. I don't want my wings to lie limp and useless because I refused to try, and I don't want the wind and the storms to silence my song, or the beating of my heart. I don't want to leave this Earth forgotten.

Yet, how many times have I softly whispered, "If I could only be like her?"

I haven't always wanted to be me or to live my life. Many times I've resented the choices I've made and the consequences they brought me. As a mother I felt I had failed. It wasn't enough that I tried and often I wanted nothing more than to vanish just as my childhood days.

I can't help but wonder, is there life after shattered dreams and a life for a mother beyond her angry children?

Yet, I will have to say, that over the years beneath wings of an angel I have taken refuge. In fever I've slept, and in prayer I've begged, "Bring solace to a mother's heart, give to her what life has taken from her, wipe her tears and gently take her hand pulling her forward."

Always believing that one day the sun would rise for me shouting from above, "Be of good cheer, my little one, for God has not forsaken you. Be willing to accept the changes in your life and believe that your children are learning."

But in fear I answered on this blessed day, "Will you shine for me tomorrow? Dry my tears and remember me again in stormy weather?"

One afternoon I was even more deeply troubled as the answers I needed continued to elude me, but as I sat down to write, I stopped long enough to watch soft breezes gently kiss the vines clinging to the arbor outside my window. Moved by silent touch, they remain the same today as yesterday and the year before, yet, am I?

This overflowing fragrant vine, filled with blooming honeysuckle, permeates the air with an enchanting scent uniquely its own. It also wraps itself around everything else in sight.

I can't untangle its limbs and tiny tendrils to separate one from another. Is it this way for me? Am I still so entangled in the lives of those I love; I've stopped living my life? Are the opinions and beliefs of others still more important than my own?

My journey has taken me to many places of the heart. I have gone from a place of sorrow to one of greater peace, but sometimes I feel disloyal. I want to offer my children a life of security and one of rejoicing because we all made it through a terrible storm. But this isn't possible. I don't live their lives and they can't live mine.

My pain as a battered woman fades in comparison to my grief as a mother. Weary and discouraged, I wanted to lay this aging woman to rest; it seemed the right thing to do. She had paid penance for all her wrong doings. Then I realized that I *was* moving forward. It wasn't enough to wait for my children to catch up with me; my ship was pulling away from the harbor. I had given up enough of me and it was time to nurture my needs and establish a life of my own.

Deep in thought, I feel the currents and whispering winds telling me I am above the valley and beyond that place of strife and to live my life in peace. High into the mountaintops and across the azure sky I'm soaring groundless and free. I've found my way, yet I'm afraid of flight, and I'm afraid of failing.

In every woman's life a time will come when she will review the life she has lived, whether it be in quiet moments when her wee children are sleeping, or in the quiet chambers of her heart while rocking her first grandchild. Why should she see it with regret?

Regret would most certainly be my soul's fatal wound. After all that I have experienced I am not meant to fail my soul's sacred mission, but it took me years to find inner-peace and to accept my life and who I am.

Many times I felt alone on my journey, but these were the times I was learning to trust in myself.

When no one else was around to comfort me, quiet, inner stillness brought me to a light that became a lantern to my feet and I'm grateful for the weaving of my life into radiant colors from threads of sorrow.

And just when I believed all darkness would consume me, faith took me one more step deeper until I reached the light of my soul. Arriving at that tender place within, feeling *deeply spiritually connected*, gifted me with my souls power to live my life according to the dictates of my own conscious.

In return, quietly my heart sings a melody to a woman's song. From years of heartache, pain taught me mercy, and loneliness taught me love. How can I not breath appreciation for all those poignant insights that taught me thoughtfulness, kindness, and humility? And how can I forget sorrow gifted me with compassion

From my trials, my heart opened to receive the love that freed my soul. Self-love abandons not the shadow, but allows room for all aspects of its self. Giving thanks, loving and forgiving brings miraculous changes, and today my soul is my light, she is my strength.

In this life, we *are* on a spiritual journey, and we suffer needlessly without knowing that there is a reason for the conditions and situations in our lives. If we would only see each road block as another doorway, each difficult situation as an opportunity to understand what we haven't been willing to learn then life on the outside would mirror what is in need of healing on the inside.

My life is not one I would wish upon anyone, but it is a life that holds eternal purpose. The times in which I suffered came about from *my resistance to understand my lessons*—I wanted change to happen from the outside, while my spirit needed change to come from within.

I would like to share this sacred experience with you so that you also can know that in all things there is spiritual purpose, and you too can learn from the heartbreak in your life and find meaning to your life.

Prayer and meditation brought me comfort as well as spiritual guidance and on this particular night; I wanted reassurance of my soul's sacred mission. For several years I felt strongly that I would help many women heal from abuse, but I was discouraged and doubted in my abilities. So I asked for Spirit's help.

Drawing from the power of meditation, I visualized light surrounding my body and as the light grew stronger, I felt myself leave this Earth plane and go deeper within feeling a love all-powerful and glorious fill my being.

Breathtakingly, my prayer was answered as light entered my darkened room. I could see silvery outlines of spiritual beings in radiant and shimmering light.

Then, I saw a misty doorway opening as an even more beautiful light came closer. The light was so radiant and the love so pure, I could scarcely breathe. I wept in awe at the glory of this being.

As she drew closer, I knew she was another dimension to my spirit. I could not deny her presence as she held out her hand.

Silent words filled my heart and I began to speak the words out loud for her: "*You are a Creator Goddess and have chosen to be here during these most difficult times to help bring healing to this Earth. You knew the knowledge you would need could only come from personal suffering. You have been through all the pain you will ever need to experience, for now is the time to take what you have learned into the world and touch the lives of those who also suffer as you once did.*"

My life passed before me, with a review of all I had experienced. I felt my own pain, and the memory of a woman's face and her worthlessness filled my heart with sorrow. I wept knowing this was not who I was, and yet all those years were spent in inner darkness.

Receiving this personal revelation changed my life dramatically. Without a doubt, I saw and felt my soul's presence.

All the strength and courage we need for safe passage is inside. When we're trapped in fear and uncertainty, this inner-knowing guides us and the Universe responds miraculously bringing to us that which we need to learn, heal, let go and become stronger. As we cleanse the inner self our body becomes a vessel of Love.

My soul's mission is that of being a Light Worker, or someone who *spiritually* teaches and heals wounded hearts. This journey is a hard road. It is often the most challenging and dangerous path we can choose, but in this walk, I've found love, bravery, truth, and triumph. I've learned that out of darkness we can emerge graceful and strong and in this there is no regret, but understanding—we are spiritual heiresses living to choose our own meaning and purpose.

Often it is necessary to break away from antiquated ideology and beliefs handed down to us and discover new truths that bring us joy and fulfillment. The way is open for each woman, man or child to discover their purpose this lifetime—there isn't a "one path fits all." Each path is individualized and often it is filled with many diverse challenges and opportunities to learn. And through it all, I've learned, we are not to be followers, but to rely on the inner voice to guide us to our own truth.

Knowing that a woman is gifted in God's Power and it is from her difficult experiences she emerges from cocoon into a spiritual Goddess brings me to the understanding that no one can tell a woman what her role is to be in this life.

From caterpillar to butterfly, each stage of transformation in the life of the butterfly is vitally important and so it is with us. While in the caterpillar stage, we are concerned with things of the earth and our vision is limited. But then a yearning to be more, explore more, and learn more awakens us from a deep sleep.

The cocoon stage is the beginning of our spiritual journey. It is here that we learn more of our spirituality and the powers we have. In the quietness of the heart, healing begins until the soul is cleansed.

The emergence of the butterfly from the cocoon state is symbolic of spiritual awakening out of the limitations of the physical world. All that has gone before strengthens our wings. Her own transformation is total. In her cocoon state, she is completely still. After she emerges, she has wings to fly and tastes a new freedom.

Because of this, I'm grateful for the whimsical memories of the child I used to be as she danced upon her stage with music sweeping her into a world of fantasy. From all that has gone before a joyous melody plays on as I reach for the stars and believe in magic and feel joy in simple pleasures. And even though yellow faded photographs, timeless in memory, reflect a young woman shaped by many voices, never once did truth fade away.

Twenty-four

Reflections of the past

It is a sad day when you find out that it's not accident or time or fortune but just yourself that kept things from you.
-Lillian Hellman

Why did Bobby behave the way he did? Why did I? It is a difficult question to answer. There were many factors involved, but perhaps the most significant answer would be Bobby was a victim of abuse and so I was.

Whether abuse is physical, emotional or sexual it doesn't matter. Since birth, Bobby experienced loss, abandonment, and rejection, physical, mental and sexual abuse—he didn't know anything else. His pain had been deeply buried. No longer feeling his pain, anger was the only emotion he knew.

Even though he was raised in a devoutly religious family, that in itself does not prevent abuse from happening, in fact, that may create a perfect place to hide behind deceptive behavior.

My life story was also one of dark secrets. All the religious training and teachings I received didn't uproot the seeds of self-loathing, but rather they reinforced them.

By telling me who I should be, did nothing to change the way I felt—If God wasn't able to accept bad behavior in his children, how could I accept the bad that was in me? The abuse in my life changed me. Without boundaries and a strong sense of self, I was afraid of anyone more powerful or authoritative and I always took the blame and internalized it—I lived inside emotions that didn't feel good, feeling helpless to stop letting people hurt me.

When I met Bobby, we were two wounded spirits giving to one another valuable life lessons. There was familiarity between us. I felt destined to marry him and perhaps, I was. Two wounded hearts seeking release from a painful past. When it didn't happen, he blamed me and I blamed him.

By the time I knew, without a doubt, that my marriage was a terrible mistake, I believed it was too late.

I was pregnant. Then later, babies were born one right after another. We lived like humble church mice, begging handouts that only instilled further humiliation. A devout belief in my religion provided a mantle to cover my shame and embarrassment. Wanting to prove that I was indeed a loving, kind, and decent human being, I sacrificed, gave service, and obeyed, but this did nothing to change what was inside me.

When I should have left Bobby, I also bought into the excuses of why I should stay. Bobby found ways to put a roof over our heads and even if we moved constantly, my children had a place to sleep in their own bedrooms. Often, I would only have to look around me and see the toys in their bedrooms or their bikes on the back porch to tell me this was also their house. When I watched my children playing, we seemed to be like every other family.

Feeling like a failure, I wanted my family to see me in a different light. But my sisters distanced themselves from me, and this also felt like personal rejection. I wanted to feel good about myself and that meant I needed their approval. If I admitted I married an abusive man that was an admission of my own stupidity.

But for them, it was painful to watch two dysfunctional people act in abhorrent ways. Screaming and fighting with one another, no one wanted to be around us. Although, never once did I start an argument with Bobby in public, I engaged in the fight with him.

Not only did my sisters distance their lives from mine, my mother played the role of an enabler. She wanted to fix my problems in anyway that she could or else she allowed my problems to adversely affected her. I hated upsetting my mother, and I didn't feel safe in involving her—I didn't trust that she would be any stronger than I was.

In the beginning, I tried to leave Bobby. I ran from him. I called people from my church that I knew, but no one wanted to get involved. Even though bruises were obvious and they were aware of why I was running from Bobby, they didn't do anything more than provide a temporary bed to sleep in. Feeling like a fool and an imposition, I quit calling for help.

In retrospect, from the beginning it wasn't so much that Bobby was attracted to me, but that I was attracted to him. I accepted his emotional unavailability and his cruelty, and allowed myself to label our painful relationship as love when love had absolutely nothing to do with it.

Today, I think of the angry words that were spoken, the beatings and humiliation I faced nearly everyday and it seems almost impossible to believe someone could treat anyone in that manner and still claim to love them. What seems even more tragic is that I lived with it for fifteen years and brought even greater heartache into the lives of my children.

No one changes because we *want* them to and no one changes because we try harder. Bobby was an angry man, and where there is anger, love doesn't exist. It's as simple as this: no one can love another if they can't love themselves; sometimes the heart has been so badly damaged they don't know how to love.

Once I left my husband, the awful truth was still waiting for me just as it was from the beginning, and today the truth is here for anyone to read.

Little lies woven together became the tiny threads that held the fabric in my family's tapestry together. When the lie was revealed, the tapestry fell into a shambled heap of ugly and torn pieces of fabric. Not one piece had been stitched together with love or truth, and the worst lie of all was the one I had been telling myself, I wasn't worth being loved.

So why do women stay? Questions multiply with each answer. It is baffling, heart-wrenching and one of the most difficult relationships to end. I stayed in my marriage for 15 years believing that leaving would be worse than staying and just the thought of telling anyone was too humiliating.

The door was always open, but I was too afraid to walk out. I wouldn't survive if I did, and my children would hate me for taking them away from their father. In my mind, I thought I was doing what was best for them. Stripped of dignity, shamed and humiliated, I was not much more than a broken spirit.

Would I have lived my life differently if I knew then what I know now? I would hope so, but unfortunately, I think most of us that are impetuous and headstrong believe we are the exception; with love we can change our man. Maybe we don't think at all, but rather settle for any body that will love us. Sooner or later we're faced with intolerable behavior, but feel helpless to change what is happening to us.

Part of the myriad of problems is also *trust*. It's difficult for abused women to trust in anyone because she has yet to trust herself. Even though she knows she should dial 911 for help or get completely away from him, the outside world appears as frightening as her own.

She also fears criticism and the pressure to leave her husband if she confides in anyone. A battered woman holds on to hope that "this time" he will change. Promises, promises are never-ending, but once she tells someone, it isn't just between her and her husband. Now her problem involves people who don't understand. A battered woman fools herself into seeing a kinder side to her partner.

When threatened, the abuser makes all sorts of promises. But as soon as his victim returns, he loses all desire and ability to be good. He can't help it. He isn't able to keep his promises even if he wanted to—he fears closeness as much as he wants it.

Often a battered woman doesn't even know she is abused. Emotional and mental abuse transfers the guilt of the abuser to his victim and because of a battered woman's predisposition or early childhood training; she doesn't see the behavior as being abusive.

Another reason women stay is because it's frightening to step out into the world as a single parent. She may not have adequate education or finances to begin life on her own. And it's frightening to admit failure. It's frightening to leave an abusive man that has the power and desire to destroy anyone who is a threat to his survival. And more often than not, an abused woman has been so controlled she may not have access to any money or keys to the car, if any exist. She is completely dependent. To live this way is a crime, it is humiliating and emotionally debilitating—is it any wonder women live in despair, become depressed, strike back, and appear just as dysfunctional as their abuser?

This irrational and dangerous behavior has a name—it's called codependency. It's a behavior many of us have learned. It's a behavior that traps us in unhealthy relationships. It's a behavior that causes us to try and control our environment.

As a woman of my faith, I understand the frustration a battered woman feels. Inside she feels powerless. She wants God to tell her its okay to leave. She has always been told whom she should be; naturally, she waits to be told what to do. She also seeks answers from the Elders in her church when in reality this only reinforces her inability to reach within and grasp hold of her power and her strength and her wisdom.

In her temple ceremony she is told that her husband is her direct link to God. Male dominance, either subtly or overtly, controls many women and emotional abuse if not physical is tolerated as women strive to hold the family together—she is the core of her family's strength. Having been taught that she is to be her husband's helpmate, she also believes it is her responsibility to see that he is successful. Is there any ground more fertile for codependency behavior?

Mormon teachings apply tremendous demands and high expectations on its members. Many feel pressured into living and appearing picture perfect, and most often they never feel good enough or that they serve enough or live exemplary lives just perfect enough, at least I know I did, and they must always answer to someone.

Many Mormon Bishops also believe families should stay together, and if problems exist in the relationship, the answer is to be obedient and live closer to the Lord, but obedience to what? If I paid my tithing was that supposed to mean God would help my husband make a living? Or if I attended the temple would the blessings magically appear in my relationship with my husband? That's like planting turnips and expecting to harvest carrots.

With every act there is a direct consequence. If a woman stays with an abusive man, the direct result will be a broken spirit, death or severe depression, fractured ribs, bruises and shattered dreams.

A battered woman isn't just another member of her congregation having problems in her marriage; she and her children are *endangered* souls. When there is any question of physical or emotional battering a woman should not be questioned as to who is at fault. If law enforcement must be notified then so be it. If a woman needs to find safety within a shelter, she must be encouraged to leave her husband. I am not saying that ecclesiastical leaders or anyone else for that matter can tell a woman she must divorce her husband, (that choice must be hers) but she must be encouraged to leave for her spiritual, emotional and physical safety as the family receives counseling. If she won't do it for herself then her children must be considered. Child Welfare Services must be notified. Doing nothing only ensures the abuse will continue.

I am not implying that abusers can't change. But I am saying it is highly unlikely, and in the meantime your immediate family is in danger. Changing behavior is extremely difficult especially when one is so badly damaged. They can't accept responsibility because that is just another assault on their poor self-image. Abuse is a learned behavior and abused children grow up desensitized to the pain that it causes. They feel their anger and most often are unable to get beyond the rage to the pain. They will generally do most anything to protect what false sense of self they have. Over time, the ego takes over and it responds to what it has learned.

How often have you been told, "You deserved it?" How often have you been told that you need to accept responsibility for your behavior as if you are the one to blame? How often have you felt responsible? How often have you felt badly when you've contemplated leaving your abuser? How often have you minimized or justified abuse, regardless of how insignificant or catastrophic the incident? Why do you do it?

Over time, the victim buys into the myth that somehow she is the cause behind her husband's abuse. Blaming causes confusion. But who is right and who is wrong doesn't matter, abuse is intolerable in any situation. It isn't appropriate or acceptable behavior to hurt someone because they said something or did something to provoke one's anger. It's that simple, abuse should never be tolerated by anyone and if it is… the question should immediately be asked, "Why?"

When we so desperately need approval, love or friendship, we may forfeit our ability to take care of our self. Neediness is just another form of fear—fear of being alone, fear of failure or the fear that we're really not lovable.

Battered women have been so victimized by their batterer that they feel worthless, and often, battered women are depressed women. One of the most difficult tasks in stopping the vicious cycle is to break through denial. In order to break through denial a battered woman must become angry instead of depressed.

It's important to remember, anger is a signal that something is wrong and needs attention, and that depression is a symptom of repressed anger and a feeling of helplessness.

A phenomenon regarding abuse is that the abused justify the abuser. It's not unheard of to hear a woman say, "How can I blame him for getting angry after what I did." The battered woman has allowed herself to become so victimized; she has completely bought into the abuser's view of what is happening. Abuse is a normal experience for them. Their sense of reality is distorted and their self-esteem has been shattered.

Reasons why women stay make no sense to those on the outside, but fear is paralyzing. It immobilizes the mind. I think of a tiny, helpless rabbit when it's been traumatized. Its body goes limp until the heart quietly stops. A woman's mind freezes in a similar manner in its attempt to survive.

To justify our fear, we find every possible excuse not to do the one thing we know we should. Isn't it time to rid yourself of all the reasons why you stay and put an end to all the justifications for doing the most unloving things you could do to yourself?

Marriage vows are the ultimate vows, but sometimes they can hinder spiritual and emotional growth. In fact, some relationships can destroy it. Abuse is immoral and sinister and a thief—it destroys everyone in its path. So when you believe you are doing the right thing by holding your marriage together, you may not understand the vows you really made.

Weren't the vows I made the same as my husband's? Didn't he promise to honor and cherish me for the rest of our lives together? Honor is respect, and love is to protect. Obviously, those vows were broken from the very beginning. Didn't that give me the right and obligation to break the vow of silence?

When you are ready to break the vows of silence, there are organizations, crisis centers and other programs designed to help families in need. At the end of this book, you will find basic information that will help assess your needs, but if your life is in danger seek help immediately. Call your local crisis hotline or your local police. Reach out for the help you need.

Shouldn't today be the first day you take the necessary steps to bring joy, happiness and inner peace into your life? It won't happen overnight, but each step you take brings you closer to the loving and warm person you are—you certainly deserve it!

Nurture & Heal Your Soul

Healing the forgotten child within
With the light of love.

A workbook and supplemental
Guide for spiritual healing

Beginning of a New Journey

Tools you will use on your journey:

1. Journal
2. Pen
3. Hand-held mirror
4. Photograph of you as a child
5. Photograph as you are today
6. Soft, healing music
7. Candles
8. Quiet place to read, meditate, and write
9. Desire and dedication

I found meditating a necessary ritual in my recovery. (You may want to read books that offer helpful meditating techniques.) These books can be found in the new age section of your local bookstores or in libraries.

Meditation is an ancient art that many have mastered. It isn't necessary to sit for long periods of time, you only need to be still and quiet your thoughts for five or ten minutes early in the morning and then once again at night.

Each chapter is optional to give awareness, offer suggestions and promote healing. Work at your own pace, with or without outside assistance, but always call upon the angels and feel their presence. You are to gain inner strength other than rely on any outside source, but angels bring comfort as will your Higher Self, and your Spirit Guide…inviting them into your heart is all it takes—quickly they will respond.

If you are currently in an abusive relationship, call 911 or your local shelter. Seek professional help. I cannot over-emphasis this enough. Do not attempt to work through the following chapters without <u>first</u> seeking safe shelter and working with a professional counselor trained in the area of domestic violence. If you are a victim of incest, rape or childhood sexual abuse you may need to seek professional help.

If you are in need of professional therapy, call your local hotline for battered women's shelters and ask if they can recommend an experienced therapist in the area of domestic violence or childhood sexual abuse.

This book can act as a sport and a tool that you may use along with counseling. If you are suffering from depression, you also need medical intervention. What you will read is not intended to replace expert medical advice. The following chapters are taken from my personal experience and they are my views and opinions.

Support groups can also be a positive influence. Don't deny yourself the benefit of encouragement and support while you are in a transitional stage. If you are a mother with children, call for information regarding groups that also include children—a list of agencies or support groups can be found at the end of this book.

Introduction

The heart understands life's mysteries,
And the cause of all sorrow.
As you journey through the heart,
You will hear the sweet melody of a woman's song,
And learn to accept your defeats
With the grace of a woman and not the grief of a child.

Every woman wants to be an expression of love. It is our inherent nature to love and nurture those around us. While many women achieve their dreams, others feel trapped, unfulfilled, and angry. Although, each soul's journey is different, a common thread we all share is that we *want* our life to be our own and to live authentically.

What makes the difference between those who achieve their dreams and those that don't? It's all in how we think and feel and in what we believe, therefore before we can change our behavior we have to change our beliefs.

Anytime we embark upon a new journey, it's frightening. We're leaving behind familiarity and even if we're dissatisfied, change can be frightening for many of us. But where does fear come from? Are we born to fail while others rise to higher levels? Should we accept discomfort as a way of life?

No one is born to fail, but we are born into different circumstances to experience many different situations and no two are alike. While I do believe in destiny—my life is a perfect example—we can get ourselves stuck in *avoidable* ruts. While you can't veer from your soul's destiny or life plan, you can certainly experience a lot of misery along the way.

Fear is instilled at an early age in our development from primary caretakers that are unable to love and nurture, consequently children grow into adults with emotional deficiencies. From pained childhoods of neglect, emotional, physical or sexual abuse, children grow into adults unable to bond with any other relationship except those that offer pain.

It's not that we intentionally carry emotional baggage with us from relationship to relationship; we just don't know how to leave it behind. In part it's because we don't know how to do things differently—behaviors can be deeply rooted.

While we may be in denial, avoidance doesn't change anything for us except give us more misery because we can't escape from living, buried unhealed feelings (you will learn more about this in subsequent chapters).

Many choose not to find healing. They choose to remain victims of their situations and circumstances, but in so doing they will continue to attract relationships and situations with the same problems as before.

Don't let that be you. The rewards of healing are worth it. Freedom and dignity, joy and inner peace grace the lives of those that are willing to walk through life with humbleness of heart.

Since relationships act as a mirror reflecting how we think and feel about our Self in one way or another, it isn't that difficult to see what we need to work on. For example: If you are attracted to those who mistreat you, your self-esteem has been damaged. When you accept unloving relationships, you associate pain/rejection with love.

Just keep in mind that fear is the master deceiver, which gives all control to the personality or ego Self. It is that deceiver that blames the other person and refuses to accept responsibility.

There is a difference between the personality and the soul. Once you are aware that *you* are the life breathed into your physical body, anything is possible. Miracles happen all the time because it is love that performs those miracles. Within the limitless bounds of Love all things *are* possible. Hearts are changed. Lives are changed. When the heart is in direct communion with the soul change is inevitable and Love is the answer—it is the only power behind all change.

There is a cleansing of the emotional body or subconscious mind that is necessary before we can change a negative belief. A miraculous transformation begins when light is drawn into the body, which will surface repressed emotional trauma, into the conscious mind.

Healing light is the Holy Spirit's Love, but first, you must open your heart or have a humbleness of heart that is willing to accept responsibility for all conditions in your life. We have to open our hearts to feel self-love, and how sad it is that many women do not love themselves.

All personal growth arises from the ancient truism *"Know Thyself."* The more you learn about your spiritual Self and the purpose of your soul's journey, the more meaning, joy, and fulfillment you will have in your life. You will never resolve your problems or life issues if you do not know who you are!

Too often we are told who we are yet we don't feel our true worth. It's important that you open your mind to a new way of thinking or to a higher level of understanding. It isn't enough to be told or prodded or controlled—you have to make things right in your life and that requires you to do things your way.

Often we allow our Selves to remain trapped in a set of beliefs that prevent us from deep inner spiritual growth. In this set of beliefs nothing changes. Behavior is repeated over and again with the same results. Consequently, we become expert doers, but without the ability to be genuine, loving and free.

Embarking upon a spiritual journey allows you to think for yourself. While each of us strive to be accepted, to be good enough, and to be honored and respected in our lives many of us don't feel that way no matter what we do or how hard we try.

One fallacy you may have been taught is that perfection is something you must strive for and someday if you *are* "good enough" you just might reach perfection.

But there is hope. Your spiritual journey will teach you a different perspective that dissolves fear. You don't have to get rid of your flaws or imperfections. Instead you can accept who you are with the understanding that you already are perfect.

People often view the spiritual path as a search for light. In truth, spirituality asks that we embrace light and darkness together in whole. We are beings of duality, this world exists of duality, and any effort to focus all our attention on perfection only serves to increase the power of fear.

Awareness gives us power. Before anyone can modify his/her behavior they must be aware of what needs to be changed. Since we are also creatures of habit *desire* is the single most powerful motivator. There are those who know just about everything including what is wrong with them, but they lack motivation in order to change.

Change isn't an overnight assignment and what is engrained in our thought patterns isn't easily modified. Therefore, desire is the motivation that makes the difference between those that rise above the challenges that they face and those that don't.

The real meaning of life comes with knowing the *greater truth of who we are* and this is the purpose of a spiritual journey. As you begin your healing journey, you will find that you aren't alone. Angels without wings will come into your life, and information will be given to you in ways you can understand as long as you continue asking questions and seeking answers.

If you desire change, your journey has already begun. Once you ask for help from the spiritual realm, light will center on you, and the angels will begin working with you. They are always with us, but believing in their presence makes them available to us.

The only roadblock that stands in your way from making a soul transformation is fear. Your past and all that has gone into creating your personality and beliefs can be the roadblocks that prevent you from achieving the happiness and success you desire. These roadblocks consist of *living, buried, negative feelings*. These *unhealed feelings* are referred to as our *Wounded Inner Child*.

You *can* erase emotional trauma from your memory and this is the purpose of a spiritual healing journey. Once called upon, the Holy Spirit will radiate light into your physical body. You must be willing to participate in this miraculous healing process because you also have the healing power inside you.

It is also important that you believe in your Spirit Self. All change comes about when we draw close to our Eternal Source. The subconscious mind can be a barrier between the Spirit Self and the personality—dissolving its power by dissolving negative energy restores your awareness and desire to continuously draw closer to its power.

Secrets of the heart aren't safe just because you tucked them away. Instead "being tucked away" gives darkness more power than your illuminating light. Bringing them into the light and your consciousness gives you the control you need. While this may seem daunting and intimidating, memories can't harm you once you face them while avoiding healing can.

As you heal all past wounds, whether they are big or small, you'll feel lighter and more joyful with greater purpose to continue seeking higher truths. The most difficult part of this journey is taking the first step.

Life holds so many opportunities for you if you can learn to move through your fears to explore and express your pure essence. And in doing so you really haven't eliminated your dark side but rather you will have learned self-acceptance. As you grow into self-love your dark side loses its power.

The following are a few of the necessary steps that will help bring healing into your life.

1. You must gain control of your life, and make important choices that will *enable* you to bring peace into your life.
2. It's important that you understand and believe *life is a spiritual journey.*
3. Take responsibility for your healing.
4. Open your heart to love.

A wonderful sight is the rainbow—after rains have fallen the rainbow begins at the bottom of the earth spanning across the heaven only to reconnect with the earth again. A woman's sorrows begin in the core of her heart reaching out to touch the hearts of many returning her pain tenfold, but a woman's song heals all pain as she finds closure to her life lessons.

Listen to the beating of your heart and you will hear the lyrics to a woman's song as you learn to accept your defeats with the grace of a woman and not the grief of a child.

Why do I stay?

Is this what life really is all about—accepting discomfort?

Are you still chasing leprechauns and hoping to find a pot of gold at the end of the rainbow? If not, perhaps you have learned to temper your longings and settle in with relationships or situations you don't particularly feel comfortable with. Many of us don't really know how miserable we are or how much of our identity we have lost until we stop long enough to really soul search into our deepest feelings.

Kermit the Frog enchantingly sings, " The Rainbow Connection," but the lyrics to the song resound in our hearts…. "Have you been half asleep and have you heard voices? I've heard them calling my name. Is this the sweet sound that calls the young sailors? The voice might be one and the same. I've heard it too many times to ignore it. It's something that I'm supposed to be. Someday we'll find it, the rainbow connection, the lovers, the dreamers and me…"

What is it that *you* are searching for? Are *you* on your way to finding it or are you impatiently waiting for someone else to make you happy? I want you to put this book down for just a moment and think about those two simple questions and ask yourself if you are on your way to finding it or if you expect someone else to fill the void within.

While leprechauns may not be real (although, I would like to believe that they are) the pot of gold does exist and there is a treasure at the end of the rainbow, but you are the only one that can discover it and your secret longings will take you where you need to go. Being divinely connected to your Spirit Self is the secret to a safe passage.

We all have the power to change our lives; furthermore, it is our responsibility to make ourselves happy, not anyone else's. While we also have our personality and character, there is a deeper power that lies within us. It is up to us to find that personal power and bring it to light.

You can learn how to bring this power into the light and strengthen it just the way you would strengthen your physical body—with motivation and exercise. You must exercise your personal power by doing two things: Believe in yourself and trust your own intuition.

Evaluate your life as it is today. What is it that you need? Have you thought about making a life-changing decision, if so what is it that is holding you back? You may not be in a relationship, and yet still struggle with issues of low-self esteem, self-doubt, anxiety, depression and loneliness.

Although, there are valid reasons for staying in relationships that hurt, such as housing and finances, *we also stay because of fear.* Fear hinders us from making significant changes. We don't trust in our ability to achieve success, find love, or to be happy. Being alone is frightening for many people, and because of fear, there are those that believe *any* body is better than *no* body.

If your issues happen to be low self-esteem, fear of inadequacy or failure then you must also evaluate the reasons you feel the way you do. Do you want to feel differently? Do you believe that you can?

I doubt there is any woman who lives with heartache that doesn't want it to end, and I doubt there is any woman who lives with insecurities, the fear of intimacy and emptiness that doesn't want her life to be different.

I'm not referring to the real fear we have of leaving an abusive man. It can be extremely dangerous for a woman when she does leave. The abuse can become deadly. This fear is warranted, it is cautioning us to be extremely careful and to seek help, but staying because we fear what will happen does not keep us any safer—our physical/emotional/spiritual Self is constantly at risk.

What I am referring to is the elusive fear that prevents us from doing the most loving thing we can do for ourselves. It's the kind of fear that immobilizes us and prevents us from ending unloving relationships or changing self-defeating behavior patterns. It's that convincing fear that tells us we won't be able to take care of ourselves or that we will be alone forever, or that no matter how much we try, we will fail. And as long as we feel this way we're right!

Although fear is an illusion, illusions are *great* deceivers. They become bigger than life once we allow them to be, but illusions are still illusions— figments of our imagination.

Of all the emotions we feel, fear is our worst enemy. While anger motivates us into doing something, fear encourages no action at all. And, if fear persists, fear becomes an entity, another personage inside us because we have given it power.

Rather than believe in our Selves, the voice in our head invariably says,

"Don't do it, you'll fail." *Stop* listening to that voice in your head—don't give it power. Trust that you when you take action doors will open bringing to you gifts of healing and sustenance and nurturing.

Most often we don't think beyond fear. *We run from fear.* We remain trapped inside fear, addictions, and unhealthy relationships. Often, this is the only life we have known, or the only feelings we have experienced.

A quote that is worth repeating is: "Sometimes we're running because we're scared, but then again, sometimes we're scared because we're running." Belleruth Naparstek

We project fear as coming from the outside. We blame others and we expect others to lessen our pain, but often we end relationships only to find someone else that hurts us without stopping long enough to understand our *pained low self-esteem* and the many unhealed aspects of our personality that are in need of healing

Perhaps you *are* ready to make necessary changes in your life, and I believe that you are simply because this book is in your hands and now that it is, you will discover an ancient truth…when the student is ready the master will appear. All that you need will come to you if you are willing.

At soul level, I don't believe we are willing to accept discomfort as a way of life. It is a way of life that is in direct conflict with our Spirit. Regardless of our circumstances or our painted-on smiles, when something is missing we feel it. Could it be a secret longing to unite the inner-wounded child with a courageous woman breathing an endless sigh?

Both inner-child and Spirit must meet in the middle of your heart and become united so that your spiritual journey can take flight. Much like the path you would follow in search of the rainbow and the pot of gold.

Once you have traveled far enough, you will also discover that the pot of gold really is the golden light of love, which is the treasure right inside your heart. And it is the rainbow's promise to provide angels to watch over you and guide you in your search for a woman's soul, her own life and all that is important to her.

Solution: For a moment, think about your reasons for staying in a relationship that hurts, or think about the reasons you settle for less than what you deserve. Think about the reasons your behavior is self-defeating and if you really want to change.

Then quiet your mind and sit very still. Don't run from your feelings regardless of what they are, but rather let your feelings remain as long as they will. As negative thoughts come into your awareness send love to your feelings. Accept the fear that you feel, accept the confusion it brings. Become one with your thoughts. Stay as long as it takes for fear to dissipate. Let the calmness inside, the spirit that resides in you; dissolve fear in its warm embrace.

Do this over and again until the feeling you have no longer poses a threat to you.

Then, ask yourself: What is it that I know I must do, but I'm afraid?

Embrace fear and understand that fear is okay. Fear isn't your enemy because it is doing its best to protect you from the unknown. Think of fear as a little entity created by you to protect you from the cruelty in life. Today, thank this little entity for doing its job because now you are ready to do those things you know you must.

Now embrace the part of you that is wise, courageous and all knowing. Believe she exists and unite the part that is frightened with the courageous one. Close your eyes take a deep breath then repeat this prayer:

Holy Spirit, I am in need of your help today. Silence my inner turmoil with sweet whispering thoughts of love and encouragement. When I stop believing in myself, gently take my hand and pull me forward.

Amen.

In childhood

In life everything has a purpose, a time and a season.
A time to be young, and a time to grow up,
And a time to return to finish what needs to be done.

As children, we learn from our feelings. This is how we determine how safe it is to love and to express our true feelings. If we don't feel safe in expressing our true feelings we will repress them and ultimately deny our true feelings.

But if verbal expression is encouraged self-love grows through self-esteem and self-confidence. They create a true sense of Self as we can only determine who we are through our feelings. The most important reason being, true feelings consist of love.

On the other hand, if we don't feel safe in expressing true feelings then we learn to say those things we really don't mean. We are more afraid of saying something that will get us in trouble or rock the proverbial family boat.

In the earliest beginning of a child's life, I believe a child knows from the deepest portion of his or her being who they really are. They desire to be an expression of this Love. But true self-expression can be stifled and blocked, which only forces a super-imposed personality to emerge. Sometimes they also learn that it isn't safe to say anything at all. They've learned to keep peace at all costs.

While feelings shouldn't control us, they are important. Feelings matter and as you will learn, feelings consist of energy or spiritual matter! In more ways than one, feelings do matter.

They matter to us because they are part of us—they express our individuality and they help us develop into our true Self, and they matter because they consist of an intangible matter that is energy. If we receive incorrect perceptions of our true identity, this negative energy will help form and shape our personality.

Over time, we accumulate more emotional pain until many of us literally exist inside a "pained" body.

Negative energy also works against the physical body in that it destroys cells and weakens the body's natural immune system and as our immune system weakens, we become ill. Every part of us suffers, our physical body, minds, hearts and souls—and we feel that suffering through personal relationships, our physical health and our relationship with deity.

So, why do we do it? Because we don't know any better! It is what we have learned. At the back of the book you will find a list of co-dependent behaviors. Co-dependency is a term used for unhealthy behavior and its cause. There are different explanations as to what this term actually means, but what it means to me is a behavior that knows how everyone else is feeling with little regard or understanding for a person's own feelings. Co-dependents live their lives from the *outside*. Living from the *inside* is too painful or difficult. Co-dependents don't know how to take care of themselves. In their need to feel accepted and loved, they are willing to do most anything because they are afraid of rejection or disapproval at their deepest level.

As you read through the list of co-dependent behaviors, make a list of what you identify with. This will open your eyes as to who is responsible for the dysfunction in your life. Then continue reading this chapter so that you will gain an understanding of the importance of *feeling* all your feelings.

Since feelings *are* important, let's examine what feelings are and what they consist of:

Feelings are receptors—through our feelings we receive messages from the outside and internalize what they mean.

Feelings are also indicators. They let us know when we are frightened or when we feel safe, when we are warm or cold, sad or happy and they let us know when we are hurt and angry.

Our feelings send us messages and if we try and make feelings go away, we lose an important part of ourselves. That emotional side is the center for giving and receiving. It is what makes us laugh as well as cry. That same part allows us to enjoy touch and to live with warmth, intimacy, and passion. Most of all, true feelings remind us who we really are.

Feelings come from our deepest thoughts. When thought and feeling come together energy is created, if this energy remains inside our emotions (either consisting of love or fear) a seed is conceived. This seed of energy expands into life, releasing that vibration into the force of creation. This is where everything begins to happen.

This energy is seen through our aura or energy field. It can either consist of shimmering and bright colors or it can be dark and filmy. Our energy field can change as our moods change, but from negative energy that is buried within the psyche, your energy field will reflect it.

What happens when we shut down our feelings? Where do they go? When feelings are repressed *we linger in the emotions created from them.* We're not allowing the natural process of feeling to happen. When we hold them inside we are holding in negative energy that can harm the physical as well as emotional body.

The heart center is also part of the soul's emotional body, and when we close off our feelings, we restrict the heart center from giving and receiving love.

Another important reason for not repressing feelings is that an emotional withdrawal causes us to lose positive feelings as well. We lose touch with our own true identity and so in its place a false Self is created. We also lose our ability to be intimate with people or trust in others.

Intuitiveness is a gift, a gift from the Holy Spirit. It is our connection or link to Heaven, and without it we feel a void, emptiness and longing. Intuitiveness is our most sacred gift. It is the all knowing source that guides us and is a constant teaching force—when the heart is free from negative feelings, our true feelings respond to a thought and we create positive situations from our feelings instead of reacting to fear.

The *subconscious* mind is an emotional reservoir and it holds our entire unresolved trauma from our past, regardless of how far that past goes and it is this unhealed energy that causes drug/alcohol/sex/food/gambling addictions. It isn't possible to rid the mind and body from these addictions without healing/cleansing the subconscious mind from living, buried, negative feelings. Or in other words, nurture the un-nurtured grown child; replace fear with love.

Energy is constantly attracting energy of its kind. Outside the body an energy field known as the soul's aura exists. Our personal world affairs, such as finances and relationships are also controlled or directed from our aura. We attract situations from which we are to learn from the energy consisting in our aura. It is from here that we can change our lives if we change the energy that surrounds us.

We can't rewrite the past, but we can pen in a happy ending. Life isn't just a lucky roll of dice for some and misfortune for another. We determine our own state of affairs. No one is doing anything to us that we aren't doing to ourselves. If you didn't receive the love and nurturing every child needs and deserves, don't you think it's about time to finish what should have been done?

There is a time and a season for all things under heaven, and perhaps your season is one of self-care and nurturing. As you gain a sense of self-love and worthiness within, you draw more Love/Light from your Source of spiritual existence. This is where it all begins—a new day and a new beginning. No longer willing to accept discomfort as a way of life, your relationships will honor your divinity—you will seek and draw relationships to you that will encourage loyalty and companionship complimenting a full expression of individual needs.

Solution: Make a commitment to yourself: *Today I am willing to accept responsibility for my happiness. I am willing to admit that I am powerless over others. I am willing to take control of my life.*

I am willing to open my heart and allow Spirit to work with me and I believe that when I do the Universe will respond bringing people, knowledge, and opportunities into my life for the purpose of healing my soul.

Blessed be.

Why do I feel this way?

Feel the movement of the clouds,
The touch of the unseen wind,
The feel of the raindrop,
And watch the glow of the sun.
It is the illumination of an unseen energy
The power of love.

As children we learn to avoid feelings. We do all sorts of things to avoid feeling what we don't want to feel until; we stop associating with our feelings, the energy that is in us. When we aren't nurturing our true identity, another personality is created as a result.

Codependents are master reactors and deceivers. No matter how they are feeling they don't associate with their pain. Instead, they feel the need to appear perfectly put together. Many personalities wear that all too obvious painted on smile. If you ask them how they are feeling they'll respond with a perfect smile that all is well, but even that smile will crack under all the pressure that is building inside if something isn't done to release it.

Can you describe the kind of woman that forces a smile? She isn't genuine. You may not feel comfortable around her—there is a sense of betrayal as though you can identify with her but you're not at ease with it. You can see the emptiness in her eyes and feel your own. The eyes are the windows to the soul and regardless of how hard we pretend to be someone that we are not; we can't hide the fact that we're not authentic.

On the other hand, we've all been around a luminous woman whose countenance portrays the ultimate beauty. She has unassuming grace, inner beauty, dignity and compassion—she is the one we either idolize or envy!

So, what really creates a radiant woman? Do you think it is because of her outward appearance? Or is it something that goes much, much deeper than that? I believe a radiant woman is one who is deeply spiritually connected—she is her soul! She lives in harmony with the sacred divine as she has become one with her divinity. Underneath the painted on smile or the fearful one, we are Goddesses! This is our true identity and there is power and radiance that glows from within once we are joined—we connect to our divine through our feelings with an intelligence that goes beyond description.

Before we can re-connect, we need to understand how we lost contact with our divine in the first place. Disconnection takes place over time when we bury emotional pain. What causes emotional pain? The cause of emotional pain is any behavior that destroys our natural and inherent innocence deeply wounding us.

Since feelings are indicators, they serve as a warning when something isn't right. Regardless of what the situation is, when it isn't right for us, we know it. We should act accordingly to protect us from harm. If we've been conditioned to associate love with pain—those that hurt us may appear to be someone that really does loves us, and we ignore the warning. Our head tells us one thing while our heart tells us another—which one do we listen to?

Feelings that contradict each other create confusion and it isn't unusual to feel as though our God has abandoned us. But what has really happened is we've separated from our Spirit. Our heart isn't in harmony with our head. We feel and think separately, therefore; the message we receive isn't clear and we're not certain as to what we should do.

Before the mind and heart can think and feel simultaneously much healing is needed. From continual stress, and stuffing feelings, and being hurt over and again, we become numb to our feelings. In the end, we're overloaded, overstressed and ready to explode. There isn't room for any emotion except anger!

Although you may feel dead inside, you can't ignore or get rid of anger, but what do we do when we get angry? Usually we blow up. Hit the ceiling. Scream and yell or throw tantrums and then when it's all over, we go right back doing the same things we did before. We've released some steam by blowing up, but we haven't healed our pain.

I can't count the many times I've heard women say they don't feel anything at all inside, and yet they keep on allowing the same kinds of behavior that hurt them over and again. They stuff all their feelings and emotions and get angry without understanding why.

I understand. I've been there! I know exactly how it feels to hold it all inside. Although, anger is a warning that something is wrong, we don't always fix it. In time, we don't even associate the real source of our pain with the anger that we feel.

Amazingly, as women we tend to have a high tolerance for misery. Living around manipulative and devious people distorts reality. It's almost impossible to see what's really happening inside the relationship.

Over time, the intensity of a person's anger turns into rage because of repetitive pain and they haven't appropriately dealt with the source of their pain. When they finally face it rage can throw their recovery into reverse. Only you know how much hurt you've kept inside and how long you've been angry. But you need to be aware that it isn't going to get any better until you do—until you resolve the source of your anger. Liberation from long periods of abuse is complex. Issues of trust, rejection and anger are deeply embedded.

Rage isn't the same as anger. Rage is a result of repeated trauma. With the intensity of a person's anger, letting go is difficult. Victims often fall prey to the "helpless victim" role because they are dealing with many complexities at the same time, severe depression being one of them.

Severe depression complicates recovery because the treatment of abuse depression is not as simple as the treatment of a common mood disorder. The victim/survivor's depression is deeply rooted in the reality of abuse and insidious cruelty.

Rather than move beyond their horrible experience, victims may put more emphasis on their horrifying abusive experience. This is where their focus is and just like an old broken phonograph record they replay their experience over and again. Rather than releasing pain the victim is reliving her ordeal in order to feel valued even if it's only self-pity.

Don't become one of them! Focus your attention on healing. You aren't helpless and you don't have to be a victim. What you want to be is a survivor. While therapy is valuable it doesn't have to last forever, and you don't have to repeat another abusive relationship in order to learn how to take care of yourself.

A common deterrent to recovery is in a victim's need to be avenged. To feel vindicated is a common need for many battered women because they feel unlovable and similar to little children they constantly need reassurance that they are acceptable and loved. Considering a battered woman's trust issue, healing becomes more complex as she faces reality.

Healing anger/rage can be complex, but if you will focus on your healing by getting in touch with your feelings/emotions and releasing anger/pain you will discover the pot of gold in your heart—the treasure of healing love. You don't have to do all the work yourself if you are willing to open your heart center to love. As you do this a spiritual healing energy is released. All that is required of you is to let it happen.

You will also find yourself working through different recovery phases. The first two initial steps you will work through are the following:

The first step is denial. In this phase it is important that you get angry and identify the source of your anger. Why are you angry? Who is it that is causing you so much pain?

The second step is shock and disbelief. You may go through periods of shock with episodes of denial or numbness. You may not know which end is up and it may be difficult to understand how you got there or if you'll ever recover. It isn't unusual to feel like you're on a rollercoaster powered at the very least by your abuser.

You may not feel in control of anything—your anger/rage may be all that you can feel. Don't repress your feelings, but don't linger in your emotions either and it's okay to be angry not only at your abuser but also with yourself. This will serve as a reminder to take better care of your Self in the future.

Venting anger is an important step that you can't bypass. I call it the purging step. During this phase of recovery a lot of healing is taking place. Finally, you're able to say, "I'm angry as hell and no one will ever do this to me again." Although it can be a difficult stage in that it is emotionally draining it's important to remember to always take care of yourself. You don't need to do anything other than just be aware of what is going on and how you feel about it. It isn't necessary to confront anyone that has hurt you during this stage of recovery—it's enough to be aware of your feelings, feel validated and supported and to do something about it.

Always remember…before you can build your life from the inside out, you have to know what you are feeling and what you need. As basic as this may sound, many of us are clueless as to what we are feeling; therefore we can't take care of our needs.

Another way that we lose touch with our feelings is from those that use emotional blackmail to manipulate us into doing what they want. They are experts at it and their behavior has probably worked to their advantage up to this point.

The following are a few questions you may want to ask yourself:

1. What control do I have over the way they feel?
2. Do I feel guilty or responsible for the way they feel?
3. Whose feelings am I feeling?

Read through the lists at the end of the book that describe emotional/ physical abuse and see how many descriptions you identify with. This list of abusive behavior may only serve to reinforce what you already know and help you get in touch with *your* feelings.

Remember, an illness in the physical body is caused by an imbalance of energy or a blocking of energy, therefore; healing the mind and body begins by healing the spirit. The more energy we let flow the healthier we are mentally, spiritually and physically.

Solution: *You need to unblock this energy by releasing it.*

There are appropriate methods to help you release anger that do not harm anyone:

- Vent with a trusted friend. When you do, talk about all the times you were hurt. Give yourself permission to feel all your feelings, and cry by feeling the denigration, humiliation and helplessness you were forced to endure.
- Put a name and a face to your inner pain. What did he or she do? How did it make you feel? Then:
- Give love to yourself as you would someone else that you care about when they are hurting. Comfort your Self. Be compassionate and validate your feelings—they are important and you are loved; you are a caring, bright and intelligent woman that never deserved to be hurt by anyone!

Another exercise you may want to try, which happens to be my favorite:

- Do you have a punching bag? Can you make one? An old stuffed animal and a bat make a strange pair, but it helps to hit something that you won't hurt to help release the anger. If you need to, imagine your spouse/partner sitting in a chair (although it is only a stuffed animal you don't mind ripping its head off). Then go ahead and take a swing.

The following is another exercise that you might feel more comfortable doing:

Sit in front of a mirror. Think of a person with whom you're angry, someone that failed you in one-way or another. They may or may not be aware of their inability to nurture, to love or to validate your self-worth, they may or may not be aware of the pain they have caused you, but it is important that you express your feelings and let them know exactly how you feel.

Look into this mirror and see the other person. Tell them why you're angry. When you're finished, tell them what you needed from them. Tell them you needed to feel protected, loved, valued and that they failed you. Tell them that all you wanted was their love and approval.

Once again look into the mirror, but this time see only you and say to yourself, *I am willing to release the need to be angry at* _____(say the person's name out loud to yourself).

If you have difficulty connecting with your feelings, the following may help you:

Hold a mirror in your hand. Stare at your reflection. What do you see? Who is the woman with the face in the mirror? Gaze deeper into her eyes, the window to your soul. Can you see pain behind your eyes? Can you see regret and resentment and anger darken the light of your soul?

Gently touch your face, and with its softness feel your pain—pain has so much to tell you. Release the waves inside your being—feel your pain—and cry! Let your soul weep from the deepest portion of your being—feel your heartache and let your tears flow.

When we're hurting not only do we feel angry, but we also feel unimportant. This is what abuse does to us and it's important that you not take on the other person's unfinished healing. It can't be said enough that victims hurt victims. This isn't an excuse, but it's an explanation. They wouldn't hurt if they weren't hurting—we can't expect them to undo what they have done nor can we expect them to understand what they have done.

Be willing to include the following affirmations in your personal belief system:

I will express anger when necessary in healthy ways because:
I feel better about myself when I am honest
My opinions are valued

From now on:
I will honor myself by expressing all my feelings
I am important and how I feel matters!
I will eliminate all toxic people and end toxic relationships
I will establish a safe-zone in which healing can begin....

Facing Fear

Do not allow fear of what if
Steal the joy of what is.

Because we have harbored fear so intensely it has already manifested itself inside our emotions—it is ever present ready to jump into action. It's interesting that the thing we fear the most in reality hasn't happened, but it has to us. We're forcing our Selves to live through it every time we face a crisis consequently, we don't enjoy the simple pleasures of life each day!

As soon as fear enters our minds, our minds take it and run with it. We literally work our Selves into a panic long before anything has even happened. If you have ever expressed fear just to have someone say to you, "There's nothing to be afraid of, it's all in your head," then you also realize that "in your head" is the worst place for fear to be.

Of all our emotions fear is the most pervasive. While anger motivates us into doing something fear encourages no action at all. It's as though we're paralyzed and can't take any action.

While existing inside a panic and reaction mode, we're always waiting for the next crisis because we have been conditioned to expect the worst. Even when the worst hasn't happened or may not happen—to us it has.

Most of us live anywhere from mild panic to extreme panic most of the time if not all the time. This feeling/emotion can stay with us for years after the abuse. When my teen-agers are ten minutes late coming home, I'm beside myself with worry. If I can't reach them by cell-phone, I call out a search party. I expect the worst in all most every situation but this behavior is emotionally draining not to mention extremely embarrassing.

Fear isn't the only obstacle we face in recovery. Running from our emotions is another problem because we've learned to *avoid* our feelings. What we don't want to feel we either deny it or avoid it.

The simple truth is: We don't know how to effectively deal with our feelings. We don't feel comfortable inside our feelings/emotions therefore; we haven't learned to trust our feelings either.

While there may be other factors involved in running, irrational guilt is also a common deterrent in recovery.

When we put our needs first guilt raises it's ugly head screaming that we can't do that. Putting our needs first feels unnatural and selfish. Our first reaction is to get rid of the guilt by getting rid of the feeling. But always remember this, you can't get rid of feelings by avoidance; you only trap the energy inside.

Again, we've been conditioned to react before we've given rationality a chance to set in! Now it's time to retrain the mind. I don't know that it's impossible to completely erase years of programming, but it is possible to offer another solution or way to deal with stress.

It's a simple solution, but effective if you can sit still long enough without falling apart or sending the police out on a 30-minute high speed chase just because your daughter is ten minutes late coming home in your car.

When you feel panic coming on allow your emotions to be just what they are. Feel rooted in the present moment. Take in several cleansing breaths and as you inhale and exhale release the energy that has been trapped. Don't focus on any particular event that may have caused you extreme fear in the past, but rather stay as focused as you can in the present.

It's important that you understand the origination of panic isn't in the present, but rather the past but you're not living in the past and you are presently safe.

If you suffer from anxiety or severe panic, make an appointment with a medical doctor. Don't be afraid or ashamed if you need help, but don't stop there. Medication doesn't cure the cause of stress disorders, but healing from the abuse will. As long as the subconscious mind still holds residual energy created from unhealed trauma you'll continue to react to it.

Solution: When fear is present, you may use a bubble of light in which to center yourself. Visualize light surrounding you until you are completely immersed inside this light. Feel yourself gravitate toward the core of the Earth— the Earth's energy will also flow from the earth into the soles of your feet traveling up through your physical body helping to ground your emotions.

When you feel yourself running, be still. Let your feelings come to you. Center yourself in the present and focus on what you can hear, smell or touch. Continue taking deep breaths until you feel yourself more centered, and then focus on what you are feeling. Ask yourself, "Why do I feel this way? Why do I feel afraid? What am I afraid of?" Be still, and let the answers come to you and feel comforted knowing that as you do, solutions will come to you. You will know how to handle the situation.

Here's a simple process to help you clear negative emotions when they arise:

Acknowledge that an emotion is present
Be still without any judgments
Take a few deep breaths and allow yourself to fully experience what you are feeling
Slowly breathe in and exhale as often as necessary
If a negative energy, such as fear or anger persists, call forth a positive feeling or love energy to stay with it
Imagine your soul embracing that part of you that is distressed to bring you comfort
Maintain this image until the emotion has dissolved

Often the emotion dissipates on its own once you acknowledge it, but if it doesn't then repeat the steps until you feel that it is gone.

With the natural flow of energy, we experience the full spectrum of our environment and our circumstances. Which means, we're not to be afraid anymore. We know we can handle what comes our way.

It helps to know that every crisis or bad situation isn't the end of the world. Terrible things aren't going to happen. We don't have to be afraid.

The following are several affirmations you can say to yourself each day:

- I will remember to feel all my feelings
- I will honor my feelings
- I will remember to take care of myself
- I will remember that loving begins with me
- I am willing to make a commitment to honor the process of spiritual growth

Trust in Divine Guidance

Intricately connected to all that is, each moment becomes a teaching moment as the Holy Spirit of Truth guides us through difficult times.

It is important that you be in a safe environment with emotional support when you do this part of your journey. I don't know that it is possible to begin healing if you are still in a crisis situation.

If you are ready, this is a good time to begin journaling with the intent to remember how you felt as a child, and what may have happened to cause you to fear love. If you have a photograph of yourself as a child, place that photograph inside your journal where it will be seen each day that you write.

Read the following questions and think about your answers as honestly as you can: How did I experience love as a child? Did I observe my parents expressing love; did I openly share feelings? Was I raised with lots of hugs? Did I feel loved and nurtured by my primary caregiver? Or did I feel uncomfortable displaying affection such as giving or receiving hugs? Did I experience screaming or fighting and much crying as a result? Was it difficult to experience love? Did I most often feel rejected? Did I feel that it was necessary to please in order to receive praise?

Try to piece together a mental picture of you inside the workings of your family structure, and at the end of this chapter begin writing about the small child you used to be.

Regardless of the atmosphere in your family of origin, you will seek out similar experiences as an adult. If as a child you looked for love and found pain, as an adult you'll find pain instead of love...

If as a child you experienced sexual abuse this will cause you to feel guilty or uncomfortable with your sexuality. If you were shamed as a child you will find it difficult to honor yourself as a woman.

Often, it isn't possible to confront those that have hurt us. They aren't ready to accept the responsibility. The most important lesson in spiritual healing is to understand that everyone did the best they could. We are all victims of our circumstances. Those that hurt others are hurting also. It is from their unhealed childhood pain they do the same to others when they become adults, and it isn't necessary to confront anyone as long as you do the next best thing—revive it to relive it and release everyone to their highest good.

Before you begin journaling, it is essential to outline your spiritual journey as to what you want to accomplish. Determine what area in your life needs your immediate attention. Then begin working on that area. If you are in an unhealthy relationship, you may want to examine the reasons why you stay or what attracted you to this person in the first place. What it is that you are expecting to happen? What changes are you waiting to see? You may also want to explore how you feel about yourself and why.

If you have issues with trust or intimacy, explore these feelings. When did you first feel betrayed and unable to trust again? What happened? Are you ready to explore your trust issues? Could it be that you are unable to trust yourself and your ability to find or attract healthy relationships?

You may find that you can't remember much about your childhood. It helps to coax your memory just like you would a frightened child—be gentle with yourself. Remember good times. Think of pleasant things you did as a child—nurture your feelings with validation. But don't force age regression. It usually doesn't work anyway. If you have difficulty or intense fear surfaces—seek professional help.

At the beginning of an entry, write what it is that you expect your writing to reveal. Share your innermost and private feelings through your writing. You are sharing this with your Higher Self, and you will also be guided intuitively. Your wise Self knows exactly what your needs are. She has all the answers to your questions.

Write in your journal each day and then at the end of the week, review what you have written. Take your time but be consistent! This isn't something that you will finish overnight, and it may be a difficult process for you, but it is important that you honor the healing process.

I know that it was a very difficult time for me. I found that it was necessary to relive the abuse so that I could release it. When we are threatened or in a situation where intense fear is present, it is natural to repress it. With any trauma, the mind is protective in that it shuts down. But the memory remains trapped in the form of residual energy. As the energy surfaces so do the memories.

If you aren't ready for this exercise, it may be enough for you to know that you are working toward a more manageable life. I've worked with women who are in an abusive situation and they want solutions to their problems, but they aren't willing to take control of their lives. We gain that control by taking one step at a time. First, you must eliminate as much stress from your life as possible and end toxic relationships. You know when you have done all that you can. There are marriages/relationships that can be saved and then there are those that you must end.

Accepting abuse, as a way of life is just another way of saying, "I don't deserve to be treated differently." Just as blaming everyone in your life for your misery reinforces self-pity and feelings of helplessness.

Spiritual teachers remind us that the first step in creating change is awakening to the power that is within us—the never-ending power of possibility. Your abilities and capabilities are endless and simply by spiritually awakening to the power that is you is the single most important thing you will ever do. You are the Goddess, the High Priestess of your life and no one has power or dominion over you—reclaim what you have relinquished.

When you change, you make a difference for many people, most importantly your children. Giving birth to your dreams and strengthening your wings is one of the most valuable gifts we give to our children. But I don't believe its reason enough for change, you must want change because you deserve it.

While journaling is rewarding in that it is enlightening, it can also be just another way to blame others. Always remember how important it is that you let go of your need to remain a victim. While moving beyond helplessness into a different way of thinking is empowering.

Journaling will also help you understand your past and the lessons you were to learn from it. When you understand your lessons you begin cleansing from the hurt you experienced and cleansing is healing.

I wish that I could wave a magic wand and send healing light your way to release you from the pain you have endured for many years. But I can't. You have to go through the journey for its own sake without focusing on the outcome. As you do you will grow in ways you never imagined.

In a butterfly's metamorphosis, each stage is vital to the butterfly's survival, most importantly; a butterfly would not exist without first going through its miraculous changes from egg to caterpillar to butterfly.

The caterpillar stage is one of limitations. It is also one of learning through experience. You may see your life as a series of bad mistakes, and yet if seen from another perspective, mistakes are only learning experiences. Be gentle with your judgments.

While in her cocoon stage a butterfly is quiet and very still allowing nature to complete her transformation. We also take care of necessary business when in our cocoon stage. Our past surfaces where we begin exploring the lessons we have gone through. And in the healing process, we gain awareness of our true identity. We also learn our soul's life purpose, which sheds light on our trials and gives reason for them.

And then the moment comes when the butterfly emerges—she has wings to fly and she tastes her new freedom knowing that her struggle to find freedom gave strength to her wings—uniquely, individualized, each butterfly is breathless in its beauty.

The butterfly transformation is symbolic of our spiritual awakening out of the limitations of the physical world. This is an exciting and empowering phase of your life, but one that you arrive at after going through each step of the healing journey.

Solution: Buy or create a personal journal. You can purchase one at most every imaginative design or discount stores. It is important that you find one that says something about you. This will be a special book that you will use daily on your healing journey.

Once you have your journal, find time to write once a day. Be consistent in your effort to write as much as you can each day. Make this your time to be alone when you won't be disturbed and journal with the intent to understand your feelings, your behavior and your relationships and what changes you want to make.

Journaling is an important aspect of your healing journey. You will be amazed at where your writing will take you. Journaling with the intent to heal past emotional wounds, you will discover many new facets about yourself, but most important you will be facing the pain you have buried.

It is also important to note: the mind conceals severe trauma from our awareness as a protective measure. To reveal this or to bring that memory into your awareness without proper guidance and support can further traumatize you.

A Time for Healing and Soul Nurturing

It is a courageous soul that takes the steps necessary to grow through adversity.

As you remember painful memory, you will also feel all the emotions involved with that memory. You may often feel as though you have collided with a train. It can feel overwhelming, but intuitively, you will know what you need so it is important that you trust in your intuitiveness.

If you need to be with loving and supporting friends or family, involve them or this may be a good time to join a support group, if you haven't already. You may even want to deaden the pain, but don't. It is important that you allow this process to happen.

To be honest, many times I was sorely tempted to find relief through either sleeping pills or tranquilizers. But I stopped myself before I started. I knew that if I didn't, I would end up where I left off years ago—chemically dependent.

You may also feel the emotional trauma throughout your whole body. It's common to feel flu like symptoms, as well as weepy most of the time. But it will pass. When you feel like this, drink plenty of water and get adequate rest. Sleep and a balanced diet are so important. No one can slay dragons without adequate nourishment for strength, and you won't be able to work through an emotional crisis if you aren't resting and taking care of your needs. You may also feel confused because you may not have vivid memory of anything in particular, but you feel emotional just the same. This is normal and part of the healing process. Your body is just releasing toxins that have been buried inside cells and tissue.

Give yourself credit and validate your self-worth. It takes a lot of courage to go through the cleansing stage—I've known many who just can't do it. They want to. They hate the way their lives are, but they don't have the courage. I'm not being critical and I'm not judging them—I realize how difficult it is. I stumbled upon healing accidentally. I don't know that I would have done it had I not started writing this book. I had no idea what was in store for me before I started and then I couldn't stop.

I agonized over many of my choices. Going back through the memory of the abortion procedure was extremely difficult. I wanted to die. I hurt so badly and all I could do was cry. And I cried. Sometimes I thought I wouldn't stop crying for all the hurt that choice had caused me, and all the self-loathing as a result. And when I stopped crying, I still didn't know if I could ever forgive myself.

You will go through similar pain and when you do, feel the arms of love around you. Know that Angels feel your pain and have never once judged you—their love will be a support to you.

When you feel the need for a break, take one. Don't write in your journal. Don't talk about the past—watch a comedy and laugh. Join life and be grateful for all that you are learning. Don't dwell on the past or remain stuck in it. Dig into it long enough to revive what needs to be released.

You may need to severe relationships with those who feel threatened by your choice to be in recovery. This isn't always an easy process—many changes may need to take place, but you must always think of yourself first. And it is okay to put your Self first!

The first and foremost important thing you can do for yourself during this time is to nurture, nurture and nurture your inner Self. Be a child again. Love that child. Sing lullabies to her pain. Comfort and take care of her—that child is you and heaven only knows how long you have felt unloved.

Be ever so gentle with yourself. If you feel ashamed remember where this feeling is coming from. It isn't because you are a shameful little girl, but rather you feel that way because someone else instilled shame. Give it back to them without the desire to hurt them as they hurt you. There isn't anything for which you should feel guilty or ashamed.

Rather than rid yourself of any negative image or feeling, allow that feeling to be as it is—replace it with loving thoughts. Whatever we resist has a way of persisting, but if we accept our negative feelings, they will dissipate as we nurture self-love. The idea is to always replace a negative thought with a positive one.

Acceptance simply quiets our fears and our releases resistance.

Solution: The following exercises can help you release any guilt or shame that you might have. When we harbor shame it is because someone else gave it to us. It isn't because of what we did or what was done to us—we were made to feel guilty. Now it's time to give it back.

The following is a meditation: Prepare yourself for meditation. Do this during a time when you will not be disturbed. Listen to soothing, meditative music. Light candles. Feel relaxed.

Take three or four deep cleansing breaths. As you inhale draw the light of love to you and as you exhale release all negative emotions of mistrust and fear. Continue inhaling love and exhaling negative emotions until you feel calm. As you continue inhaling and exhaling, draw all your scattered emotions and feelings inward until you feel centered. Continue breathing until you feel completely relaxed.

Visualize a long, winding staircase. See yourself walking barefoot toward this elegant, marble staircase and begin descending one step at a time. Feel the coolness of the steps as your bare feet touch the marble. Feel the smoothness of the railing. Hold this railing as you carefully walk to the bottom of the stairs. At the end of the stairway is a beautiful garden filled with trees, birds, butterflies and flowers. In the middle of the garden is a flowing stream of crystal clear water. Walk closer to this stream and listen to the running water and the soft melody played in harmony among all the living creatures inside the garden. As you walk away from the stream you see a garden bench.

Sit down on this garden bench and watch a small child with long, beautiful hair laced with ribbons. Notice how the white, flowing cotton dress wraps around her tiny legs as she slowly comes to you. Reach out your hand and draw her into your arms.

Smell the freshness of her body as she snuggles in the warmth of your care. Ask her why she is crying. Listen to her as she expresses her innermost feelings. Validate her feelings and let her know that you care and that you understand.

Tell her that you will protect her if she is ready to confront those people who have harmed her.

Visualize this person move toward you carrying an empty basket. As this person comes closer, feel the fear of this small child and reassure her that she is safe and protected. No harm will ever come to her again. You will be her Earth-angel and be there for her.

Tell her that it is okay to say whatever it is that she is feeling and that she no longer has to carry this pain. When she is through saying all that needs to be said watch carefully as this small child takes from her heart all the pain she has carried and places the pain inside the empty basket.

Feel the lightness of this small child and feel her inner-strength and personal power return as she gives back all her suffering…listen as she tells this older person that it isn't her pain any longer—she did nothing to deserve this pain and it doesn't belong to her. Watch as this person turns around and walks away carrying all the pain that he/she inflicted upon this small child.

Carefully place this small child with her feet firmly upon the ground telling her that you will always be there when she needs you. All that she needs to do is call out your name.

You are now ready to leave this peaceful garden knowing that you can return anytime that you are needed. Walk toward the stairway and retrace your steps upward feeling the coolness of the steps and the softness of the marble as your hands and fingers hold to the rail.

Feel yourself growing lighter knowing that you are this grown child and no one can ever hurt you in this way again—you are stronger now, but you will always be there when this small child surfaces again and calls out your name.

Blessed be.

Here is another exercise that you might want to try:

On a slip of paper write the person's name that is associated with your pain. Write what this person did to hurt you.

The list can be long or short. You may write as much as you need, just be sure to include all the pain that you have carried over the years and how this pain affected you and your choices.

Then put the slips of paper into a small container in which it can safely be burned. Strike a match and burn the paper along with the pain and shame and guilt. Take all the time you need. Cry and let your tears flow for all the years you have held this pain inside. This is your moment to be remembered, as you were before you felt betrayed or defiled, shamed or hurt in any other way. As the paper burns, watch the smoke carry your pain away from the center of the bowl, which symbolizes the center of your heart—feel your pain lifting and exiting from your heart. Then take the ashes outside of your home and toss them into the wind, as you return know that you are whole again—you've released another burden and it doesn't belong to you anymore.

This is your time to nurture yourself as you would a small child. Wrap yourself in a warm, cuddling blanket. Give yourself permission to cry, as often as you need to.

Although, the following isn't anything new or something you haven't heard before, spending time alone is the only way to feel in sweet communion with your soul. Create your unique healing rituals. There are different ways of doing this, and I will suggest a few, but you can create ways of your own also:

- Fill your tub with fragrant bath oil, light candles and listen to soft music and as you soak in the warm water take time to be one with your body and all that it offers you. As you run your hands over your body feel the softness of your face and how your eyes express what is in your heart. Feel your hands and remember how tenderly they cared for a newborn baby or wiped tears from a child's face. Feel your fingertips and know that they carry loving energy to heal with their touch. Continue running your hand down the length of your body and feel each part that responds and know how much pleasure, love and joy you receive as a woman. Your body is a gift and not one you should ever see with shame.

- Spend time doing something (even if it is one simple pleasure) that you enjoy doing each day. Buy yourself a treat, an ice-cream cone or a small crafted angel to grace your nightstand and remind you that you are loved dearly.

- Exercise and eat a well-balanced meal. Drink plenty of water and include healthy foods into your diet. Eliminate alcohol, sugars and caffeine as much as possible and make a commitment to nourish and be good to your physical Self.

- Disengage from toxic friendships and make a commitment to eliminate negative energy in every possible way. In a later chapter you learn more about letting go and detaching from harmful behavior, but for now think of ways you can eliminate stress and negative influences from your life. Make a list of all those people, places and things that create negative energy, and begin the elimination process.

Although painful memory may have surfaced, it doesn't always come when we think it will. Now that you have invited the *all-glowing light* of the Holy Spirit into your heart it acts as a spotlight clearing out all the pain inside and this may be just the beginning. Give yourself time and be patient. Allow the process to continue. More memory and residual negative energy will surface when you are ready.

Often on my healing journey, I listened to those same, softly, spoken words, *"Oh, little one, if you could only see what we see in you."* Those simple words encouraged me in ways nothing else could, and I will say them to you...*Oh, little one, if you could only see what the angels see in you, then you would know how vitally it is important to heal the past and find the real you.*

Today, I want you to close your eyes and envision a circle of angels in your presence. Feel yourself draw close to them. They are with you and they desire only to enlighten, love and support you on your journey. And if you could only see what they see in you, I have no doubt you would see a beautiful soul.

Blessed be.

Detachment

Worry and obsessing is what keeps us so entangled in the lives of others that we forfeit our power to think, feel and take care of our needs.

etaching from people and the behavior that hurts us is another important step you will take in recovery. Perhaps I should just say that all steps are important, but each step plays a unique and different role in keeping you safe.

Unmanageability can creep into your recovery at any time if you haven't had enough time to establish firm boundaries and a safe place inside that says *I don't have to do this, or I don't have to allow behavior that hurts me.*

That's what this chapter is about—letting go, and detaching from the over-involvement in the lives of those people whose behavior hurts us. While detachment is necessary, it doesn't mean that we need to stop caring about a loved one. It is the behavior from which we have to detach.

Read through the list of co-dependency at the end of this book. Check those behaviors you identify with then describe how this behavior harms you.

Think about the certain situations or people in your life today that you may be overly involved with. How are those situations affecting your peace of mind and your happiness? Then ask yourself:

- Why are you overly involved?
- Do you feel it is your responsibility?
- What would happen if you didn't worry or get yourself overly involved in that person's certain situation?

Loving others doesn't have to hurt. We *can* detach from the suffering of those we care about. In fact, it is essential to our well-being that we do. It may be in a loving way or it may not be, but we have to detach if we want to recover from a behavior that hurts us all.

Over-involvement doesn't appear to be dangerous in its earliest stage. In fact, over-involvement feels natural and necessary even though it has become an obsession for us. But just because over involvement feels familiar and a behavior we have lived with doesn't make it any less threatening. And you know what I mean if you've been overly involved with behavior other than your own. It doesn't feel good and often we're not aware of our behavior until we suffer enough from it.

Often we think, "After this I won't help them anymore," just to repeat our behavior over again as they repeat theirs. Enabling even once only ensures that the behavior will continue. But if their problems or behavior bothered them as much as it does us, do you think they would continue? Can we make them stop if they don't want to? It is a simple fact that we can't, so why do we keep trying?

This is where we make an error in judgment—we want them to change badly enough to believe we can do it for them. In reality we want them to stop so we can stop hurting!

While detachment is difficult, we can make it easier on everyone by staying finely tuned to our feelings and our needs. When we cross that thin line of caring and enabling, we feel it. It is a behavior that causes us to get angry, make threats and demands, which of course we don't carry through.

Enabling is a helpless way to approach any give situation and sometimes the one we are helping doesn't want our help or they don't want to take responsibility for their lack of responsibility. When its time to butt out we need to do so gracefully.

Detachment is another word for objectivity. When you are overly involved or believe that it is your responsibility to fix or rescue someone whose behavior is out of control, you lose your objectivity. Nothing within the situation appears clear and that's because we mess things up when we get involved.

Obsessive behavior hurts everyone. Many of us fool our Selves into believing we are helping. But just like stepping into quick sand, we lose our sense of objectivity quick enough to sink into a whole lot of misery. We're overly involved before we know it. And then we get our Selves entangled to the point that we stop living our life or infringe upon their right to learn.

Ask yourself the following questions:

- Is there a person in your life that is causing you excessive worry?
- Is your behavior controlling?
- What would your life be like if you detached from that person's problem?
- What *can* you do that would be helpful and beneficial?
- What lessons are they to be learning?
- Are you preventing them from learning?
- Who are you really trying to help?
- Could it be that you don't have enough faith in the learning process?
- Perhaps you feel that something terrible will happen if you don't help?
- Are you feeling their fear or is it your own?
- Is there something in your present situations and circumstances that you could be learning from? Perhaps this is a time for your learning also.

Detachment means allowing each situation to follow its natural course without trying to control the outcome. It also means *acting* in a responsible way instead of *reacting* in ways that hurt everyone. Allowing those we love to experience the *consequences* of their irresponsible behavior is actually a higher demonstration of love.

Make a list of any past situation in which you obsessively worried, what was the outcome? Did you live through it? Did things turn out okay? What did you learn?

Spend the next few Moments seeing everyone around you as part of you. Each giving to one another lesson to grow from. Let go of your need to force the outcome of any given situation. Be willing to let them be as they are. With loving thoughts for their highest good send love to them.

For a moment, visualize God's loving hands taking this person and his/her problems and placing them under His care. Now visualize the Holy Spirit surrounding this person with radiant and shimmering light filled with His love and protection.

Let God's loving hands release your hands away from the situation while telling you that everything will be all right. As you do this know that you are releasing them to their highest good where they can learn and move on.

If this is difficult for you, breath deeply until you can let go of your resistance—have faith and understand that loving others is part of letting go.

Once we learn to disengage from over-involvement, we start-facing problems realistically. We know what we can do to help and we know what we can't do. Care enough to step aside and see the situation from a different perspective. It may not seem the same when you see it as another opportunity for them to learn an important lesson—don't take that lesson from them.

You will know when your help is necessary and when help is actually help and not hindrance. Sometimes, one of the most loving gifts we can share is that of self-mastery. We all need to know that we can believe in our Selves under any situation. Abuse destroys self-confidence, but we won't gain it back if we aren't allowed to stretch our wings and try.

It isn't possible to make things better for anyone; they have to do it for themselves. Help them to see this—let them know that you do believe in them. Give them support and encouragement rather than criticism.

You may need to practice detaching every day. Quite often I have to remind myself to let go of my need to fix everything. It's just not my responsibility and it's okay! Sometimes my daily mantra consists of: detach, detach, detach.

Solution: Practice repeating the Serenity Prayer when you are in doubt:

God grant me the serenity
To accept the things I cannot change,
Courage to change the things I can,
And the wisdom to know the difference.

Safety in Boundaries

Creating and enforcing safe boundaries
is another way that I nurture and care for myself.

C an you remember how many times your boundaries were invaded today? How often do you feel resentful when you give in to something you would rather not do? Or say yes when you should have said no? How often do you feel taken advantage of? The list could be endless. Boundary invasion is common—those around us don't respect boundaries and we let them get away with it. Often, we don't respect boundaries either. We see our help or interference as necessary. Sometimes boundary invasions appear insignificant, so we let them slide, but the firmer you are in setting appropriate boundaries that help you feel better about yourself, the safer you will feel.

When we haven't learned necessary life-skills, the line between enabling and caring isn't clear. We aren't sure when giving ends and co-dependent behavior begins. After all, isn't it our responsibility to take care of others and make sure they are happy, but what about our needs? Who looks after them while we are busy taking care of others?

Because we live around those who haven't healthy boundaries it is imperative that we be the first to establish a safety zone.

This chapter may seem redundant to that of "detachment," and perhaps it is, but I feel that it is important not only to establish firm boundaries, but also to *emotionally disengage* from the pain caused by inappropriate boundaries. Not only do we need to set appropriate boundaries, we need to practice stepping outside the emotional drama created by a crisis.

Something that helps me when I'm close to going over the edge is to stop everything that I'm doing until I can figure out what I'm doing wrong.

When you reach a point that you don't know who is to blame or you are trying to accomplish the impossible—STOP running. STOP doing and STOP ignoring your needs and start listening.

The moment we cross over the line of caring and enabling we start giving in. Our boundaries soften until they are pushed way out of our safety zone and we feel completely helpless and angry. There is always someone ready to take advantage of our benevolence. So, stop doing it. When this happens, don't just get angry do something about it. You need to take time-out to re-evaluate *your* behavior. But be gentle with yourself and reestablish your position.

For a moment, explore your personal boundaries and ask yourself how firm your boundaries are:

1. *When you need to say no, do you hopelessly give in?*
2. *Are you afraid to say no because of what might happen?*
3. *Do you say yes just to win someone's approval?*
4. *Are you afraid of taking control?*
5. *Does your happiness depend on other people?*
6. *Do you have difficulty asking for what you want?*

Evaluate your answers and determine if any one of the above is causing conflict in your life. It really is okay to think for yourself and create boundaries that keep you safe. It is okay to say no and take control of what is happening inside your world. Things just don't happen to us we allow things to happen.

What boundaries do you need in your life today? Take one step at a time; make a list of what is important to you and a priority of what changes need to take place now.

In order to have appropriate boundaries you must be aware of what feels right and what doesn't. You also need to be clear about what boundaries you are setting with yourself and with whom you are setting the boundaries. Then determine how firm you need to be, what your reasons are for placing that boundary and how flexible you intend to be.

When we are unbending in our expectations and in our demands, we don't give our Selves' room to consider the other persons needs and their feelings and what is reasonable. Inflexibility causes a great deal of conflict. Although, we believe we are right and that what we ask of other people is appropriate, being flexible, yielding and understanding opens the doorway to communication. We don't always see things as clearly as we think we do.

Remember that you set your own boundaries and you are responsible for enforcing them. Boundaries are not to hurt someone or deprive them of their right to live the way they choose, but rather to set appropriate guidelines that help you both experience the result of your choices.

Remaining firm in the long run may involve *tough* love measures and so you must be prepared when tough action is needed. While it may be difficult to enforce consequences or to ask for help remember that giving in only ensures a future reoccurrence. Be willing to love not only yourself but the other person involved enough to say, "It's time for both of us to be self-responsible."

Frankly, my kids have perfected timing down to a science. They know exactly how long it takes before I cave in and let them have their way. I won't deny that this step is my most difficult and resented step.

As I have said many times, it would be much easier to recover from co-dependency on an island—alone!

You may also find this chapter to be "a work in progress" so when you give in you aren't alone. Just keep trying. You can't expect any more than that. You're learning just as I am and when we haven't had that example growing up developing the skill later on isn't easy.

Sorting is another necessary part of healing. You need to sort through feelings almost daily until it gets easier to identify what is yours and what isn't. We pick up energies from other people when we don't have firm boundaries or a safety zone around us.

Make a list of the all the feelings that you have right now about the situations in your life and ask yourself: What fear am I experiencing? Where is it coming from? Am I anxious? Where is it coming from? Continue with your list of feelings/emotions depending on what it is that you are experiencing at any given time.

If you are worried about something directly related to you and you have control over it, then own it. If you are anxious over something that is outside your control, then disown it. It isn't your problem and no matter how much you want to you can't resolve it.

With *unhealthy boundaries* we focus outside of ourselves and usually live anywhere in between discomfort, apprehension to absolute misery. Often, we just wait for the next disaster to happen and the behavior causing the pain isn't even ours.

When in recovery one of the most challenging aspects will be in keeping yourself safe long enough to recover. You have lots of work to do on yourself without having to worry about your children.

If your situation doesn't include children then focus on the relationships you are involved with. Boundary invasion isn't limited to any particular relationship—it's in the way we interact with everyone. And you will need to evaluate how boundary invasions affect you day to day.

There are rewards for setting limits and healthy boundaries—you start living your own life.

The following are a few common boundary questions:

- Isn't it my responsibility to make my partner/children happy?
- Isn't it selfish to set limits?
- How do I set limits and still be a good person?
- Why do I feel so guilty when I say no?
- Sometimes I know what is best for others to do, isn't it my job to care for them?
- Do I feel compelled to take on more than my share?
- Do I feel better about myself when I do?

Not only is it *not* your responsibility to make others happy, it is impossible. You don't have that kind of power.

Since each situation is different, you must judge each by its own merits. If you are being selfish with your time, your money or your possessions, you may need to re-evaluate your motives. I believe we instinctively know when we are being self-caring vs. selfishness.

We may also confuse love with need. I think many of us find some distorted pleasure in giving our Self a little pat on the back as though self-sacrifice is an honor.

There are those situations in which tough measures have to be taken. One mother, completely exasperated and at the end of her rope said, "If I take the keys away from my son, he threatens to burn down my home."

"If I enforce any consequences, such as grounding my son from going out, he punches holes in my walls." Does this mean we give in and hand over the keys or let our son/daughter come home whenever they choose? No, it doesn't. But we will have to take the necessary steps to enforce harsh consequences.

If your home involves teen-agers with substance abuse, here are a few examples of common boundaries you might want to think about.

- *I will not allow anyone to verbally or physically abuse me*
- *I will not allow substance abuse in my home*
- *I will not use my home as a runaway center*
- *I will not lie to protect anyone*
- *I will not finance anyone's chemical dependency*

- *I will not allow criminal behavior in my home*
- *I will not rescue anyone from the consequences of their behavior*
- *I will take action when necessary*

It isn't realistic to blame ourselves when our children or someone else we care about suffers. But we can enforce necessary boundaries that protect the family and seek help. Enabling our children is actually interfering and taking away their spiritual growth—they need to learn how to work through their messes and face whatever consequences they bring upon themselves. This is the only way they learn.

Solution: Prevention is the best solution. If you are involved in an abusive relationship don't look the other way when it involves children. They are life's little sponges and while you may think they aren't absorbing much of anything, they are absorbing everything. It is proven that even children who don't experience abuse but witness it repeat the behavior.

Mothers with *children at risk* need to be involved. From school activities and church activities and homework. Communication is crucial. A support group for the children is essential—venting, talking, sharing and releasing fears must happen before they act out their pain/anger in unhealthy ways.

Children/adolescents/teenagers need to know they are loved, valued and respected and they need to know that they are not to blame for the split up of the family. When abuse is involved they need help in sorting through their hurt. How can they possibly understand their emotions if they keep them bottled up inside?

Make a list of the behaviors you are not willing to put up with. Involve your children. Let them participate and ask for their cooperation.

With each rule establish a fair consequence if broken (and then stick to it).

If your home-life is unmanageable, get in touch with your local crisis hotline and ask for referrals to an outreach program in your area such as tough love.

Choice and accountability is important, but a parent that is strict, demanding and controlling may not have any more success in raising emotionally healthy children than a parent that is permissive—children certainly react differently, but they need to feel their own power in a gentle and loving manner.

They need to know that they will be held accountable for any negative choice that they do make, but that they do have choice. Too often parents enforce choices upon them without realizing how detrimental it is to their well-being.

Forgiveness

Oh love divine, give solace to my hurting heart
Stay with me in my hour of need.
As the seed of love becomes my guiding star

When we have been deeply wounded, a place is created for God's Love in the garden of the heart and love will bloom from each tiny compassionate seed that is planted, if we nurture and cultivate seedlings of forgiveness.

I don't know of anyone that hasn't or doesn't need to do forgiveness work during different stages of their spiritual growth. We can't get through life without the need to forgive or be forgiven. But ultimately, those that give us our greatest challenges teach us our most valuable lessons. It is here inside these difficult lessons we learn the most about ourselves, and I don't know that we can understand the power of love if we aren't tried and tested at our deepest level.

And many of us are greatly tested! Heartbreak and betrayal are part of life, but when we're hurting it's difficult not to resent our trials, and feel targeted for all the bad luck that could possibly happen to anyone.

But you always have choice—it is the mind's free will or ability to think and no one can ever take that from you. When you hear the word "free agency," some may think that it means, "I can do anything I want..." Regardless of what we do, there is a direct consequence as a result. We can't escape from our actions in that there is a divine order to all existence! Mother Earth is divine order in action. There is perfect-ness in Her balance and rhythm. Chaos is a result of any imbalance or interference with Mother Earth's perfect divine order. Likewise, in spirit there is a perfect order to all that happens to us. It is when we interfere with those happenings with bitterness; we restrict the natural flow of energy that keeps us balanced and in harmony with our true Self.

As difficult as it may be to believe that all we need to learn and to spiritually develop comes our way, but it is true. Nothing happens by chance. In fact, your life is guided by an internal blue print—you were born into your situation for a purpose, and it isn't because you are just an unfortunate soul, it is because your situation is perfect for you in order to evolve.

Throughout life you will continuously attract specific relationships/ situations in which you can gain experience and knowledge or an opportunity to help someone else. Sometimes, we attract unnecessary heartache because we didn't learn from a previous experience and we're stuck in our progress. When this happens, suffering is a flashing red light warning you that you are not in harmony with your spirit. You are refusing to learn and move on and "bad things" are happening as a result.

You may be asking, "But what does this have to do with forgiveness?"

It has everything to do with forgiving. We play a role in every life that we touch. Either we are giving or we are receiving necessary life-lessons. There will come a time when we are in need of forgiveness and when we will need to be forgiving.

It is from our heart center that love radiates encompassing the physical body with miraculous changes, but what opens the heart center? Where does love begin? Love is a basic instinct it is inside us. It isn't that we need to be taught *how* to love, but fear has a way of changing God's Love, the only love we understood before fear taught us differently, and we're on a discovery journey to re-experience it.

I have no doubt that this planet is Spirit's worst nightmare. It's a dark and menacing place for any soul to navigate their way around. Horrific acts of violence and cruelty happen daily and then with limited understanding we are asked to forgive because God said we have to.

It is my understanding that God doesn't command or expect any of us to do anything. He gifted us with the gift of free will and He can't interfere, but there is another side to this commandment and one that I wasn't taught in Sunday school. I had to figure this one out on my own and only after much heartache and suffering.

The sword we hold above our enemies is the same sword that will pierce our own hearts and souls. All that we think or see in others comes from a personal belief. What we see in someone else is only a reflection of either a personal attribute or a personal flaw. Likewise, what we can't forgive in others is simply an un-forgiven act of our own. We can't escape personal responsibility for every thought and action—it is part of God's divine plan and perfect order in all things and it is the only way *we* learn and spiritually grow.

How we act on the outside mirrors everything inward that we try to deny. But its impossible to sweep any negative concept we have about our Selves under the rug—the truth is in our actions and our voices because it is in our hearts. This is a frightening concept. What faults do I see in others? Whatever they happen to be they only reflect my own self-image.

Most of us are stubborn mortals that don't like being told what to do—we learn our lessons the hard way, but do we have to? Is this a necessary part of life or just something we're forcing upon our Selves?

All we need to do is ask ourselves a few questions such as, "Why is it important to have the heart of a little child? What is it about children that we are to be more like? Could it be their willingness to forgive? Could it be their humbleness of heart? What about their innocence and love that they have for everyone? Sometimes, it's a real shame to grow up leaving behind a world of enchantment, especially since the world we enter is less loving and kind.

Bitterness destroys the soul's innocence and beauty. What should be love emanating from the heart fear has taken its place. How dark it must be for the spirit to live in a house without love and this is what happens when we cling to our resentments and bitterness and anger because we can't forgive and let it go.

But what about crimes committed against innocent children? Why do they suffer at such a tender age? Is there a life lesson to be learned inside such treacherous deeds as child sexual or physical abuse? What about murder victims? Are they responsible? What possible life-lessons can be learned from heinous crimes such as that?

Before I answer those questions, let me first say without understanding the purpose for each soul's journey or knowing what the soul experienced before this lifetime, I don't know that there is a comforting answer or one that brings closure to its victims. We don't always have all the answers and we're not given a complete picture that explains horrific acts of violence.

I can only teach from personal experience. At a young age, I was sexually abused. How often did it happen? I'm not sure that it happened more than once, but I do know the abuse changed the direction of my life. Does that mean I veered off my chosen path because of it? Not at all, had it not happened, I wouldn't be the woman I am today, and I rather like who I am. Each life-changing event was a necessary part of my soul's journey. Had none of those events taken place, I wouldn't be fulfilling sacred commitments today—they were necessary for my spiritual development.

Although my life is one of many trials, how many times have I been given an option or a way out? Never at any time was I forced to enter into an abusive marriage or situations that would give me necessary experiences for the writing of this book. In awe and disbelief, the workings of Spirit mesmerize me in its simplicity, complexity and incredible love and support.

How can I not forgive all that has gone before? I have been blessed! Not only spiritually, physically, emotionally and materialistically, but with awareness and personal empowerment. Life can only get better as I continue my soul's journey. Would I do it over? Yes, but I sure hope I don't have to.

The soul takes a tremendous risk just entering the earth plane. This isn't a safe place to be, but we are given all that we need both from this side and the spiritual realm to find our way safely home.

What makes life more difficult for each of us is our negative self-image. We really don't identify with the Spirit's that we are. We don't claim or understand the dynamics of Spiritual Energy. Spirit consists of an electromagnetic field powered by the mind.

Inside our hearts are life's gardens. From the emotional bed of our soul we're always planting seedlings. Secrets of the heart really aren't secrets. We experience our secrets of self-loathing, fear of failure or inadequacies in daily life.

Personal belief is a potent seed especially when rooted in fear. Fear is what we know best. But most often, we aren't consciously aware of those negative, buried, living feelings. It's even possible that nothing overwhelming traumatic happened to you and yet a seed of self-worthlessness was instilled just the same. That's when we have to stop what we're doing and reflect upon what's really happening to us and ask our Self what is in need of healing. What's going on inside that is causing us pain or causing us to judge or condemn?

Reasons may vary, but the theory is the same. If we haven't forgiven our Selves for something that we have done, we will attract those who are or will be in need of forgiving. If we are angry we will attract angry people. If we believe money is the root of all evil, regardless of how hard we try we won't have money. Even if we have money but hoard it eventually we will lose all that we have gained. Whatever it is that we believe and send forth into the Universal Mind, the Universal Mind responds—I don't think there is anything *free* in the divine order that makes the world go 'round. What we send forth returns. But the mind is different in that we have the power to think in anyway we choose and change our experiences. No one can take this from us. Free will is a gift from our Creator.

No one is doing anything to us that we don't allow happen. No one is hurting us if we aren't already hurting and we can't experience loving relationships if we don't love our Selves. Herein lies the mystery to love. Most of us don't love ourselves enough to really love our neighbors—we may think we do, but do we really *feel* love without hesitation, without exceptions, and without expectations?

Each step in healing is essential, but important as each step is, *forgiveness* is the only one that can truly release us from the past. If we do all the others, but fail to understand the power and wisdom in forgiveness, we simply go in a circle back to where we started.

When our happiness is dependent on receiving restitution, or an apology from someone who has hurt us, we then give that person power over our well-being. I've known too many people who can't forgive and their bitterness reflects in their countenance. Their burdens are double because it isn't just their pain they carry they carry the other's as well.

Another aspect of forgiveness is that once a negative experience takes place both people are affected. As long as we harbor resentments our hearts are connected. We are joined together until that psychic tie is severed. While you may think you have removed yourself and fled as far as possible away from someone you hate or resent—you're just a heartbeat away.

Forgiveness is a powerful word in that it stirs passionate feelings and emotions in each of us, but regardless of one person's views over another no one has your answers; they haven't walked in your shoes or lived your life. No one understands your pain and they can't expect you to be just as they are. There are wounds of the heart that seem unforgivable. Nothing will ever repair the hurt that has been done and its blasphemy for someone to judge another's pain. This is not my intent. Crimes of the heart take time to work through and more time to heal.

This journey we know as life really is the heart's journey to re-discover and understand the power of love. How then does forgiveness free us? Think about your answer and make a conscious choice to bring more light to your pathway and by doing this you will find how forgiveness illuminates the greater pathway of understanding.

We all need to do forgiveness work. Anyone who has a problem loving and forgiving is stuck in this area. Yet, traditionally, we think forgiveness has everything to do with people who have harmed us, but a lesson we are to be learning is that there is no guilt in anyone because only *love* is real.

Solution: Make a list on two separate sheets of paper. On the first sheet, make a list of all those people with whom you harbor ill feelings. Then answer the following questions: What is it that they did? Write your answers along side their name, and then underneath that explain what happened as a result of their actions. Then give yourself some time and think about how you felt about yourself as a result.

When you are finished ask yourself the following questions:

- What difference has harboring ill feelings toward this person(s) made in your life today?
- Have you forced them to pay for what they did?
- Did you feel better as a result?
- Do you need an apology before you can forgive?
- Can they really make amends for what they did?
- Would it make any difference if they did?

When you are ready, write a letter to those who have hurt you. Express to them what they did to you. Understand that they may not be able to acknowledge or express their sorrow but that you are ready to move on in spite of it. You don't have to mail your letter. Often, recovery takes place without anyone else involved. Your healing shouldn't be contingent upon them, if it is, you are giving them power over you as a willing participant.

On the other sheet of paper, I want you to be really honest with yourself. This exercise may be more difficult, but I want you to make a list of all those things you have done that caused you to feel ashamed.

- How responsible do you feel if your children suffered abuse?
- Do you suffer from depression?
- Do you (or did you) neglect your children as well as yourself as a result?
- Do you feel guilty?
- Do you feel ashamed?
- How angry are you toward the people in your life who have harmed you?
- Could it be that you are this angry with yourself?
- Do you often think about getting even or punishing them in some way?
- Do you realize that when you feel this way you are punishing yourself?

After you have done that, write a reconciliation letter to your Self. Express any anger you may have for any mistake you made. Express your unwillingness to trust in your ability to make healthy choices that will bring love into your life. Write about all the guilt your choices have brought you.

Prepare a time and a special place to hold a weeping ceremony.
Call upon the angels of healing—ask that they attend you.

With all your heartaches, grief, and sorrow embrace all the pain you have suffered.
Gather to you the love that has been absent from your heart.
And cry for all those things that matter.
And for all those things you cannot change.
Feel the arms of love comforting you. You have nothing for which to feel ashamed.
Allow this love into your heart as you softly whisper... I am willing to forgive myself.
Then gently, lovingly say, I am forgiven. Do this as often as you need until you no longer feel a resistance to the words I AM FORGIVEN.

You make a difference the moment you decide that today you will act with love, speak with love and honor the divine that you are.

Song of the Soul

All things Bright and Beautiful

He who is thankful in all things shall be made glorious,
And the things of this Earth shall be added unto him.

A soft melody awakens the earth from a babbling brook flowing gently down stream and as we become one with Mother Earth that melody touches our hearts and awakens our senses—we are more than our physical body, we are more than our thoughts and our needs—we are Spirit flowing gently through the stream of life renewed by feelings of joy and all things bright and beautiful.

Joy as the energy of love is of the highest vibrations on this earth, and according to the universal Law of Attraction, as we think we vibrate. And as we vibrate we attract. With this thought in mind, do you know what it is that you are thinking most often and attracting?

Take your time to think about your most often thought about thoughts and the feelings you entertain. Are your thoughts filled with anticipation? Or are they filled with remorse and self-doubt?

Perhaps this is a good time to close the book and put your head down on your desk, just like you did when you were in kindergarten, and think about your thoughts and feelings and what they consist of. Once you have evaluated the workings of your mind then resume reading—I'll still be here.

Vile weeds are noxious, negative thoughts growing in the soul's garden and you can't get rid of them just because you want to—something must first take their place.

While you can't always make all the changes you want in life, a change of heart changes everything. And this is where you need to start today—with a change of heart.

There are many reasons why living with joy creates miracles. With the light of love/joy, you have the power to burn away impurities in your emotional system, dissolve worry, anxiety, grief and other negative emotions and strengthen your immune system as you discover and move into a more joyful inner world. As you resonate with joy, love draws you to a more meaningful life, releasing you from a painful past.

In your search for happiness you will be drawn to those things that will open you to new ideas. Not allowing old negative thought patterns deter you is one of your greatest challenges.

Spirituality teaches that we are beings of duality and that we should embrace all that we are. With this concept in mind, we can't rid our Selves of negative thoughts—they are part of us. Instead we must learn to co-exist simultaneously with both personality and spirit. But we give less power to our ego-self when we're consciously thinking and creating from a higher realm of wisdom.

The conscious mind is always searching for its source of existence. If we don't interfere with this instinctive nature, and just do our part to weed out doubt, our thoughts become a creative source. As Spirit you are the conscious mind, a co-creator with your Maker, so how are you using or abusing this power?

How do we become more consciously aware of what we are thinking? First, we have to live inside our feelings being alive to them and second; we have to stay focused in the present and third, we have to continually work on healing living, buried negative feelings so that we can release them. Spiritually, you have the power to do all of it!

With each new phase in recovery, you will discover more truths about your Self as you are challenged to keep going forward. Ultimately, the more you know about and express your authentic Self, the more meaning, joy and fulfillment you will have in your life—living with a joyful, thankful heart keeps you focused minute by minute until you create a new habit and a new way of thinking and feeling.

Magic wands don't exist with the power to turn pumpkins into coaches or mice into prancing horses, but we have magic of our own that will turn gloom to joy, confusion to clarity, helplessness to empowerment and distress to inner-stillness.

And this power is a happy heart! One that is willing to paint their world with bright and cheery thoughts rather than dismal and shallow ones. You have the power to decide how you will experience any given situation in life. There isn't any force outside you that has that power.

Of all the many things we can't change, we *can* change our attitude. One of the difficulties we find in changing behavior is in getting rid of our habitual negative thought patterns. The subconscious mind responds with instinct and habit. As thinking and behavioral patterns deepen, they become stubborn habits to change. While the subconscious mind has its own power it is a servant of the conscious mind. It follows orders by acting on whatever is fed to it. But one thing it cannot do is distinguish between what is real and what isn't.

Your conscious mind is the gatekeeper, and for personal power, you must always be aware of what you are allowing to enter through this gate before it ends up in the subconscious mind. Old habits are like unwelcome guests, they show up unexpectedly and you can't get rid of them fast enough just as old negative thought patterns have a way of turning your life upside down!

The way to change a negative thought pattern is to stay centered in the present moment. You accomplish two things when you stay focused. First, you build self-esteem. You have the power and the control of outside influences. No longer a boat without a rudder, violent winds won't wash you up against the reef or abandon you on a foreign island—you will be at the helm deciding where you want to go and what you want to experience.

Second, you will be able to focus on the journey, not the destination! Joy isn't something we arrive at when we reach the finish line. Joy comes from taking the journey and learning from it.

Too often, we search outside our inner-world for fulfillment and happiness when it is in our lives all the time. Joy, the energy of love is the essence of our true identity waiting for us to express it openly.

Create joyful situations. Be young again and be creative—bring the heart of innocence into what you are doing and how you are feeling. When you're discouraged see life through the eyes of a little one. They refuse to stay mad or sad for very long.

Sometimes we need a real kick in the behind! And if it's not a swift kick, then at the very least something that will snap us out of depressed thoughts into reality. This moment is the only thing that is real! It's the only moment that matters—do something positive with it and be happy that you have this time in your life to make a difference.

Knowing how powerful our thoughts or feelings can be is frightening. Especially when we recognize how gloomy they are most of the time. For those that have suffered through long months and perhaps years of depression, we know all too well the affects of this illness. Everything in life appears in its worst condition. From the moment we wake up to the moment we fall asleep, our thoughts go anywhere from hopelessness to severe desperation.

The workings of a depressed mind are complex. With any length of time our negative thought patterns only deepen. Uprooting them is more difficult and I don't know that we trust in miracles of wonderful happenings. The worst happened before and we believe the worst will continue to happen to us—it's our fate.

While medication is helpful and it may be necessary, it isn't a long-term solution. We have to change the way we think and feel and respond to life. First you have to change a belief before you can change a behavior.

From depression to recovery is a thin line between severe anxiety and inner-peace. Rebuilding your emotional and physical health isn't easy. Relapse is real, but bringing joy into your inner-world makes a difference. You can't live in the past if you stay focused in the present, and you can't be afraid if you understand the true purpose in each situation that happens. Just as you can't be miserable if you dwell on happy thoughts—being grateful *is* dwelling on happy, cheerful thoughts.

Which brings me to another topic, and that is balance. Life is overwhelming for many of us. We have outside stressors working against us all the time and that doesn't include stressors brought on by the seven dwarfs of menopause. If I'm not careful, before I'm aware of what is happening I'm irritable, cranky, exhausted, bloated, grouchy, bitchy and as Suzanne Somers says, all dried up!

We need balance in our lives. We need to be aware of what is happening—how we think affects our physical body and negativity disrupts its natural rhythm. When you feel your inner-world start tipping, take time out and listen to what your body is telling you.

With the many challenges battered women in recovery face everyday, they need as much stability, focus and support and energy they can get. Discouragement only serves to rob us of the energy that we do have.

When my writing challenged me to dig deeper and dream higher I wasn't able to do it. I didn't know how. There was an unseen barrier I couldn't break through. That is until I stopped trying to force my mind into thinking something it wasn't ready to accept.

My dreams weren't going to happen *someday* because they already had. Believing you already have something creates that situation in the near future without awakening the unfriendly foe of opposition. For example, in my head I envisioned myself as a published author. I gave thanks for my work and the opportunity to play an enormous part in the healing of many hearts. How could I possibly fail? Joy burst forth from a tiny seedling planted in my heart by desire. Never once did I use the word "if," but rather my book "is" published. I envisioned my work in print spreading throughout the country from hand to hand and heart to heart.

An old Chinese Proverb says: If I keep a green bough in my heart, the singing bird will come. To me, the green bough is the willingness to believe in miracles and trust in an unseen power. And all that is required is an open heart to feel the joy that is inside you and bring it to life and as you resonate with joy, love and happiness you automatically draw to you a more meaningful life.

There is a myriad of fascinating discoveries we make on the road to recovery—opening the heart to love, letting go, and establishing safe boundaries that help us maintain well-being are all part of the journey, but there is also something more that happens: We return the heart to love. And from a warm heart a life of happiness blooms where you are planted.

If the writing in this chapter sounds like Pollyanna speaking, it's not. I'm the one who has complained and criticized anyone who sounded like Pollyanna! But it would be nice to have her ability to see the good in everyone. Since Pollyanna is a fictional character in a story, we take what she presents and apply it in our lives.

And so my challenge to you is: Count your blessings and bring more joy into your inner-world every day. It has to be a priority—chronic depression alters the mind and it affects how we deal with problems even when we're no longer depressed—everything in life is over-exaggerated. We're either going to one extreme or the other. As if we can't live without drama or a crisis. I think most of us pen in a little disaster each day in our day planner just to remind us that we are needed.

Through many tears, I've felt my Savior's Love while writing this book. Words cannot express the gratitude I feel for the healing I couldn't find any other way. The gifts of the soul have become priceless treasures in that I know peace abides in the heart of the one who loves.

Certainly joy, love and inner peace is meant for each one of us, regardless of our meager circumstances. As you travel your humble journey, many challenges lie ahead, but when you become discouraged remember the song of the soul. It is a song of the highest devotion, and when sung from the depths of your heart, the Earth shall lay its treasures at your feet.

Change happens when we stay fully aware of every moment of every day, and, so, the assignment for today is to *cherish the moment.*

In your healing journal: at the end of every day count your blessings and write them in your journal. Without fail, enter seven things in your journal that you are grateful for *each day.*

Bring laughter into your life. You will find balance when you are kind and loving toward your Self.

What simple pleasures can you do that will lift your spirits? When you need to, think of them during the day. Look for new discoveries about yourself you didn't notice before.

- Make an affirmation and tell yourself everyday, "I am loved"
- Awaken the child within that loves to giggle and make funny faces
- Run barefoot in the grass blowing bubbles
- Squeeze mud from your garden through your toes
- Sip magic punch that makes you invisible
- Giggle when you should be serious
- Paint whiskers on your face
- Wear your clothes inside out
- Whatever you decide to do—have a happy day and remember: you are loved!

If someone hasn't told you lately that you are loved, I'm telling you now. You, dear one, are loved more than you have ever known.

Healing with Light

God's Pure Love

Beneath wings of those that love, light fills the earth today.
Open your heart to receive God's bounteous blessings,
And heal your soul with radiant light.
With the heart of a child,
Invoke the spirit of innocence and beauty
And return the heart to love.

ealing with Light works hand in hand with the chapter, *"Why do I feel this way."* When you open the heart in search of a better life, you also invite God's All Shining Light into your life. It isn't something that you consciously do, but rather something that just happens.

If there is anything that I have learned, it is about the power of love, and how it turns lives around and heals the wounded soul. Every chapter that I write the word Love, Light and Energy is interchangeably used. There isn't any way to escape from it. Love is the essence of our spiritual being and with the Light of Love the physical body can be healed. You don't have to do anything special such as perform a ritual using a specific dialogue—you just need to ask for help and acknowledge that there is a Higher Power.

The ego is self-sufficient and all knowing and needs no one while the soul is without arrogance. This is why therapy in itself doesn't work for many people. We use the same mind that got us into trouble in the first place to resolve our problems.

Light is flooding the Earth today. Many are awakening to their spiritual calling and many are responding to the yearnings in their hearts. This is a New Age—a spiritual age, and you can take full advantage of the Light that has entered our dimension by opening your mind and hearts to it.

Inside the energy of Love are minuscule particles of a healing substance. All you have to do is open your heart to experience more love in everything that you do.

When I first realized the power in the light that I was using in healing, I was amazed. I had never *felt* such power. In my youth, I had been taught about those who had the power to heal the sick, but not once did I feel this power when used.

Today, I have no doubt we all have the power to heal if we develop the ability to use it. A tiny mustard seed exists inside us and as we erase and heal all negative energy inside us, this tiny seed of faith begins to grow.

Women in the early history of the Mormon Church developed their spiritual gifts and they used this spiritual power to literally heal the blind and the lame. I don't know of anyone since that time that has used this same gift in such a remarkable way. But we have the same power and we can begin tapping into this power by calling upon the Holy Spirit to assist us.

Desire cultivates the seed of faith and this is something I consistently worked on. Each night I spent time in silence and in prayer asking for guidance, and I always received more than I expected.

Each answer came with an intense feeling of Love and sometimes the Love that filled my heart lifted me higher into another dimension that wasn't affected by the negativity on this Earth plane. So moved by an intensity of emotions, I wept. The Love I felt was the pure love of Christ. It opened my mind to see the reality of how each of us is intricately connected to one another, and what we do has a tremendous rippling affect. Feeling a Love so powerful and pure changed the way I had once believed.

When this Love begins to enter your being by way of visualized light it will change everything about you because the power of this light awakens your Spirit and rekindles the love that you are. Only then can you really understand that nothing outside of love is real. What we go through in this life is temporary, but necessary. We can't arrive at the gates of Heaven without taking the journey.

The Light of Love is two-fold in that it is healing and enlightening. As we heal from our past, we evolve to another level. Line upon line, we are given what we are in need of. When we are ready, our Higher Self takes us to a higher plane; it is our wise Self that is constantly aware of our needs. Intuitively, we feel the promptings we are given and intellectually our minds also open to receive further understanding.

When we understand our depth of energy, the energy brings itself into physical form through the neurosystem of the body. We are all Spirit, which is pure energy, and our body is a frequency of color. Our chemistry is electromagnetic energy and when an imbalance occurs in our spiritual make-up it is manifested physically. To reverse illness either emotionally or physically we have to intensify spiritually.

Deepening our spiritual connection restores our physical vitality and health. Intensifying spiritually is the only way we heal the soul's tabernacle—our physical body. Alone our awareness is limited to what we have learned from others.

As you go through each step of healing you are assisting your soul in undertaking your spiritual journey—you aren't alone and you will receive the guidance that you need. This has always given me comfort. Sometimes we feel isolated and completely alone as we let go of the past including our old, familiar belief system.

Light will continue working it's way throughout your body changing the infrastructure of your cells—cleansing them from the residual negative energy or inner darkness. This inner-darkness is sometimes referred to as the veil that separates you from your spirit. Bringing light and love into your mind, heart and body thins the veil drawing you closer to your Spirit and the wisdom therein.

As you draw in more light, your wise eyes begin to see beyond the illusions and myths, and yet all that you have learned is part of life's sacred journey and each life lesson leads you into the sunrise of tomorrow. Imbalance only occurs when we prevent spiritual progress or the learning process from rising to greet us on our spiritual journey.

But today is a new beginning; you are making way by clearing out the past for your soul to be your navigator as you are opening the heart center to feel the love from your true Self. Uniting Spirit's Mind with the intuitive feelings in your heart brings power and stability into your life under any circumstance.

This can be an exciting time in life if you let go of your need to control everything that happens. We don't know what the outcome is going to be in any given situation, and sometimes we complicate situations by trying to enforce a certain one. Letting go is important just as it is important to believe that when you do you will be drawn to those things that are for your higher good.

Always remember that your life is mapped out—it always has been, and your soul knows what it needs to finish your journey.

I know the way isn't clear-cut in the beginning, and it can be frightening when you are asked to believe in a power that you can't see. But you must trust in the healing process and know that every step you take is necessary. All that you need on your journey will come to you. Do not fixate on anything in particular; just be open to receive internal guidance, and be patient. When it is time for new changes to be made in your life—you will feel it.

Intuitively, you will know what your body needs to heal. Sometimes, other people will come into your life to help teach you. Books will fall from the shelves (theoretically speaking). But you will be drawn to those things that will offer you the information that you are seeking.

As you work with light you will notice that light accomplishes the exact opposite result of stress. While stress depletes the body of necessary vitality, light replenishes it. Whatever it is that you take away from your body replace it with the energy of love.

Not only are you healing your body with light you are also healing your mind. This is an important aspect of your journey also. Anyone who has experienced a loss of personal power is in need of this light.

Empowerment is an energy surge. You have your own level of energy or empowerment and by working with various colors you draw to you an essential source of life that is healing. In reality what you are doing is aligning your spiritual body and clearing your chakras of grimy film or negative energy.

Chakras are energy openings in your body. You have one just above your head, one in your forehead between your eyes, one in the center of your throat, one in your heart area, one at your solar plexus, one in your stomach and one in your reproductive area. These spots are where energy moves in and out of your body. They are not physical, but run through your body from front to back and top to bottom. When fully balanced and working properly your physical body is well-balanced and healthy.

When you are drawing light to you for personal empowerment draw upon seven colors: red, orange, yellow, green, blue, purple, and burgundy. These colors are words; they are the energy that gives power to your words.

In this short crash course of "healing with light," it isn't possible to cover all there is to know, but I can give you enough information to begin working and when you are ready you will intuitively seek more understanding.

Solution: You can help the healing process by visualizing rays of shimmering light flowing through your body. Visualize your body as a grid with tiny lines flowing in every direction. Down ray light showering from above and visualize it flow through your body filling each tiny line with its power.

- Early in the mornings spend time drawing to yourself blue-white light. Visualize it all around you forming a protective bubble. Emerge yourself in this bubble of light and feel its healing energy penetrate your physical being. Then draw this light into your physical being by an opening in the crown of your head and feel it flow through you saturating your entire body. Feel its warmth as it flows through your head and into your arms and hands and into your heart center as it flows downward into your legs and feet. Visualize each sparkling particle of this light healing your cells and tissue lifting all negative energy until it is dissolved. When you take a shower, visualize streams of energetic blue-white light cleansing the aura around you. If you are nervous or feel frightened—cleanse this energy from the outside of your body as well as the inside.

- When you take a bath, visualize deep rose, the healing light of love, in your bathwater as it flows from the tap. Soak in this light and feel it comforting your tired body. Feel the light soothing your heart center and releasing any hurts you might be experiencing. Appreciate your body and give thanks for it. Ask that the light help cleanse all guilt and shame that you may be feelings—sense your sensuality and be grateful that you are a woman.

- When you retire at the end of the day, spend time again with the light of love. Draw it into your awareness, and visualize all the colors in the rainbow dancing as tiny particles around you. Whichever color you feel most attracted to, draw that color into your body. Ask your Higher Self what is in need of healing and let the answers come to you. Then begin working on that area in your body that needs your attention.

- When you are feeling angry, visualize rays of the orange-red flame of purification, and draw this light into your body through your crown center. Ask that this light dissolve any anger that you may be feeling. Feel this energy dissipate into the flame of purification.

- When you have used the orange-red flame of purification, cleanse your inner-self with the blue-white flame of life to recharge your energy centers.

Believe in the power of light and believe in the power of love and believe in Angels. They are people who come into your life when you need them most! Beneath their wings you will find the help you seek as you open your heart to miracles—that's what this life is all about.

A Woman's Song

From her cocoon, a woman of strength emerges—breathtaking as a butterfly, with wings of faith she flies. Owning her power, her life has new meaning and the silent longing she feels is simply her spirit invoking a child's dream writing the lyrics to a woman's song.

child's world captures the heart of the soul, and a child's dream reveals the soul's desires and it's sacred destiny. It is here that the map of fate is outlined so clearly and cleverly that in our heart of hearts we have no doubt, in faith we are to follow our secret longings.

Although it is just a short whisper in time that we are children, a child's heart teaches us what we are to remember. And long into our later years, it is this heart we are to recall and to embrace and recapture it's vibrant meaning.

To return to love is to embrace the heart that is warm and inviting. No matter what went before, we still long for something more, and to feel passionate about something that is within our reach, and to give from the depths of our soul.

Can we deny ourselves this truth? Can we really leave this Earth forgotten? Will we stand by and allow the wings of our soul to lie limp and weak because we failed to try? I believe the fatal wound of the soul is regret—regret not for what we did, but for what we failed to do.

On your healing journey, if you will always keep your heart open, you will discover the joy of womanhood, and the polarities of both male and female that you must unite within your being. There are no guarantees in life– we are here to learn and choices must be made. Often, we don't know the way to go, or what will be for our highest good. The wounded inner child can hold us back if we allow it; old myths can linger from antiquated dogma if we fail to reach inside for further light and wisdom.

But beyond this, you must know that you are a Goddess, an heiress to God's Kingdom. All that He is He bestows upon *all* of His children—We are to pattern our lives from the example of the Savior and walk in his footsteps, yet how far do we follow behind afraid to open our minds and believe the unbelievable, and to reach for the unreachable star?

We are Gods and Goddesses, Priests and Priestesses, dreamers and seekers and our lives did not come about by chance, nor were we born into adversity without purpose, and most importantly, we are not without the knowledge to understand why or the power to heal.

Your journey may parallel mine, often frightening and confusing. I've grown weary when the way hasn't been clear—perhaps for way showers, it is to be this way…we tread a path unknown to us all.

But still I have no doubt that we have our own special purpose on this Earth. Many times we think we know what it is, when in fact it's what *we want*, not what Spirit had in mind. Perhaps this is why you haven't spread your wings just yet because there are other plans for you.

For a moment, close your eyes and visualize one of God's most exquisite creations, the butterfly.

We are just like butterflies. When the inner child is healed, and our true Self is revealed, we emerge from the cocoon of our learning as strong women of adversity. In love, and wings adorned with compassion, we spread our beautiful, rainbow colored wings and fly.

The beauty, intricacy in shape, size and color, distinguishes each butterfly in its uniqueness. Consider its beauty and grace as it spreads its wings to explore and experience life naturally—flowing gently in the air in perfect harmony and rhythm as the wind rises beneath its wings.

God created the butterflies and He created you. He gave you life so that you could celebrate your individuality, and discover what it is like to be a woman through feelings of sensuality and passion—there is no one on this Earth just like you.

With extraordinary vibrant colors, delicate and fragile, butterfly wings carry them safely through gentle breezes or turbulent winds. And yet so filled with grace, the butterfly does much more, it tells the story of your life and mine.

Imagine yourself inside the darkness of a tiny cocoon. Could it be that a metamorphosis *is* taking place? In time, the butterfly emerges, but in order to survive the butterfly must squeeze through the opening on its own. As the butterfly forces itself through the opening, the substance needed for its strength is forced into the wings. If the cocoon were to be broken from the outside freeing the butterfly, the butterfly would never rise with the wind or float serenely through the air or dazzle the eyes of the beholder.

Inside your cocoon a weaving of beautiful colors *is* taking place, the culminating of spiritual colors from sorrow gifting vibrant life inside your wings. It is the souls tapestry with intricate colors that glimmer, colors that tell your life story of agony and ecstasy, failings and triumph.

The child within is forever changed inside her cocoon; a woman of wisdom now speaks in truth. When we least expect it the spirit awakens. No longer sleepwalking, the soul softly whispers in remembrance of a child's dream and the heart sings a melody to a woman's song.

Sweet melodic lyrics tell of your story and how from years of heartache, pain taught you mercy, and loneliness taught you love. How can you not breath appreciation for all those poignant insights that taught you compassion, and humility? A woman of adversity awakening into a spiritual woman filled with grace is as wondrous as the butterfly.

To be deeply spiritually connected is the arpeggio, and the wonder of Spirit's Song. It's a joining of heart and soul in a love affair. It is to know yourself more intimately, to love more abundantly. It is the song that releases inhibitions and embraces femininity—as we love who we are, we share that love—as we open our eyes to our divinity, the world around us responds. And above all, it is an owning of our personal power relinquishing it to none.

Today you are faced with a myriad of challenges. You may feel overwhelmed with the many tasks in front of you but if you do one thing, and that is reclaim your personal power, my dear one, you will walk in grace until you feel whole and restored again.

A woman with a voice is a deeply spiritual woman who honors all life and all opinions and choices—she simply chooses what is right for her. We make a difference in the lives of others only when we make a difference in our own. And while it is important to take a strong stand in order for changes to be made—the change we seek is within. We don't have control over outside forces and we can't rely on them to give us equal rights or personal power.

Women have been subservient since the beginning of time and because of this many fight back. Sometimes they go to the extreme and I don't blame them. But even if a man in authority bestowed special powers upon me, I still wouldn't have any—no one gives anyone something special anymore than they can take it away—it is from within we find it and nurture it into a remarkable spiritual power.

Being is a wonderful aspect of life. Be loving, be kind, be forgiving but most of all be yourself. You are your own authority and always remember this: If you seek you will find, if you ask you will be given. There are no secrets about heaven, or the spiritual kingdom. All souls are created equal no one is more special or self-righteous or more powerful.

Too often we live the life planned for us and at some point we stop living the life we were meant to live. Take back your power and reclaim your place in life. You have many wonderful qualities necessary to make your dreams happen.

And if you will recapture the heart of a child and her innocence, all things shall be made possible—you are a Goddess and a Spiritual Heiress. Believe in your dreams and reach for that unreachable star.

No one has the magic book that tells people how to live and no one discovered the only sacred path we must all follow—if you live with love you will find *your* way. Your spirit is always seeking its source and she will guide you.

The mystical *alchemy of grace* is that it creates a luminous moment. The moment we grasp hold of something we thought we had lost or something we've never believed we owned. It is the moment we wake and realize we have spun sorrow into gold.

Nothing is as important as living deeply from the heart and nothing is as important as fulfilling our dreams and living life passionately. Your dreams may not be to have your name in glittering lights, but to love and nurture little souls, spread peace with loving thoughts, walk in faith and hold your head high. We touch lives around us all the time—what mark do we leave behind?

Do we not all Dream? Do we not all long to be passionate women? Do we not long to feel the Earth beneath our feet and feel deeply connected?

As a little girl, I will always remember watching the heavens from my bedroom window, believing the moon was the doorway into Heaven. In my waking dreams, I entered through this doorway and in wonder gazed at the stars around me. Bound with the Earth, the Universe was one with me and I knew my life was one of sacred promises.

Not long ago, I wrote this poem that I would like to share with you. It was written during a time when my future felt dim and the way seemed dark and lonely:

> *Close to my heart is the beginning of time,*
> *For this was the moment my dreams were born.*
> *Filled with passion, my heart still chimes,*
> *For something of which I mourn.*
> *In forgotten memory and restless tears,*
> *My sacred dreams still burn within,*
> *Pleading to break free from the sepals of fear.*

I don't know that we ever forget our childhood dreams, the innocence and wonder of being young. Although, for many, childhood does not hold happy memories, still dreams exist in the heart of every soul. We have our secret longings that speak in morning's sunlight and dance the night away... these are as much a part of the soul's repertoire as the unavoidable and formidable darkness.

The soul's journey through darkness reveals the light within, the everlasting light that draws us closer each time we fail, and when heartache drowns our soul in anguish, this light eternal is who we are.

If you could only see what the angels see in you then you would also know of your uniqueness and feel your great worth. You would see your life inside the cocoon as a necessary aspect of your life, and then you would see the opening just the other side of healing feelings. It is the darkest just before morning light, and this is the way it feels just before our soul begins to soar, our fears are silenced, and the seed of dreams begins to sprout. It's a moment we dare to truly believe in ourselves. It's the moment we begin creating our life and our identity from our childhood dreams

Even though it can be a long way home, spiritual growth is the single most important mission you can undertake on your journey into recovery.

The only thing required is that you show up each day willing to live in a way that you feel honored and respected. You must be willing to trust in divine guidance. Be still often and listen to your heart sing, and follow the voice within. This is the secret to a safe-passage as you journey.

There is a magical realm inside the heart with wonders the mind cannot conceive, treasures the world cannot offer. It is a place to converse with the angels and feel their love. It is a place to move away from fear and open to your deepest love.

Today, find a quiet moment and fill the air with soft music. Light a candle in remembrance of your pain. Cry a mother's tears, feel a woman's grief, and then remember your dreams. Awaken in your hearts gentle compassion—all is forgiven—all is well—you are born again.

Feel the presence of angelic beings. Feel the fluttering of their wings as lovingly they gather round you. Listen as they instill feelings once forgotten. *Who are you? Do you really know? Where did you come from? Is there life inside your physical body that seems to have a life of its own?*

Whisper sweet invocations to your seed of dreams and believe that dreams really do come true. It is always a new dawn in early morning light, and a time to reinvent, redefine, and rediscover new aspects about you.

And, just before the curtain falls on a life you wish to leave behind, and a new life begins, pirouette like the little girl you used to be, the one who graced your childhood days. Dream her dreams and reach for the stars, and find that magical place inside.

Feel your uniqueness, and feel your power. Feel your Wings spread and in your heart give thanks for a Woman's Song—a song of strength after tears have washed away years of pain. And as night falls, cover your soul with a blanket of dreams for tonight, my dear reader, you are beneath the wings of beloved angels.

Blessed be...

A Time to Say Good Bye

Every morning as I work with heavenly beings, my heart is filled with their love; I will miss the mornings we have worked together. They have filled my life with challenges, which have forced me to grow; they have placed golden opportunities before me and given me the courage to use my creativity. They are dear to me, and our hearts are forever entwined with the love we have shared.

A message from the author

In writing my story, my greatest concern has been that the physical abuse would diminish the effect of emotional abuse. But the truth is, the line between verbal and physical abuse is a thin one. Many verbally abusive relationships will never cross the physical abuse line, but don't be deceived; the absence of physical abuse does not make a verbally abusive relationship any less destructive or acceptable—verbal or emotional abuse is not okay. A broken spirit doesn't hurt any less than broken bones. Furthermore, in not putting a stop to verbal abuse may enable your relationship to escalate into physical violence.

It is my heart's most fervent prayer that leaders in all faiths will unite and help put an end to domestic violence. Women that have been taught to stay within their fold and seek guidance from their leaders must receive the help they need: A safe place to go, counseling from those trained in domestic violence, financial assistance, assistance in drug abuse intervention and rehabilitation. How each organization spends its money received from members varies from church to church, but I don't see enough money being spent to save the family. Nothing is as important as helping families be safe, and to help them recover from abuse so that they can enter into society productive and well adjusted. It is true that the family is being destroyed and there isn't any faith that is immune to physical or emotional abuse.

Women must begin owning their power and relinquishing it to none this is the only way abuse ends in the family. Women can't change their abusive partners and we can't change religious organizations soon enough or assume that they will understand the complexities of the problem, especially in a male dominated society. Women have to take their rightful stand as beings of equality in all things and to be their own source of wisdom and knowledge.

They must understand that they have spiritual gifts that offer them the power to heal, bless and guide their lives—faith is the key to all gifts!

If you are being abused and have turned to your ecclesiastical leaders for help only to be turned away in one form or another, you are not alone. Women tell me heart-wrenching stories daily—they aren't receiving the help they need from ecclesiastical leaders and yet they don't know where else to turn. This is what they have been taught. Drastic changes need to take place and together we can make that happen.

If you are being abused it is up to you to stop the abuse.

Do all *you* can to find a safe place. Call your local crisis center hotline. Make preparations to leave. Don't minimize the danger that you and your children are in and protect yourself from any further pregnancies. While husbands or partners make promises they can't keep, women become pregnant and this only further complicates a dangerous and complex situation.

Realize the role you play in the abusive situation. When you stay you enable. When you believe in empty promises you prolong the inevitable. When you continue to do all you can to be a better wife you are depleting yourself of vital energy that you need to take care of your Self.

Understand that depression is part of the battered woman syndrome. We do all that we can to end the abuse, but it is never enough and I believe deep inside we know it will never be enough—depression is another sign of resignation.

If you are ready to begin your healing journey—follow the steps I've outlined in the book and as you continue your journey into recovery, journal as often as you can. Take a break when you need to, but always keep your heart open to love. Taking care of yourself is vital to recovery. You may need to learn how to love and nurture yourself, but once you get started it becomes a natural response in any given situation. You are important and how you feel is important— loving our Selves is where our outlook in life changes.

While I still face many challenges, there is peace in knowing that I do control my destiny. Always looking in all the wrong places for inner-strength to face each challenge drove me into despair. The victim's role felt familiar while reaching beyond hopelessness and fear seemed foreign. I've learned that there is peace in letting go of those things in which I have no control.

Faith is an important element in my life. I know that every situation works itself out to everyone's highest good, and that in life there are always second chances.

Sending loving prayers your way as you journey.

What is abuse?

erbal and emotional abuse also involves controlling partners. What does controlling mean? Controlling is in reference to people who try to run other people's lives. Controlling people insist and persist to get their way, and they get upset when they don't get it. They have learned emotional blackmail techniques—whatever it takes to get you to do what they want they will do, especially if it causes someone else to feeling guilty.

In a controlling relationship, both the abused and the abuser tend to be "controlling." Think about the different ways you respond to your partner's emotional abuse. Perhaps you throw yourself into the pity pot the moment your partner does something that upsets you. Your reaction may also involve the silent treatment as you withdraw into yourself.

Often, as children we learn to withdraw when we are offended. This dark hole becomes a place to lick our wounds and to feel sorry for ourselves. Sometimes this is the only solace that we find. While we may see this as "self caring," in essence we are hurting only our Self.

It is important to understand (so that we can free our "selves") that not all relationships are meant to last forever. In relationships, we come together for different reasons. The key to understanding our relationships is to look within for the cause of our unhappiness.

Our relationships mirror to us the pain that we brought with us into the relationship—it is here that you start working on your Self. Although, there are relationships that can be mended (and I am not referring to those where physical violence is present), when relationships are over they are over. Nothing we do changes that, but prolonging it hurts everyone.

I also believe that once we stay beyond any reasonable period of time, misery adds to misery until it's *impossible* to ignore the situation. Codependent behavior is an illness in that it is progressive. As the situation worsens so does depression. And *severe depression* is a warning that you've got to stop hurting yourself.

Be willing to accept personal responsibility (regardless of what has gone on in your life before) that you have unhealed issues of childhood sexual or physical or emotional abuse. This statement may trigger an immediate response of *not me my childhood was ideal*. I have loving parents. Nothing is wrong with me, it's just that I keep attracting jerks or losers or abusive men, etc. The simple truth is victims attract victims.

As your resistance to seeing inside your Self dissolves there are many things you can learn about yourself. It doesn't mean that you don't have loving parents or a supportive family, but it does mean there was some dysfunction in the way the family interacted with one another.

What controlling techniques are used?

Often there is a honeymoon cycle where love and affection are given to confuse the victim. When the perpetrator senses he/she is losing control, or perhaps they recognize they have gone too far, they begin to shower their victim with flowers, gifts, or apologies until the victim once again is rendered submissive.

It is all about power, control, and dominance, but never is it about love. Relationships vary in intensity and some do not involve physical violence, it is also the emotional/mental or verbal abuse that is clandestinely used to keep a victim under control, submissive and compliant.

Abusers often show extreme possessiveness of their partner, wanting their partner to account for their whereabouts, how they spent their money, or what they did with their time. Sexual abuse further serves to weaken the spirit of the victim. The abuser must show he has total authority and control over his partner.

Sometimes we think it is okay to be told what to do because maybe we have been taught women should be more submissive—or we believe the man is the head of his family. But any behavior that diminishes the feelings of Self worth in another should never be allowed in anyone's relationship.

It isn't okay for your partner to be jealous because he loves you and he wants to be protective. And possessiveness isn't okay because you belong to your partner. These are signs of a controlling and abusive partner. Love never involves physical or emotional abuse in any form.

Emotional and verbal abuse is disrespectful behavior. It is a behavior that often is overlooked, and it is common for the abused partner to have little or no idea that they are being treated poorly. What has happened is that the victim identifies with the abuser. The abused often feels guilty for the behavior of the abuser. For example, "How can I be mad at him after the way I behaved?" This is a common response from many victims.

There are several reasons abused people allow others to hurt them:

1. They don't recognize abuse as being abuse. For example they make excuses for their spouse or partner, such as, he/she had a bad day or he/she didn't really mean what they just said.
2. They lack survival skills or they feel guilty when implementing a plan of escape.
3. They are depressed.
4. Self-esteem is so low it feels "normal" to hurt.
5. Women with children who are unable to support themselves face real financial concerns and this keeps them trapped.
6. Problems with the legal system and the abuser's ability to manipulate the system and appear to be the victimized one.

Are you in an abusive relationship?

*L*ook over the following questions. Think about how you are being treated and how you treat your partner. Remember, when one person intimidates, hurts or continually puts down the other person, its abuse whether it is physical/emotional/mental or verbal.

Does your partner

- Embarrass or make fun of you in front of your friends or family?
- Put down your accomplishments or goals?
- Make you feel like you are unable to make decisions?
- Use intimidation or threats to gain compliance?
- Tell you that you are nothing without him?
- Treat you roughly—grab, push, pinch, shove or hit you?
- Blame you for how he feels or acts?
- Make you feel like there is no way out of the relationship?
- Do you try not to do anything that would make your partner angry?
- Do you feel like no matter what you do your partner is never happy with you?
- Do you always do what your partner wants instead of what you want?

Does your partner:

- Ignore your feelings?
- Disrespect you?
- Ridicule or insult you and then say he meant it as a joke?
- Give you the silent treatment?
- Criticize or call you names?
- Humiliate you at home or in public?
- Give you a hard time about being with friends or family?
- Roll his or her eyes when you talk?
- Make sure that what you want is the same as what he wants?
- Tell you that you are too sensitive?
- Hurt you when you are feeling down?
- Try to control decisions, money, even what you wear?
- Threaten to leave you?
- Threaten to throw you out?
- Promise never to do something hurtful again?
- Manipulate you with lies?
- Destroy furniture or punch holes in the wall?
- Hit you?
- Cause conflict just when you feel your relationship is improving?
- Say things that make you feel good only to say something that destroys your self-confidence?
- Act selfish and accuse you of having the same behavior?
- Frequently say things that he/she later denies?
- Accuse you of misunderstanding what he/she says?
- Treat you like you are a sex object?
- Interrupt you frequently?
- Listen but doesn't hear you?
- Provoke you to rage to prove you are the unstable one?

Your situation is critical if the following applies to you:

- You hope things will change especially if you are loving and patient
- You feel emotionally unsafe
- You are physically in danger
- You find yourself being careful of what you say
- You voice your opinion less and less

- You make excuses for your partner's behavior
- You don't feel it is okay to talk about your problems with anyone else
- You find yourself doubting your sanity
- You find yourself walking on eggshells
- You long for a softer and more loving companion
- You doubt your own judgment
- You doubt your abilities
- You feel trapped and helpless

Abusive individuals typically have anti-social behaviors. This detracts them from seeking help for their behavior. This person blames the other. Their problems are perceived as coming from the outside. What they want and need are impossible to receive from anyone other than themselves. They receive satisfaction from blaming/beating up their victim (as in, they deserve it.) They receive satisfaction from affairs, substance abuse, gambling, etc. Unlike the victim who spends so much time in a place of guilt, the abusive-antisocial person does not. This is all part of an individual who simply does not care.

Controlling partner:

"Controlling" refers to when people try to run other people's lives. They make a fuss when they don't get their way. They use tactics that make you feel guilty to manipulate the situation.

Controlling people insist, persist or get angry when they don't get their way, until they do get their way.

About Co-dependency

ictims of controlling partners are codependent: They seek to achieve closeness with the person they are trying to control.

Their objective is: Let me take care of you so you will love me.

Abusers are counter-codependent: These people attempt to diminish their own pain by dictating what the other person should or shouldn't do. This is so they will feel better about themselves. The codependent victim sees this as caring and then rejecting.

The objective is: It is your job to take care of me and you'd better not fail.

Controlling vs. Self-Control:

Self-Control implies the ability to control one's responses and the ability to recognize and interpret their internal messages. They know when something is right for them and when it is not.

Controlling partners give their partner the control over their happiness and well-being. For example: One partner tries to impose controlling rules on the other partner's behavior.

Common behaviors of codependents:

When you think about it, some of the nicest people are co-dependent. They always wear a smile. They are giving and never refuse to do a favor. They are happy and outgoing and they understand others and have the ability to cause others to like them. Not that anything is wrong with this, unless the giving is one-sided or unless the giving is so excessive it hurts the giver. If this is the case, then the giver is co-dependent. The other side to co-dependency is "interdependent." In this relationship there is an equality of give and take. You know the other person will be there for you. Interdependency means that you don't have to give until it hurts or causes you to feel resentful.

Co-dependent behavior is not easy. It takes a lot of work. Typically co-dependent individuals have low self-worth, depression, anxiety and a lot of guilt. Giving allows them to feel useful. Rather than self-approval, they need to win the approval of others and often they do this by giving and then feeling resentful when giving does not win the approval they seek. This approval provides some resemblance of self-esteem, while the abuser's mindset is survival. They expect others to hurt them. Co-dependent people self-judge harshly. They have a strict code by which they must live. They also have great difficulty in accepting anything from others. They don't feel deserving. While they are extremely critical of their own behavior, they make excuses for the intolerable behavior of others.

Co-dependent people misplace their anger. They get angry when they shouldn't and express their anger inappropriately and they don't get angry when they should. They have very little contact with their inner-world and, therefore, have no idea how they really feel. Usually, they don't want to know, this awareness gives rise to painful emotions they don't know how to deal with. It's easier to live on the surface, portraying a world that is idealistic rather than deal with the stuff that is going on inside. If they were asked to look inside what they would feel and experience is emotional starvation. They have been so busy taking care of the needs of others that they have completely neglected their own.

A trap that co-dependents fall into is the one that sees the softer side to the beast. Even though it may not be possible to deny the hurtful behavior it is easy to say, "if you only knew him like I do…" Co-dependents are loyal to a fault and rationalizing is their way of enduring. They also put up with relationships that are abusive or not fulfilling because being alone is perceived as empty and depressing. Being alone is distracting—no one else is pulling them away from feelings they don't want to address—to them any relationship is better than NO relationship.

It also just doesn't occur to the co-dependent person that it is NOT okay to be disrespected and hurt and it is NOT okay to put up with abusive behavior NO MATTER WHAT. Instead, they blame themselves and justify the other person's behavior by thinking they must deserve the treatment they are getting. This is preferable to facing the truth that the person they want to love them is hurting them.

Co-dependents are addiction prone. Any behavior such as excessive eating, shopping or drinking is just another way of dulling the senses. It is a way to avoid knowing themselves. Intimacy is also avoided, since intimate feelings require familiarity and comfort with ones inner-world; it is easier to shut off that aspect to our Selves.

There is a price we pay for our own self-sacrifice. It is a sacrifice that creates severe depression and destroys the spirit and our self-esteem in a vicious and downward spiral. Codependent people don't even know how angry they really are—until they explode.

I believe that many of us are waiting for that magical Moment when our partner is transformed and healed through our persistent care taking. This does not happen, no matter how hard we try.

So why would anyone spend so much time and effort in co-dependent relationships? The answer to that is because they don't know any other way. How does an individual become co-dependent in the first place? They received good training early in life.

Any dysfunction in the family predisposes a child to codependent behavior. Since children are naturally programmed to seek love and approval, this becomes part of their need for survival as much as their basic needs. When a parent or family member is dysfunctional, the child tends to focus on the needs of their caretaker, rather than their needs. In a nutshell, codependent thinking tends to develop any time a child is growing up in a home where safety is not a given, either in expressing feelings, or where life is not carefree. In other words, a codependent in training learns to walk on eggshells. The child learns to be extra sensitive in reading thoughts and feelings of others. These interactions may take place silently or implicitly, but either way, the child learns to ignore the Self's inner needs.

Codependency involves a habitual method of thinking, feeling, and behaving toward our Selves and others that cause pain. It is also important to understand these behaviors are self-destructive. These habits can lead us into, or keep us trapped in destructive relationships and they prevent us from finding peace and happiness with the most important person in our lives—ourselves. But the positive side to codependency is that these behaviors belong to the only person we can change, and that is our Selves.

Each person is different; we think and feel differently. You must identify the behaviors or areas that cause you problems and then decide what you want to do about them.

The following is a list of codependent behavior:

Codependents may:

- Think and feel responsible for other people and for their feelings, actions and choices and for their needs, well-being or lack of well-being
- Feel anxiety, pity, and guilt when other people have problems
- Feel compelled—almost forced—to help that person solve their problem, such as offering unwanted advice, fixing their problem or their feelings
- Feel angry when their help isn't effective
- Feel resentful that their needs aren't met
- Don't know what they want or need, or if they do, tell themselves what they need isn't as important
- Try to please others
- Feel safest when giving
- Feel insecure and guilty when others do give to them
- Find themselves attracted to needy people
- Over commit themselves
- Believe deep inside that other people are somehow responsible for them
- Blame others for the spot they are in
- Say other people make them feel the way they do
- Believe other people are making them crazy
- Feel victimized, angry, unappreciated, and used

Have low Self Worth

- Come from troubled, repressed or dysfunctional families
- Deny their family was troubled
- Blame themselves for everything
- Find fault with everything, including the way they feel, think, look and behave
- Reject compliments
- Feel guilty when they do things for themselves
- Think they are not good enough
- Are afraid of making mistakes
- Tell themselves they can't do anything right
- Feel they are victims
- Have been abused physically, emotionally, or sexually, neglected, abandoned

- Feel ashamed of who they are
- Live the lives of others
- Receive artificial feelings of self-worth when they help others
- Believe good things will never happen
- Try to prove their self-worth
- Need others to love them
- Settle for loveless relationships as long as they feel needed
- Become afraid to let themselves be who they are

Have problems with Obsession

Many codependents:

- Feel anxious about problems and people
- Think and talk a lot about other people
- Lose sleep over problems
- Never find answers
- Worry about the silliest things
- Think and talk a lot about other people
- Check on people
- Neglect their own responsibilities because they are so upset about someone else's problems
- Become lethargic and without energy
- Think and feel responsible for other people or their feelings, thoughts, actions, needs and well-being
- Feel anxious or guilty when other people have problems
- Find themselves saying yes, when they mean no, doing things they really don't want to do, and taking on more than their share

They are controlling

Many codependents:

- Live or have lived with people that were out of control, causing the codependents sorrow and disappointment
- They are afraid to let others be who they are and allow events to naturally happen

- Try to control people through emotional blackmail such as using guilt as a way to control behavior
- Feel controlled by people and circumstances
- Don't see or deal with their fear of loss of control
- Think they know best how things should turn out and how people should behave
- Don't feel happy, content or at peace with themselves
- Look for happiness outside of themselves
- Feel controlled by events and people
- Get frustrated and angry
- Eventually fail in their efforts or provoke people's anger

Dependency

- Become dependent on whoever they think can provide happiness
- Feel they need people more than they want them
- Feel terribly threatened by the loss of anything or person they think provides their happiness
- Didn't feel love and approval from their parents
- Don't love themselves
- Believe other people can't or don't love them.
- Often seek love from people incapable of loving
- Try to prove they are good enough to be loved
- Lose interest in their own lives when they love
- Worry that their partner will leave them
- Often seek people that are incapable of loving
- Desperately seek approval
- Equate love to pain
- Worry whether other people will approve or like them
- They are afraid to look inside for the source of their problems
- Don't believe they have the ability to take care of themselves
- Feel trapped in relationships
- Tolerate abuse in different forms
- Leave bad relationships only to form new ones with similar dysfunctional behavior
- Center their lives on other people
- Fear they will never find love

Poor communication

Codependents frequently:

- Blame
- Coerce
- Threaten
- Beg or bribe
- Have trouble saying what they mean
- Don't mean what they say
- Have difficulty asking for what they need
- Think, say and do what will please others
- Talk too much
- Avoid talking about themselves
- Have difficulty asserting their rights
- Have a difficult expressing their feelings directly and honestly
- Apologize too much
- Let others hurt them
- Get angry and become totally intolerant
- Take themselves too seriously
- Find it difficult to get to the point
- Don't know what the point is
- Eliminate NO from their vocabulary
- Say everything is their fault
- Say nothing is their fault
- Have a difficult asserting their rights
- Believe their opinions don't matter

Trust issues

Codependents:

- Don't trust themselves
- Don't trust their feelings
- Don't trust their decisions
- Think God has abandoned them
- Blame God
- Lose faith and trust in God
- Trust in other untrustworthy people

Codependents have sex issues:

Some codependents:

- Are caretakers in the bedroom
- Have sex when they don't want to
- Try to have sex when they're angry or hurt
- Refuse to enjoy sex because they're so angry at their partner
- Are afraid of losing control
- Have a difficult time asking for what they want in bed
- Withdraw emotionally from their partner
- Don't talk about it
- Feel sexual revulsion toward their partner
- Force themselves to have sex anyway
- Lose interest in sex
- Reduce sex to a technical act
- Make up reasons to abstain
- Have strong sexual fantasies about other people
- Consider or have an extramarital affair

Many codependents also:

- Feel scared, hurt, and angry
- Live with people who are very scared, hurt, and angry,
- Are afraid of their own anger
- Are frightened of other people's anger
- Think people will go away if they get angry
- Place guilt and shame on themselves for feeling angry
- Feel increasing amounts of anger, resentment, and bitterness
- Feel safer with their anger than hurt feelings
- Wonder if they'll ever not be angry

Codependents also tend to:

- Be extremely responsible
- Be extremely irresponsible
- Become martyrs, sacrificing their happiness and that of others
- Find it difficult to feel close to people

- Find it difficult to have fun and be spontaneous
- Have an overall passive response to codependency: crying, hurt, helplessness
- Have an overall aggressive response to codependency: violence, anger, dominance
- Combine passive and aggressive responses
- Laugh when they feel like crying
- Stay loyal to their compulsions and people even when it hurts
- Be ashamed about family, personal, or relationship problems
- Be confused about the nature of the problem
- Cover up, lie and protect the problem
- Not seek help because they tell themselves the problem isn't bad enough
- Wonder why the problem doesn't go away

Progressive

In the later stages of codependency, codependents may:

- Feel depressed
- Become withdrawn and isolated
- Feel hopeless
- Experience an eating disorder (over or under eating).
- Become addicted to alcohol and or other drugs
- Abuse or neglect their children and other responsibilities
- Plan an escape from a relationship in which they feel trapped
- Become violent
- Become seriously emotionally, mentally, or physically ill
- Think about suicide

How do we get our Selves into abusive relationships and then stay? From childhood conditioning, we may not have learned how to associate verbal, mental or emotional abuse as unacceptable behavior. We tend to excuse, justify or minimize what is happening inside our relationships. We tolerate varying degrees of abuse believing that it isn't that bad and that how we are reacting to the abuse isn't that bad either. Also, the un-nurtured grown child, coupled with codependent behaviors is at a high risk to become involved in abusive relationships and remain trapped.

Children grow up in homes where the primary caregiver isn't able to emotionally nurture them. Later on the "un-nurtured" child has difficulty relating to and bonding with other people. Not only do we see grown children in dysfunctional relationships but also there are many who have a craving for sugars and other foods that are "comfort" foods. We also find our Selves excessively worried about how others see us.

The *un-nurtured grown child* never feels good enough, pretty enough, smart enough, thin enough etc. Sadly, but truly, many of us have been unable to accept our Selves just as we are.

The problem is, nurturing isn't something one finds from the outside—we have to learn how to self-nurture, self-love, accept and heal our pained low-self esteem.

Lists and Checklists

The following pages have information that you can use to assist you in making decisions and taking necessary steps:

Make a list & keep it close by
Important Phone Numbers:

I will have important phone numbers available to my children and myself:

Police
Hotline
Friends
Shelter

I can tell (neighbors) about the violence, and ask them to call the police if they hear suspicious noise coming from my home.

If I leave my home, I can go (list four places):_____ , _____ , and

I can leave extra money, car keys, clothes, and copies of documents with

To ensure safety and independence, I can: Keep change for phone calls with me at all times; open my own savings account; rehearse my escape route with a support person.

Suggestions for increasing safety when the relationship is over:

I can: change the locks; install steel/metal doors, a security system, smoke detectors and an outside lighting system

I will inform _____ and_____ that my partner no longer lives with me, and ask them to call the police if s/he is observed near my home or my children.

I can obtain a protective order; I can keep it on or near me at all times aswell as leave a copy with_____.

If I feel down and ready to return to a potentially abusive situation, I can call for support or attend workshops and support groups to gain support and strengthen my relationships with other people.

Checklist
Items to take

- Identification
- Birth certificates for my children and me
- Social security cards
- School and medical records
- Money, bankbooks, credit cards
- Keys—house/car/office
- Drivers license and registration
- Medications
- Change of clothes
- Welfare identification
- Passport, green cards, work permits
- Divorce papers
- Lease/rental agreement, house deed
- Mortgage payment book, current unpaid bills
- Insurance papers
- Address book
- Pictures, jewelry, items of sentimental value
- Children's favorite toys and blankets

Women helping battered women

Help your friend recognize the abuse.

Point out the different types of abuse in dating relationships. Tell him/her how abuse happens and hurts more over time.

Express your concerns.

Tell your friend you are glad she/he confided in you. Let your friend know you are sorry this is happening to her/him. You can never say the following phrases too much:

- I'm worried about you
- It's not your fault
- I'm glad you told me about what you're going through
- You deserve better
- I'm here for you

Support your friend's strength.

Point out how your friend is able to take care of herself/himself; encourage your friend to spend time with others and take time away from the relationship.

Be accepting.

Tell your friend you are worried about their safety let your friend know you are there for them and mean it. Don't become upset if your friend is not ready to break off the relationship yet. Try to see that your friend is dealing with some difficult emotions: love and security from a partner, and fear from the abuse. If your friend wants to stay in the relationship or keeps returning to the abusive partner, hold back from telling them they are wrong. Help your friend see they are not to blame for the violence and that changing their behavior will not stop the abuse. Help your friend recognize the abuser's excuses for being violent.

Work on a safety plan.

Help your friend think of ways to be safe. Look at patterns in the abuser's behavior to figure out when the abuser is explosive or violent. Find local resources that can offer additional support.

Be there, listen, and stay there.

You may feel like a broken record no one is listening to. Keep supporting your friend. Avoid blaming; she/he will know you are standing beside them. When they are ready to end their relationship, continue to be supportive and try to get them involved in activities. It takes awhile to get over any relationship, even one that is violent. Help your friend resist the pressure to get back together.

Reach out for help.

Go to a trusted friend with what you know. Call area resources for ideas on how to help your friend. Crisis lines are available 24 hours a day and you don't have to give your name.

Keep educating yourself on domestic/dating violence.

If you are frightened or frustrated, get support for yourself. Remember, you can't rescue or solve all friends' problems.

About Depression

Causes of depression

Personality type: people who are highly self-critical, very demanding or unusually passive and dependent may be prone to depression.

Biochemical functions: Shortage or imbalances of mood influencing chemicals in the brain are thought to play a role in some cases of depression; certain medications, illnesses or infections can also lead to depression.

Environmental influences: Unfavorable family, social or working environments can cause depression as can serious interpersonal conflicts, loss of a loved one, neglect as a child, etc.

Genetic patterns: Depression is not inherited, but the tendency to suffer from some type of depressive illness does run in certain families; some studies indicate that a biochemical tendency to depression may be genetic.

Types and Symptoms of depression

Mild depression: Changes in behavior and attitude, general slowing down, neglect of responsibilities and appearances, loss of appetite, agitation, pointless over activity, poor memory, inability to concentrate, and irritability, complains about matters that used to be taken in stride.
(May not need professional intervention)

Moderate depression: Emotional flatness or emptiness, inability to find pleasure in anything, hopelessness, loss of sexual desire, of warm feelings for family and friends, exaggerated self-blame, guilt or loss of self-esteem, sometimes leading to suicidal thoughts or actions.

(May need professional intervention)

Severe depression: Sleeping disturbances, such as early morning wakefulness, sleeping too much, insomnia, chronic fatigue, lack of energy, unexplained headaches, backaches, similar complaints digestive upsets; stomach pain, nausea, indigestion, change in bowel habits, inability to function, emotional, despondent and suicidal.

(Seek immediate professional intervention)

Manic depression: extreme highs and lows

Everyone experiences some or all of these symptoms at some time. But when symptoms are severe and lasting so pain and problems outweigh pleasure much of the time, then it's time to get professional help.

Know the signs

Substance abuse

Know the warning signals that may indicate your child is using alcohol or other drugs. Even though these are indicators of substance abuse keep in mind that these and other signs may also have other causes.

- Drop in academic performance
- Lack of interest in grooming
- Withdrawal, isolation, depression, fatigue
- Aggressive, rebellious behavior
- Excessive influence by peers
- Hostility and lack of cooperation
- Deteriorating relationship with family
- Change in friends
- Loss of interest in hobbies and sport
- Change in eating or sleeping habits
- Evidence of drugs and paraphernalia: pipes, rolling papers, medicine bottles, eye drops, and butane lighters
- Physical changes: red eyes, runny nose not due to a cold, wheezing, bags under eyes, frequent sore throats, bruises from falls.

Hotlines for Victims

National Domestic Hotline
www.ndvh.org

Rape, Abuse & Incest National Network/National Sexual Assault
RAINN
www.rainn.org

Abuse Hotline & Resources
(800) 4-A-Child

How To Report Suspected Abuse
(800) 422-4453
(800) 2-A-Child

How To Get Help
(800) 799-7233

Parents Anonymous
(800) 352-0528

Tucson Centers for Women And Children
www.tucsoncenters.com/gethelp/

Domestic Violence Hotline
Arizona
Crisis Centers and Intervention
24 hour Crisis Hotline
(480) 784-1500

National Sexual Violence Resource Center
(877) 739-3895 (Toll Free)

National Domestic Violence Hotline
(800) 799-SAFE
(800) 787-3224

Alcohol Abuse Hotline
(800) ALCOHOL
Child Abuse Hotline Directory
(If you are stressed to the point of harming your children)
(800) 4-A-Child
www.therapistfinder.net/help/childhelp

Please send any questions or comments to the author at:

Janice Farnsworth
P.O. Box 1488
Payson, AZ 85547

http://www.beneathangelwings.com